Lifebook

For my children.
And for us.

Andreas Jetter
Lifebook
50 chapters about the world and good life

Bibliographic information from the German National Library:
The German National Library lists this publication in
the German National Bibliography; detailed bibliographic
data is available on the Internet at http://dnb.dnb.de.

Text and illustrations: Dr. Andreas Jetter
www.dr-jetter.com
@Andreas_Jetter

English translation: Brigitte Litzenberger
Revision: Dr. Andreas Jetter

Photo in the foreword: Antonino Zambito

© 2020/01/08 - Dr. Andreas Jetter
Production and publishing:
BoD – Books on Demand, Norderstedt

ISBN: 9783750433991

Foreword

In this book, I am trying to present all the essentials about the world and life from my point of view. For each of the 50 chapters, there are self-drawn illustrations and voluntary tasks for self-knowledge and for the implementation of the content into one's own life.

Figuratively formulated: With this book, in about 18 years, I have tried to make a chandelier out of the many small lights that have come up or met me.

More about the book is described in the first chapter, "Introduction," about a shared use in the second and about myself and about the development of the book in the last chapter.

If anyone sincerely believes that this could be a new "Life-Bible," let me tell you that I seriously think that it is formally and contentwise even a very good one. ☺ All the same, I am open to improvement.

I wish the reader in any case: Joy and success in this world and in their lives. If my book can contribute to this, it is an honor and a joy for me.

Stuttgart, January 8, 2020

Dr. Andreas Jetter

Table of contents

Foreword   V
Table of Contents   VI

1. Introduction
                        My picture, facts, expectations,
                            self-study, companions? 1
2. Discussion group and
   assembly
                             My discussion group and
                                    my assembly? 9
3. Creation of the world
                           My father and his parents? 17
4. Universe
                           My mother and her parents? 25
5. Earth
                                  What shaped me? 33
6. Life
                            My story up until today? 41
7. History
                          My worldview and self-image
                            and my meaning of life? 49
8. Technology
                               My probable future? 57
9. Environment
                            My local environment? 65
10. Human
                                      My body? 73
11. Mind
                       My strengths and weaknesses? 81

12. Feelings

My likes and dislikes? 89

13. Insight

My goals and wishes? 97

14. Problems and chances

My feelings, my thoughts;
problems and chances? 105

15. Commandments and values

My commandments
and values? 113

16. Language

My beliefs? 121

17. Personality

My personality? 129

18. God and symbols

Who is God to me?
My symbols and external image? 137

19. Nature conservation

My pets, domestic plants, and
my nature conservation? 145

20. Time management

My daily and weekly schedule? 153

21. Work

My job? 161

22. Money

My money? 169

23. Things

My things? 177

24. Health, breathing and drinking

My breathing and
my drinking? 185

25. Eating

My eating? 193

26. Sleeping and dreaming

My sleeping and dreaming? 201

27. Body moving

My exercise? 209

28. Mind training

My mind training? 217

29. Recovering

My physical life force? 225

30. Motivating

My mental life force? 234

31. Prevention

My prevention? 241

32. Healing

My diseases? 249

33. Beauty

My beauty? 257

34. Leisure

My leisure activities? 265

35. Family and relatives

My family and my relatives? 273

36. State

My state? 281

37. Economy

My economy? 289

38. Faith community and other communities

My faith community and other communities? 297

39. Norms

My norms and contracts? 305

VIII

40. Responsibility

My dealing with mistakes and
my responsibility? 313

41. Friends and
acquaintances

My friends and acquaintances? 321

42. Man and woman

My gender and
my love partner model? 329

43. Life partner

My life partner? 337

44. Love

My mental and physical love? 345

45. Children

My children? 353

46. Course of life

My whole life in an overview? 361

47. Death

My will and testament and
my living will? 369

48. Apocalypse

Subsequent time, my most beautiful
experiences and contributions? 377

49. Annual circle

My vacation and annual circle? 385

50. End

My time until the new beginning? 393

Advent picture   401
Christmas picture   403
New Year picture   405
Afterword   407

1

1. Chapter: Introduction

In this first chapter there is an introduction to this book and some ideas on how we can work with it.

Let's get started: In this book, I will give you **all the essentials about the world and about good life** from my point of view. It will be about how the world came into being, how it functions and what its future probably looks like. And we will look at all essential areas of life, such as eating, sleeping or family.

I am trying to be correct, most complete, and helpful. The content will be a summary of the most essential wisdom of our time, occasionally supplemented by my own ideas.

Why this book?

At an early age, I wanted to do something that would make the world a better place. I think this book can help. I've also learned a lot, a lot of ideas have "bubbled out" of me, and I want to pass them on in this compact way.

Learning regularly works in such a way that even as a child, one looks at the world, copies it, thinks about it, tries it out and finds one's own insights. Nevertheless, you cannot work everything out for yourself, and an understanding framework also helps you to recognize specific things.

Who is the book for?

First of all, I am writing this book **for my** own **children**. I do not have any as I am writing this, unfortunately. But now, I have the time and the ability to share what I can share through such a book with as much love and wisdom as possible.

My challenge: I don't know when at what age and where in the world my children will read this book. That's why I want it to be suitable for everyone. Especially for older children or teenagers, because they can still change a lot in their lives. And it may and should become a dear and loved companion through life.

Just as I would do with my children, I will address you in a trusting tone throughout this book. Because of the better readability, male forms in the book, which I occasionally limit myself to, are basically valid for all sexes.

If I am not your biological father, I can perhaps become something like a "spiritual father" who gives you a spiritual home through this book. It would be nice if I may be that person. Thank you.

I could have used such a book, especially as a child and teenager, and I still use it today. From this point of view, this book is also suitable for me.

So it is basically written **for us**.

How is the book designed, and why so?

First, I am dividing the content into **50 chapters**, about one for each week of the year.

Each chapter has about ten minutes of **text** read aloud, long enough for content, short enough for concentration.

The original version contains **illustrations** drawn by me. Each chapter has one in color and one in outlines for coloring - not only for children. And not perfect, but just like a father can do for his children. By the way, this applies to the whole book.

Each chapter has **tasks** at the end. Many things that are very important for you and your immediate surroundings, I can't know. The tasks help us to recognize ourselves better, to supplement the content, and then to implement it. Because only by reading, there will be little improvement. Of course, the tasks are voluntary. The choice of doing them at all, in spirit or in writing, alone or with others, is up to you. You don't always want to think about everything.

With the tasks, it might be useful to look at what it looks like now, to think briefly about what it was like and what it will probably be like, and then to decide what should be specific now. The original version of the book contains space for written answers. I recommend to write down the essentials in keywords, perhaps first on concept paper, then cleanly into the book. If you are afraid that others will read the contents, you can keep the book somewhere safe, use abbreviations, or record individual notes somewhere else.

The chapters are designed so that they can be understood independently of each other, what makes them an excellent weekly **stimulus for discussion groups** or **meetings**. Like the book, these may be independent of other world views or religions. The content is my point of view, in principle everybody is allowed to keep or develop their own opinion. Different views can also be left as they are.

If a topic is not so familiar to you, the content may seem a bit compressed. Maybe ask someone familiar with it, explore it for yourself, or be happy that you don't have to deal with it much more. If you already know a topic well, then some things may seem natural to you. Be satisfied that you already know so much, that repetition prevents forgetting and that you can experience this chapter in a comfortable and relaxed way.

To understand the contents to a large extent and then use them automatically, this should be good regularly.

Can one single author explain everything?

For most things, there are specialists who have the advantage that they hopefully know and can do a lot in their field. What they often lack is an overview. They see causes and solutions in their area – sometimes, even when they cannot be found. And many basic things in their field become so apparent to them that they no longer even talk about them, although that would be important for understanding.

On the other hand, I am also a specialist - the one for the overview. And together with the tasks, everyone becomes what they need to be if they want to live well or even survive - the specialist for their lives.

The tasks at the end of the chapter

Task 1.1 **My picture?**

When we paste or paint a picture of ourselves, the first thing we see is who is very important in our book of life.

Task 1.2 **My most important personal data?**

Let's start with self-knowledge by name, birthday, profession, place of residence, accessibility, affiliations, interests,...

Task 1.3 **My expectations for this book?**

Where do you stand in terms of knowledge and quality of life on a scale from 0 to 10 now? Ask this again after completing the book.

Task 1.4 **My self-study?**

When, where, and how will you use this book?

Task 1.5 **My individual book companions?**

Individuals can look at us from the outside, contribute their thoughts and feelings, and motivate us. This can be a friend, mentor, or a professional life consultant or coach. Who suits you best?

1.1 My picture:

1.2 My most important personal data:

1.3 My expectations:

1.4 My self-study with this book:

1.5 My individual book companions:

2. Chapter: Discussion group and assembly

A book is a lonely thing. In the last chapter, there is the idea of using it together with one or more companions.

In this chapter, we look at how the texts can also be used as impulses for discussion groups or assemblies. Here all people can meet in a connecting way, because the topic of this book is vital for everyone, regardless of age, profession or interests. Content and community can also complement family. I am writing this at the beginning so that you have this possibility of use already in mind when continuing to read.

The discussion groups

The following is a brief description of how I imagine the course of a joint discussion group:

First of all, we would deal with one **chapter** of the book, for example, chapter 25, "Nutrition." Someone reads the text aloud, or everyone reads it for themselves. Also, all participants are given some time to think about it for themselves, to do the tasks at the end of the chapter spiritually or in writing or to color the outlined picture.

Secondly, we would follow up with a short **round of discussions**, in which everyone, in turn, could express their opinion on the topic and say something about their tasks or show their picture. For example, one can tell the others what is essential to them in their diet.

They can also tell how they are doing and what is bothering them most at the moment.

Thirdly, there is an **open discussion**. Individuals can present exciting opinions, ideas for implementing the tasks, or the things affecting them in more detail. Perhaps someone has been away on a trip, is starting a new job, or is presenting a problem that is currently bothering them. There can be feedback on this. Here it would be good to be careful with quick advice and talk more about what you feel, how you see things, or how you would probably act in this situation.

Such a discussion group could typically consist of up to ten permanent **members**, be open only in exceptional cases, and be held, for example, within a family, a circle of friends or colleagues, an association, a self-help group, a religious community, a house or a neighborhood.

It is good if the discussion group in which the first chapter is dealt with takes place in the week in which January 8th falls, and each further week the next chapter takes its turn. So it nicely matches the calendar year and other groups and assemblies.

Such a discussion group has **many advantages**: Through the **impulses** given by the book, a group mentally gets through all the essential things once a year and does not always discuss the same topics. When we say something in front of others, it can be more precise and more memorable than just thinking it through quietly. Thanks to the

feedback we get views and information from people who have probably known us for some time and live with us in our time and place. If we give feedback, we may feel valuable. And in the third part, the open section, the group has the opportunity to really talk about everything that seems important to them. We can share successes and beautiful experiences in the group and be happy and proud. During difficult times the group can give comfort and courage. And they can **motivate** you to go on.

Also, we get to know each other better, strengthen the sense of belonging, and can even have leisure activities, friendships, or mutual help **outside the group**.

The assemblies

If we share the texts with many people and would like to meet many people in this way, it works best in an assembly. And if many people are there, the gathering could be nicely organized through informative lectures or cultural and festive interludes.

The assembly could be regularly open to all interested people and only exceptionally be closed to the general public. The organizers of the meeting should decide for themselves whether or not to set up a collection box for a donation to cover the expenses. However, preparation and implementation may be shared by several people. I have considered the following ten points regarding the joint procedure. Try and see if they work well for you:

First: Welcome. Someone says "hello" and maybe briefly something about who is there, why we are here today, or what will be special.

Secondly: Attunement. Here, for example, we could sing or speak something together, listen to a piece of music or meditate on the picture of the chapter.

Thirdly: News. If many people are already gathered, someone or several of them could share what is new or essential for the group.

Fourth: Crossover. In terms of content, like the attunement as an element between news and reading.

Fifth: Reading. Someone reads the text of this week's chapter out loud. If the first chapter is dealt with in the week in which the 8th of January falls, and the next chapter is dealt with in the following week, then, also here, you can get well through the year and deal with the chapters parallel to the discussion groups and other assemblies.

Sixth: Middle. The focus could be on deepening the topic. In the nutrition chapter, perhaps a sermon on the subject, a lecture, a panel discussion, a play, a film, hints on excellent local shopping opportunities, or matching spiritual or transcendental elements. Other views than those represented in the book are still allowed. While they may be unnecessarily unsettling, wrong, or bad, they can also help to improve possible mistakes or simply be different points of view.

On special holidays, commemoration days, or on certain occasions, however, a meeting with a suitable reading and "middle" can also be held.

Seventh: Reflection. In a short time of rest, everyone can think and feel meditatively for themselves.

Eighth: Finish according to the attunement.

Ninth: The farewell perhaps with hints to what will follow and there hopefully also follows:

Tenth: Encounter. It would be nice if afterward, there was something to drink or a snack and the opportunity for mutual encounters. Here we can also exchange more private information, make new contacts and deepen old ones.

The tasks at the end of the chapter

Task 2.1 **My discussion group?**

Task 2.2 **My assembly?**

Is there anything like this near you? Where?
If not, could you start something? With whom? Where?
If there are some: Which ones do you visit? When? Where?
Who participates? How does this typically work?
What are your advantages or disadvantages?

What can you do, what do you want and what will you do in each case?

2.1 My discussion group(s):

2.2 My assembly(s):

3. Chapter: Origin of the world

After having learned something about this book and its possible use in the first chapters, we will now look at the beginning of everything in the topic origin of the world.

This world is the foundation of our lives, and we are part of it. If we understand it sufficiently, we also understand what we must accept as unchangable and what we can change and how; what we can use and where we should protect ourselves. These insights will also provide regularly an accepting inner peace.

The first tasks help us to become aware of our personal origins and of ourselves.

The growth

Let's think about how our world might have come into being. Let us imagine that in the beginning there was **nothing.**

Something can only grow out of nothing if what is created is still nothing together. Let us assume that an organizing force or **order energy** grows and at the same time, **chaotic energy** in the same quantity, so in balance (energy and ballance principle). If both are equally strong, order and chaos, they together cause what exclusively exists: Nothing. Nothing has only taken another shape. What would be the perfect order? It would exist if everything were concentrated at an infinitely small point. If you are looking for something, you will find everything there. And the chaos would be perfect if everything was infinitely dispersed.

But what should order the one energy and what distribute the other one? The answer: A small part of each other's energy (mixing principle). Two **mixtures** are created: At the point of origin, order energy which organizes a little chaotic energy, called **dark matter**, around it **dark energy** that is chaotic energy which distributes some order energy.

The formula of the world would then be: Nothing (0) = the sum of all order energy (E_o) + the sum of all chaotic energy (E_c) = dark matter ($9\,E_o + 1\,E_c$) + dark energy ($9\,E_c + 1\,E_o$). (9 is then a variable > 1.)

With the distribution of the energy, the three-dimensional **space** in between is created. We can measure **change** since then with a comparison change, the time.

Let's think further: While the dark energy is able to spread easily, the dark matter at the point of origin becomes denser and denser, until the excess of the order energy finally becomes so strong that nothing can escape any more, although the chaotic energy striving for distribution continues to form.

The Big Bang

Around the year -14 billion, there is now so much chaotic energy in the order energy at the place of origin in the smallest space that the system becomes unstable and explodes. This was the end of growth. At the same time or afterward, the dark forms of energy are transformed mainly into much stronger, so-called bright forms of energy. It is possible that new bright energy and bright anti-energy are partially destroyed.

What remains: Background radiation, the new bright forms of energy, the rest of unconverted dark matter that has spread, and the remaining dark energy, far out in the universe.

Up to here, these are, more or less, my ideas, which I haven't read anywhere before, what follows is mostly science plus my own thoughts; so:

The new bright energy has the characteristic that it is concentrated in smallest centers, in so-called power-bearing particles and also in mass-bearing particles.

The newly created strong **electromagnetic energy** causes the ordering attraction of different charges and the somewhat chaotic repulsion of the same charges. And, by the way, because of the interaction with light, the new energy is also called bright energy.

A large part of the new energy is **stabilized** in **atoms**. An atom is approximately one-millionth of a millimeter small. The simplest atom is the hydrogen atom (H). Its atomic nucleus behaves as if it consisted of a positively charged proton and up to two neutrons that are not charged to the outside. Both act as if they each consisted of three quarks. A smaller, negatively charged electron seems to orbit the atomic nucleus at a great distance and on determinable orbitals. Larger atoms have more protons and neutrons in their atomic nuclei. The number of electrons and protons in the atom is the same so that an atom is electromagnetically neutral to the outside.

A new **strong nuclear force** causes the atomic nucleus to remain connected with its repulsive positive charges. Bonding of the electrically negative electron with the positive nucleus probably prevents its speed. A **weak nuclear force** acts during the conversion of protons into neutrons. An attracting **gravitational force**, which is perhaps an original remainder of the order energy, acts clearly beyond the atom.

Particles react with each other. A reaction probably takes place when the system gets closer to its original state: more order on the inside, more chaos on the outside. Smaller atoms can merge to larger atoms, for example, two hydrogen atoms to helium (He). Also, here, order gets bigger inside; chaos-energy is released on the outside.

Several atoms can form associations with free-moving electrons, so-called **metals**. By overlay of their electron orbitals, they can also combine to form **molecules**. If the so-called "outer shell" of the atoms becomes "full," this is probably more orderly. "Atoms," which exceptionally have about one electron more or less than protons, so-called ions, can "orderly" combine to outwardly neutral **salts. Liquids** also arrange themselves; depending on the polarity of the substances, they are regularly either polar water-soluble or neutral fat-soluble.

How can systems that become more orderly on the inside increase chaos on the outside? The particles can first develop a stronger natural oscillation. We say: The **temperature** rises. This regularly leads to expansion of the substance. Most substances are solid at low temperatures, liquid at medium temperatures, and gaseous at high temperatures.

Then there is the **radiation**. In electromagnetic radiation, a photon probably moves in waves, or as a wave in an electromagnetic field, at high speed away from its point of origin. Depending on the wavelength, it can be gamma or X-rays, ultraviolet, visible or infrared light, or radio waves. Whole particles such as electrons, helium cores, or neutrinos can also be emitted.

Free (chaos) energy can also cause endothermic, as activation energy the beginning of exothermic **reactions** or their back-reaction; **move** bodies, even against other forces, or fuse atoms larger than iron, which requires (chaos) energy.

Reactions, by the way, change the appearance, never the total amount of energy.

The tasks at the end of the chapter

After so much physics and chemistry now to one part of our own origin, respectively lineage:

Task 3.1 **My father?**

Task 3.2 **My paternal grandfather?**

Task 3.3 **My paternal grandmother?**

Maybe you could at least: Note down name, date of birth, job, qualities and your relationship.

3.1 My father:

3.2 My paternal grandfather:

3.3 My paternal grandmother:

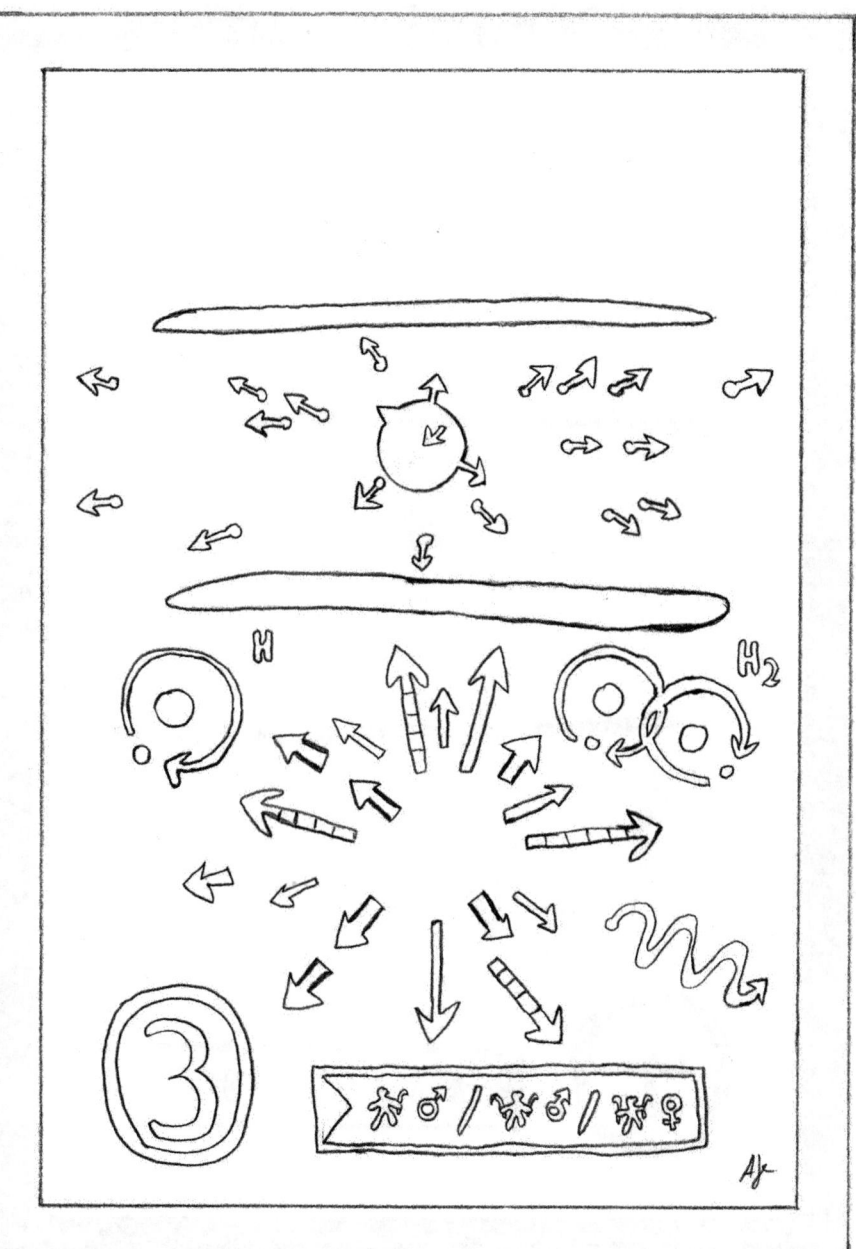

4. Chapter: Universe

In the last chapter, we looked at how the materials of this world might have been created out of nothing. The task was about a part of our fatherly ancestors. For the task of this chapter, we look at our direct maternal ancestors, and in the text of the chapter, we look at how the small elements of building material grew to become the big one, the universe.

Even though the chapter may be very astronomical, I believe it is good to at least briefly deal with it. so that we can then calmly devote ourselves to what is closer to us than the stars.

The stars

The stars were probably formed like this: The remaining dark matter has an ordering effect, and the gravitational force causes the newly formed hydrogen atoms to attract each other. As a result, they gather in large gas clouds that assume globular shapes under their gravitational force. If the gravitational pressure inside is high enough, two hydrogen atoms can each fuse to form a helium atom. The (chaos) energy released as a result heats up the environment and thus prevents also large gas globes from collapsing under their gravity. A part of the energy is radiated, and a part of the radiated energy we perceive as light. In the sky, we then see a star shining.

If there is a lot of helium in a star, it may happen that three helium atoms become one carbon atom (C). The larger a star is, the faster this happens. A carbon atom has six protons and regularly six neutrons in its nucleus and six electrons in its atomic shells. This seems to be much more orderly inside than the three helium atoms before. If this carbon production takes place quickly in massive stars, the (chaos) energy released to the outside is probably so high that the star explodes, for example, into a supernova, releasing large amounts of light and further radiation in a gamma flash.

Under the extreme pressure and the considerable energy of the explosion, a multitude of new atoms of different sizes is formed by nuclear fusion or fission.

The remnants remaining from such explosions can clump together again under the influence of gravity or dark matter and form new stars or non-luminous celestial bodies.

Our solar system

Around the year -4.6 billion, our solar system is probably created like that. Around 99 percent of the matter in our solar system was collected in our star, the **sun**. If a lump of matter flies past the sun, it will be attracted by the gravitation of the sun. To put it simply: If the gravitational force and centrifugal force of the lump's own motion are in ballance, the lump will rotate stably around the sun.

This was probably the case with our **Earth**, a planet that became almost globular under its gravitation.

The Earth is flying around the sun with seven other planets. Four stone planets near the sun and three gas planets further out. From the sun, the Earth is the third planet.

The Earth itself is brightly illuminated on the side inclined towards the sun, and dark on the side facing away from it. Within one day, the earth rotates around its own axis, which is almost perpendicular to the sun. This creates day and night.

In about 365.25 days, the earth rotates once around the sun. Since its axis of rotation is not completely perpendicular to the sun, in fact, it inclines once with the northern hemisphere, once with the southern hemisphere in the direction of the sun during its orbit. That is how the seasons develop. If the northern hemisphere is inclined towards the sun, it is summer, while in the southern hemisphere, it is winter.

If a planet itself is orbited by a celestial body, it is called a **moon**. Our moon was probably formed around the year -4.5 billion as a result of a collision with another celestial body. A lunar orbit lasts a little less, a moon phase a little more than 28 days. We see what the sun illuminates. Above all, its gravity causes high and low tides on the earth.

Meanwhile, there is not much left on the trajectory of the Earth that could still collide with us. If a meteoroid does burn up when it enters our atmosphere, we see it as a shooting star.

The galaxies and the universe

Under the influence of their gravitation and probably also the dark matter, the stars and the non-luminous celestial bodies are gathered in clusters of stars, so-called **galaxies**. There are over 100 billion galaxies in the universe. Much of what we see in the night sky are not stars at all, but galaxies or even **galaxy clusters**.

Our galaxy is the **Milky Way**. In it, more than 100 billion stars and other celestial bodies move in a spiral around a center. Our sun is located in the outer third of a sidearm. In the center, itself is a so-called "black hole." This is a celestial body that appears to be black because it has so much mass in such a small space that no light can escape.

In the whole **space,** almost everything moves away from the Big Bang location, also due to sluggishness. Because there was still a lot of ordering dark matter at the place of origin in the beginning, it slowed down the speed at first. Since we, further outside, fly through more chaotic dark energy, it accelerates the rate of expansion. Altogether there is probably more dark energy than dark matter (ratio 7:3).

How do we know all this?

Most of it might be correct in this way or in a similar way. If you want to examine it in detail, please do so with other, scientific literature. I would like to name a few things:

1. Dark energy and dark matter in the universe were proven by their interaction but their non-interaction with light / electromagnetic radiation.

2. Based on the type of light incidence of points of light from the universe, one can determine that almost everything moves away from us, the further away, the faster. Consequence: Everything started at one point.

3. If you shoot helium nuclei at a 2,000 atom thick gold foil in a vacuum, 99.8 percent of them arrive directly on the other side. Consequence: Atoms consist of almost nothing. Energy gives them effect.

4. Theories about the function of the universe, such as the theory of relativity and quantum mechanics in addition to the standard model of particle physics, already made it possible for predictions to be made, that later could be proven, such as the existence of black holes or the existence of some elementary particles and how atoms and molecules react with each other.

5. Historical dating, which is important for later chapters, is done, for example, unsing the age of the rock stratum in excavations or using the radio-carbon method.

The tasks at the end of the chapter

Task 4.1 **My mother?**

Task 4.2 **My maternal grandfather?**

Task 4.3 **My maternal grandmother?**

Maybe the same again as in task 3: at least note down name, date of birth, job, qualities and your relationship.

4.1 My mother:

4.2 My maternal grandfather:

4.3 My maternal grandmother:

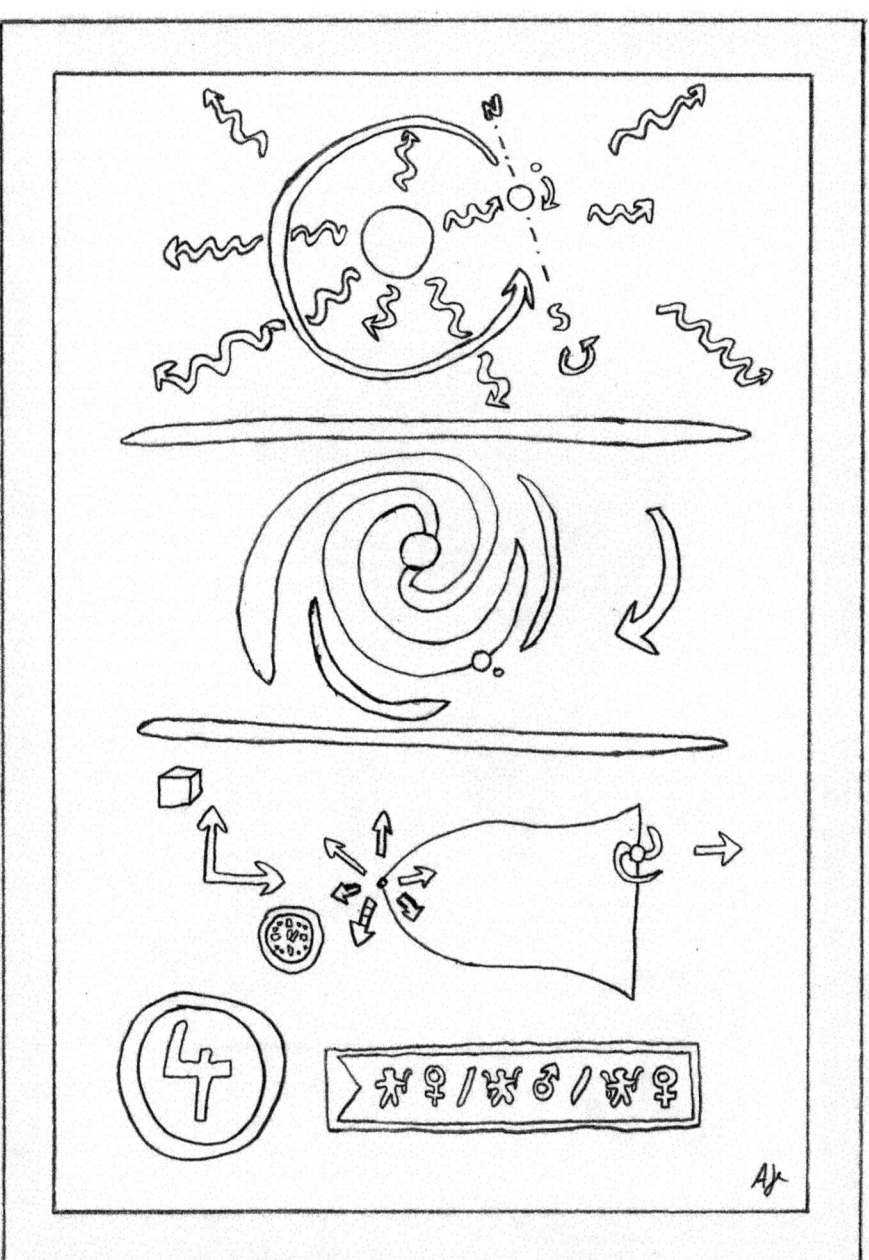

5. Chapter: Earth

In the last chapter, we saw how our solar system with the planet on which we live come about. In this chapter, we take a closer look at the origin and functionality of our home planet, so the topic is: The Earth.

The interior of the earth

At the beginning of its existence, our earth is probably very hot and liquid. The heat still comes from the process of formation and perhaps also from exothermic reactions that take place inside the Earth.

At the earth's surface, the material cools down by radiating heat, it becomes hard and forms a solid and growing thicker **earth crust** around the year -4.4 billion. It is between zero and 90 kilometers thick.

Temperature and gravitational pressure increases towards the center of the earth. The deeper you dig a mining shaft towards the center of the Earth, the warmer it gets.

Under the **Earth's crust**, the mantle is partially liquid and further inside flowable. The outer **core of the Earth** is liquid, the inner core solid, and at the center of the Earth at a depth of 6,371 kilometers, it is probably over 5,000 degrees Celsius hot.

There are circuits and currents in the Earth's interior. If particles heat up, their natural oscillation increases and with it their space requirement or pressure. Particles heated in the Earth's interior therefore push upwards, where the gravitational pressure is lower, and they can expand better. Under the earth's mantle, this is reversed, the mass cools down and sinks again. Circuits are formed.

The earth's surface

The currents in the Earth's mantle, on which the Earth's crust floats, pulled and keep pulling at it. As a result, the earth's crust is torn into many plates, which in turn are moved a few centimeters every year. Over many millions of years, this can have significant effects. When the Earth's mantle currents push earth plates apart, entire **continents** can **move**. For example, America and Europe-Africa are still moving apart today. If two earth plates collide, the Earth's mantle can expand upwards. A **mountain** is formed. This is still the case today with the collision of the Indian Plate with the Asian Plate, which extends the Himalayas. One plate can also submerge under another, which can form large **ditches**. For example, the Pacific plate sinks below the Philippine one and creates the Mariana trench.

If the plates move abruptly, because tensions that were built up are released, we feel this as an **earthquake**.
Liquid earth mantle material or melted earth crust material can come to the earth's surface through cracks or holes in the Earth's crust, particularly frequently along plate boundaries, through **volcanoes**.

On the cooled earth crust, the water could gather in the valleys. Today, about 70 percent of the earth's surface is covered by water. Salt is dissolved in the seas and **oceans**. Only around three percent of the Earth's water is available as **freshwater** in clouds, rivers, lakes, ice, and groundwater.

Especially the tides and temperature differences cause **ocean currents** in oceans.

Underwater, earthquakes can generate pressure waves that make **tsunami** waves on the coast.

The atmosphere

Some substances are present in gaseous form as **air** due to the temperatures on earth. Dry air today consists of about 78 percent nitrogen (N), 21 percent oxygen (0_2), and other gases, such as carbon dioxide.

The earth's gravity pulls the air to the earth's surface. It is, therefore, usually denser at sea level. The sun's rays heat up the earth's surface. In turn, the air heats up. If you ascend, the air becomes colder and colder. At an altitude of about 15 kilometers, the temperature is sometimes around -50 degrees Celsius. Then the air heats up again to around zero degrees at an altitude of about 50 kilometers, because the ozone (0_3) absorbs solar radiation and warms up as a result. Further up, it becomes colder and then warmer again, until in about 500 kilometers there are no more air particles.

Since air refracts different parts of light varying intense, the sky appears blue during the day, which refracts strongly, and orange-red at sunset or sunrise. A rainbow is different refracted light in the rain.

The **magnetic field**, which is probably caused by movements and friction inside the earth, protects us from the solar wind, in which entire electromagnetically charged particles are hurled away from the sun. Because of their electric charge, they are led around the earth or to the poles where they shine as an aurora.

Weather takes place in the lower atmospheric layer. Wind occurs when air pressure balances out. Also here, warm air will rise, and cool air will fall. The rotation of the earth, as well as temperature differences on the earth's surface, also have an influence.

Since water, for example, has a higher heat capacity than rock, it absorbs solar heat more slowly but remains warm longer. That's why on the coast, the wind regularly blows from sea to land during the day and from land to sea at night.

If two winds meet, hurricanes can occur. Tropical cyclones can reach wind speeds of 300 kilometers per hour. They arise when the water temperature above the oceans along the equator reaches at least 20 to 26 degrees Celsius depending on the air temperature, and certain wind conditions exist. Then a lot of humid air will rise spirally, from which a lot of rain will fall.

In general, precipitation occurs as follows: Water also evaporates slightly below its boiling point. Warm air absorbs more humidity than cold air, a maximum of four percent. If warm, humid air rises, it will cool at higher altitudes, and so be able to bind less water. The water then condenses drop by drop and clouds form. If the clouds continue to cool, if they hit cold wind or if they become too full, the water falls to the ground as rain, frozen as hail or snow. If clouds accumulate on mountains, where they are then pushed upwards by wind or thermals, i.e., rising warm air, it often rains heavily, as for example, during monsoon rains when the wind blows clouds against the southern Himalayas in summer.

And what clouds are in the sky is fog or haze above the Earth.

Thunderstorms occur when rising warm and humid air takes along single electrons of the surrounding particles. In an electron beam, the lightning, the charge separation balances out again. The air which heats up quickly and strongly around the lightning generates a sound wave, which we hear as thunder.

Erosion means that earthquakes, temperature changes, wind and rain, sometimes also plants or animals, slowly destroy mountains and land masses and regularly flush or blow these into the sea.

The task at the end of the chapter

Our parents and grandparents influenced us genetically, and they and other things also influenced us in life. Therefore the question:

Task 5 **What influenced my development?**
  (Essential people, places, events, ...)

5. *What influenced my development?*
   (Essential people, places, events, ...)

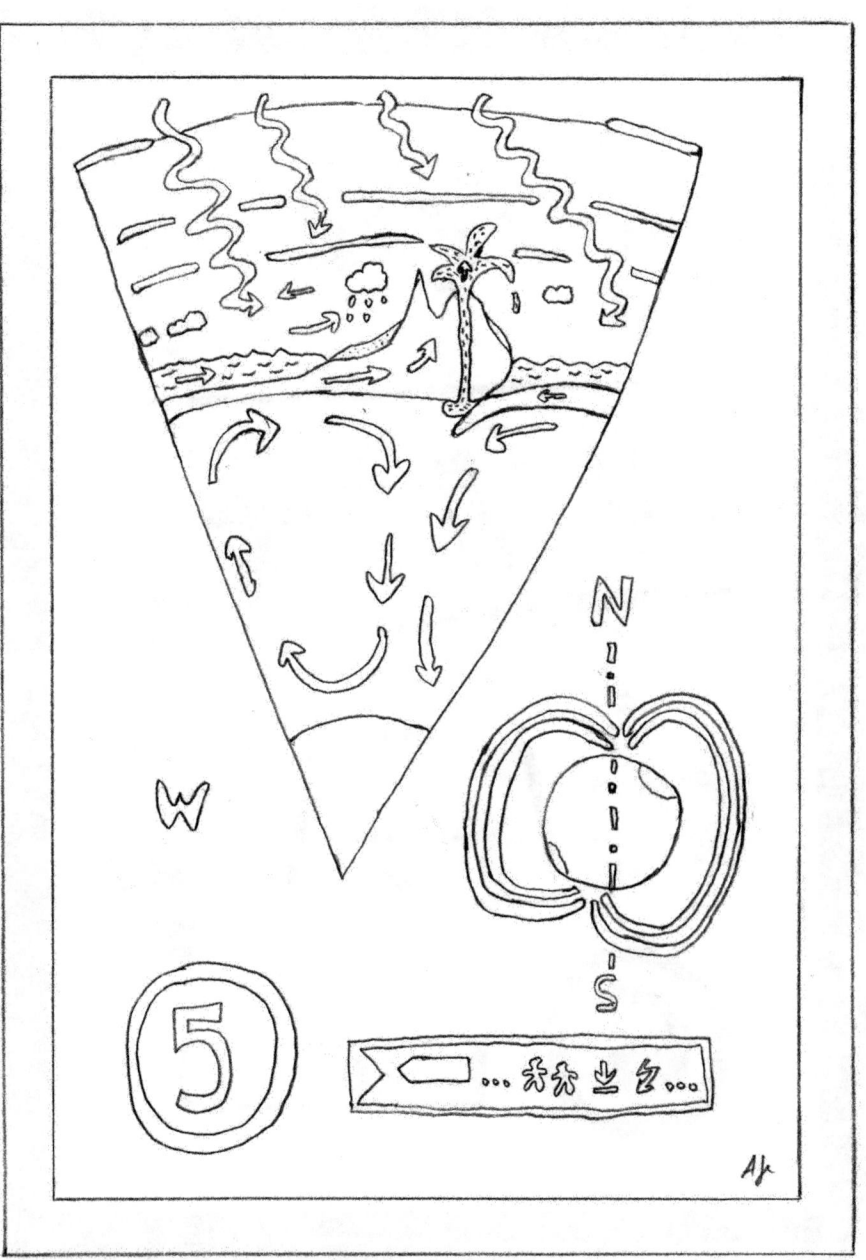

W

N
S

5

6. Chapter: Life

As we saw in the last chapters, we live on a stable, changing earth that revolves around the sun. We will now look at how, with the help of the Sun, it was possible to create on Earth what is the subject of this chapter: Life.

From inorganic to organic building materials

A prerequisite for the creation and development, for the evolution of life, at the beginning of our Earth, is both the presence of water and the fact that the earth orbits around the sun in the so-called "habitable zone." This is the distance at which it is warm enough due to the amount of solar radiation that water is not only present as ice, and cool enough that it is not only present as water steam but also as liquid water.

Chemical reactions, for example, in the saltwater of the primordial sea and especially along volcanic vents, or caused by the energy of lightning strikes, could have created new substances, probably amino acid molecules. Further chemical reactions out of these could result in larger protein molecules.

One type of molecule, **DNA**, is capable of copying itself. DNA is a long, double-spiral molecule strand consisting of two parallel strands that are connected in the middle by molecular bridges. There are only four bridge ends: Guanine, which connects to cytosine, and adenine, which connects to thymine. DNA molecules can separate at these bridge ends. If sufficient building materials are available, the counterparts can attach themselves to the open ends and complete themselves together to form a strand again. In this way, the molecule has doubled and therefore multiplied.

From chemistry to biology

Now it would be advantageous to have something around the DNA strand that protects it from damage and provides it with new and suitable molecular building blocks. The solution is a **cell** with DNA, for example, in the cell nucleus, and around it cell plasma in a cell membrane. In addition to DNA duplication, the cells also multiply by cell division.

But how can a cell build up around DNA? Well, there is another molecule, **RNA**. It has the characteristic that it only builds upon parts of the opened DNA, breaks away again, and then causes the formation especially of other proteins, which in turn form the cell.

The information about which proteins are formed and how is contained in the sequence of the four different DNA bridge ends. This is like the letters in a word. An information unit on the DNA strand is called a **gene**. They could initially have been created by randomly stringing together the DNA building blocks. In fact, most of the DNA in the cells still have no construction manual. All living beings on earth function according to this principle.

Copy errors, chemical reactions, or radioactive radiation can repeatedly lead to changes in the DNA and, consequently, also in the cell. This is called **mutation.**

We can imagine that most changes lead to deterioration, but some to improvement. What functions survive and multiply, what does not function or no longer functions disappears. This is called **selection**.

High-level organisms also develop offspring from a mixture of DNA strands that are twice present and can even selectively switch individual genes on or off.

Fossil remains of the first traces of life date back to around the year -3.75 billion. The very long time and the extreme number of molecules and living beings made many changes possible.

Over time, microorganisms emerge. **Fungal** cells can utilize nutrients in humid environments. **Plant** cells can do photosynthesis, which means to convert carbon dioxide (CO_2) and water (H_2O) with the help of the sunlight into sugar ($C_6O_6H_{12}$), which they use to build up temselves and to produce energy. The waste product is oxygen (O_2), which can be dissolved in water and air like carbon dioxide. **Animal** cells can feed on others, digest them, and in the mitochondria of their cells, gain energy to live from the back-reaction of sugar with oxygen to carbon dioxide and water.

From single-celled organisms to larger organisms

Several cells have combined to form **multicellular organisms**. Life developed this ability relatively late. Multicellular fossils can only be identified in the oceans from around the year -550 million. In multicellular organisms, cells can specialize in a division of labor, be stronger together, and when a single cell dies, the multicellular organism itself can survive. These advantages also apply to **groups** of living beings.

Sexuality enables the exchange and combination of genetic information and thus the faster dissemination of life-supporting genes. Also, the choice of partner allows targeted selection. Relatively quick reproduction and then relatively early **dying** accelerates the improvement process, and the old are no longer in competition with the young. In humans, for example, a natural reduction in hormone levels and the shortening of telomeres during cell division - in addition to damage caused by highly reactive radicals - result in aging and self-destruction in death. Also **intelligent** life forms have an advantage. They can outwit less capable ones and solve new life problems themselves.

From the **water**, life developed later on **land** and sometimes, as with whales, also back. The **air** is also used as a habitat.

Plants absorb sunlight and carbon dioxide via leaves and water and nutrients via roots. Stems serve as a connection. In the battle for sunlight, bushes and trees with wooden trunks grow beside herbs and grasses. Some, such as algae, mosses, and ferns, reproduce without blossoming. Blooming plants use wind or insects to transport their pollen. Some form fruits that animals eat and thus distribute the seeds they contain.

In the **animal** kingdom, for example, fish, amphibians, reptiles, birds, insects, and mammals are created. Different organs in the body perform various tasks. For instance, gills in fish and mostly lungs in terrestrial animals draw oxygen from the environment. Birds and mammals keep the body temperature constant. Some hatch offspring from laid eggs. In insects, this often results in a worm or caterpillar that pupates and then transforms into the actual insect. Mammals give birth to their young alive and initially supply them with milk.

All species must master **metabolism** for energy production and detoxification, **protection** from the sometimes dangerous environment, and **reproduction** to survive with each other and sometimes against each other and to develop de-facto towards a better life.

The task at the end of the chapter

Task 6 **My story (my curriculum vitae) until today?**

Note briefly how you have evolved into the vibrant person you are today. Think again about the three previous tasks and complete it chronologically.

6. My story (my curriculum vitae) until today:

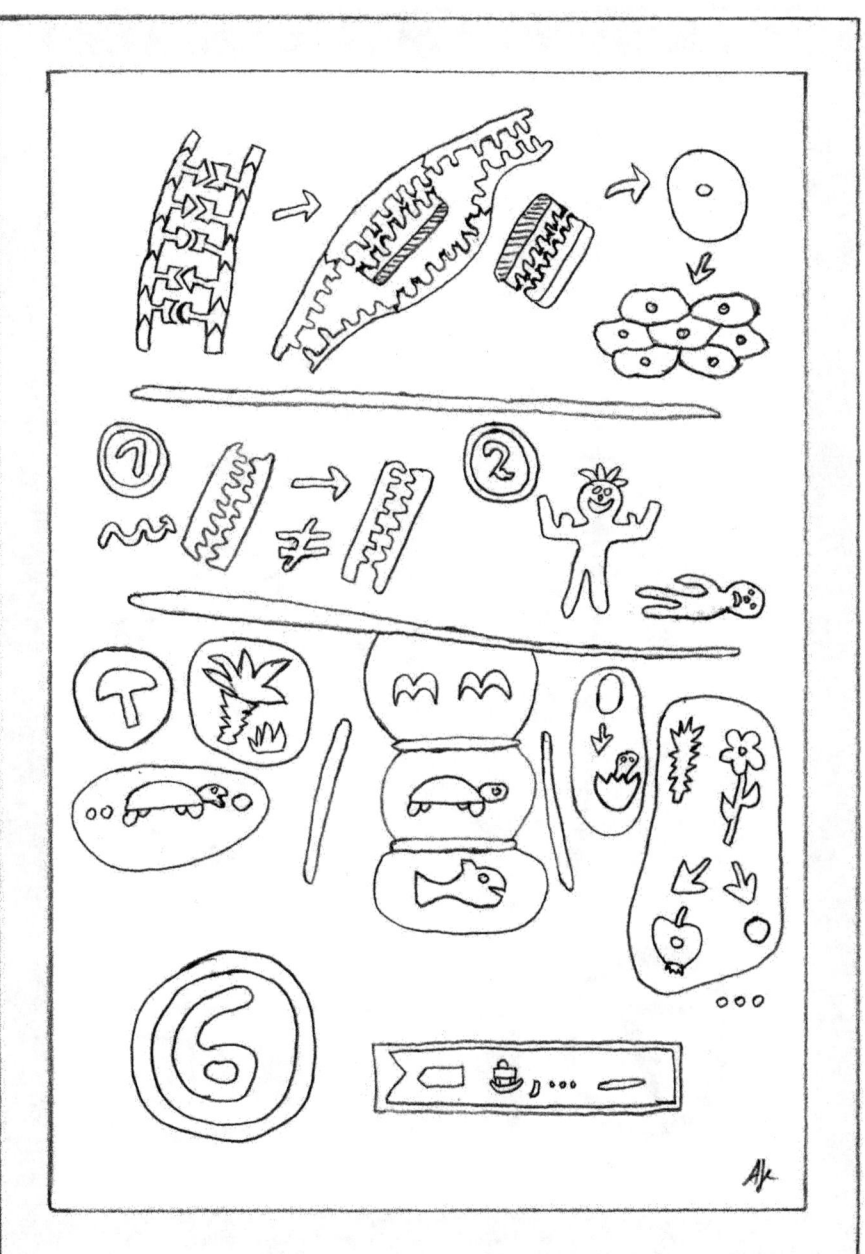

49

7. Chapter: History

The task of the last chapter was to give an overview of your story, your personal history. In this chapter, we look at the history of the world and especially of humankind. With this, we will also complete the part of your story between the origin of the world up to your grandparents, your parents, and you.

I repeat: From nothing arose dark energy, with the Big Bang about 14 billion years ago also bright energy. Galaxies were formed, in one of those our solar system emerged about 4.6 billion years ago, in which life originated on our planet Earth.

The Prehistoric Age

Different kinds of living beings develop, and most of them eventually become extinct again.

Continents migrate, separate, or combine. Some seabeds form mountains, erosion removes them again, and deposits can become new layers of rock or oil. Massive volcanic eruptions emit ashes and greenhouse gases and can cause cooling, warming, and extinction of species worldwide. Photosynthesis breaks down carbon dioxide and brings oxygen into the air; it creates the ozone layer that protects against radiation. Changing solar activity has further influences.

As a result, there are always severe **climate fluctuations.** Since -2.4 billion there are ice ages, in which the polar caps and partly nearly the whole earth are covered with ice.

There are also temperature fluctuations within ice ages and warm periods. The amount of ice on Earth changes the sea level. Coasts can sometimes be land, sometimes seafloor.

Warm water binds less oxygen than cold water. In very warm ocean parts, animal life can no longer breathe, the water can "tip over," form rotting gases and make life more difficult even on land.

Larger species of animal life can be found in the sea at around -550 million. On land, plant life develops from approximately -450 million, later also animal life.

Around the year -250 million, Siberian volcanic eruptions probably cause the most massive mass extinction to date. Dinosaurs became extinct after an asteroid impact in Central America around the year -65 million.

From **vertebrates** living in the water, **mammals** develop on land and from there, very reliably in Africa, until at the latest -5 million, human-like creatures. They begin to walk upright, using tools, fire, and perhaps even language.

By -160,000 at the latest, they will have become Homo sapiens, **man** today. Other human species, such as the Neanderthal, are now extinct.

The Stone Age

The people probably live in **smaller groups**, maybe 20 to 60, with a chief and druid, and from **hunting**, fishing, and **gathering**. In the center east of Africa, i.e., in the area of the equator, the temperature is similar throughout the year, often a little over 20 °C warm.

Fruits, herbs, or animals can be collected and hunted all year round. Simple objects such as spears, arrows, stone tools such as fist wedges, blowpipes, wooden objects, or skins help with hunting, transportation, and probably also with the defense or expansion of own hunting and gathering areas opposite other groups. People live in huts, caves, or tents. To this day, you can find remains in caves, excavations, moors, or underwater.

If not enough food is found, some will starve to death. So the groups must not become too large, so that nature can provide enough food for everyone in an accessible environment or that you can quickly relocate. If groups divide and one moves further, two groups of a tribe emerge. If some people want or have to leave a group, they may start a new clan.

Humans also spread outside Africa. Different languages, cultures, and races develop in and from different tribes. Religions arise from spiritual intuition and from attempts to explain the world with the otherworrldly, to give hope, and to strengthen rules, power, and community.

To the end of the last cold-period, in which the north-polar glacier-ice reaches as far as to Central Europe, groups start with **agriculture and cattle-breeding** from approximately -8000, in the area of the "fertile crescent" probably somewhat earlier. Now, food can be produced and stored for times of need and cold winters, also thanks to breeding higher yielding animals and plants. The surpluses are sufficient to feed **craftsmen** who can, for example, specialize in processing food or making clothes or living space.

The Age of Civilization

New materials: Ceramics, copper, charcoal, bronze, glass, iron, and new techniques: Potter's wheel, wheel, carriages, improvements in the ship, house and bridge construction, **state structures,** and around -3000 the **script** let the first advanced civilizations of antiquity develop.

Inventories and riches now make looting worthwhile. Walled **cities** and societies with nobility and clergy at the top emerge. They were responsible for security and order in palaces, fortresses, and castles, or for religion in churches, monasteries, and temples. In return, farmers and craftsmen, some of them slaves, provide the authorities with taxes and services. However, soldiers are not only used for protection, but also for maintaining power, **war**, oppression and exploitation.

From about 1500, in Europe, this period is called "modern times," the 1000 years before the Middle Ages, Europeans continue this policy of submission for almost 500 years with ships and firearms even in colonies. In Europe, letterpress printing and universities emerged in increasingly secularized states. **Globalization** is increasing.

Particularly from around 1800 onwards, **knowledge** and technical skills increase at an accelerated rate. The theory of evolution is published, the understanding of how life functions and develops becomes more precise. Larger and larger **factories** emerge, as well as engines, reinforced concrete, plastics, explosives, forms of electrical energy use, telephones, cars, and anesthesia.

From 1900 onwards, conclusive explanations of the structure of matter and the origin of the world, such as the theory of relativity and the Big Bang, quantum mechanics, or the standard model of elementary particles, arose. Airplanes, vaccination, antibiotics, psychotropic drugs, the pill, radio, television, computers, the Internet, and mobile phones are added.

Nationalist thinking and technology led from 1914 to 1918 to the First World War and from 1939 to 1945 to the Second World War with the dropping of two atomic bombs. Politically, the world was divided into a capitalist West and a communist East until about 1990. The tendency is toward democracy with a social market economy. There are approximately 200 states. Through the use of technology, a single farmer can feed over 100 people by the year 2000. The number of people and the environmental and natural damage caused by them is rising dramatically.

The tasks at the end of the chapter

Task 7.1 **My general worldview?**

Task 7.2 **My gerneral self-image?**

Task 7.3 **What gives meaning to my life?**

Who are you, and what do you live for? Just give it a try.

7.1 My general worldview:

7.2 My general self-image:

7.3 What gives meaning to my life:

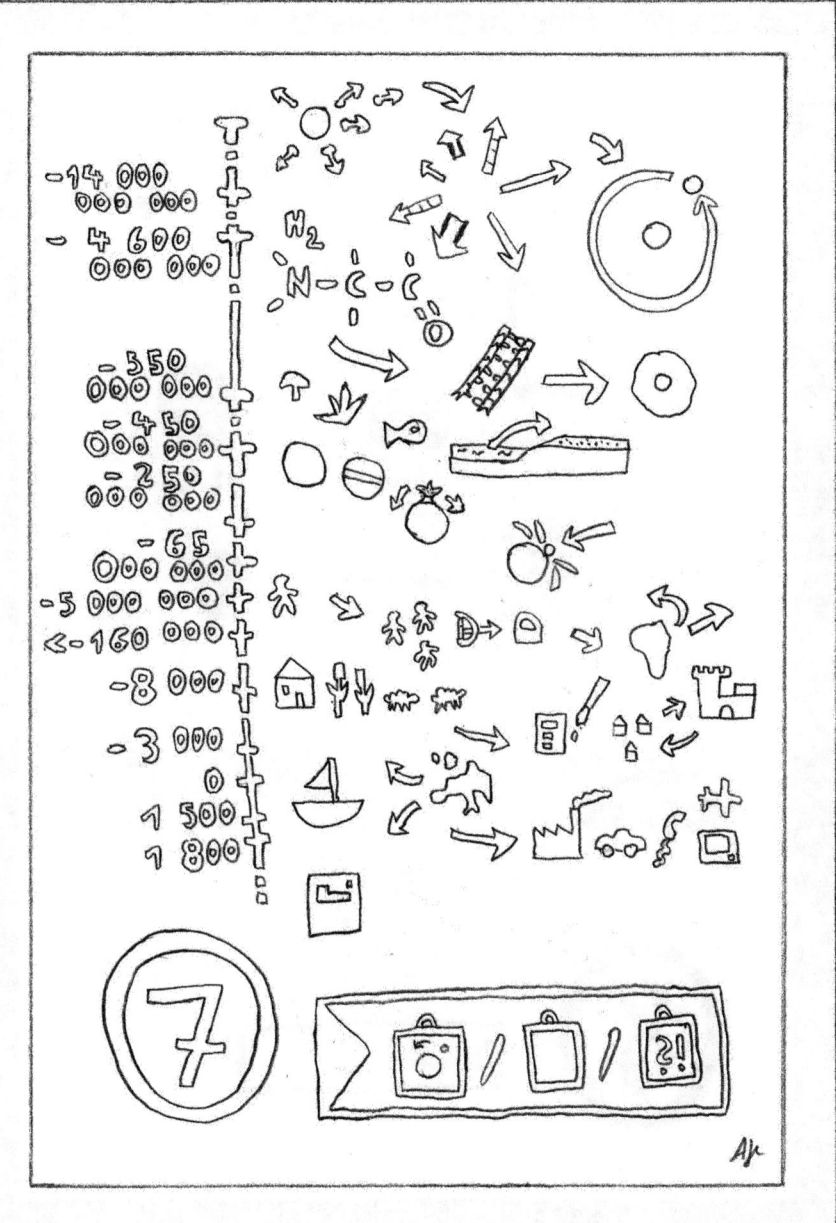

8. Chapter: Technology

In the last chapters, we examined the evolution of the world. We humans have something that we can use to intervene very potently in this development, and we are now going to look at it: Technology.

The tasks in the last chapter were not easy, and probably everyone has to find his own answer or leave it open. In this chapter, the question that stands out for me, is, who do we want to be as human beings? The ones who use the intellect of the most intelligent living creature on earth and with it our technical means to exploit and destroy the world, or to preserve our common habitat and, where possible, to make it even more livable?

Again, I can only present this topic in excerpts. Maybe it is repetition for you, perhaps you want to know more, maybe you are glad that this is it? Let's see.

The bio- and nutrition technology

First, let us look at two things with which humans intervene, specifically in the evolution of living beings.

For **breeding**, selection is used. Only specially intended specimens of plants or animals are reproduced. For example, we humans have bred dogs from wolves or cereals from grass.

In **genetic engineering**, mutation is induced purpurposefully. Viruses are used to modify the DNA of a first cell from which a new living being with the new characteristics grows. In this way, for example, firmer, more durable tomatoes were produced.

Techniques for **cultivation**, irrigation, fertilization, and pest control increase the yield. And **processing** techniques such as grinding into flour or cooking often make food more edible.

Mathematics

Mathematics is a mental technique for solving problems logically, detached from individual cases. It works with **numbers**, for example: 0, 1, 2, 3, 4, 5, 6, 7, 8, 9, 10, 11, 12, ... and mathematical **rules**, for example:
  Adding: $1 + 2 = 3$, subtracting: $5 - 2 = 3$;
  Multiply: $3 \times 2 = 6$; Divide: $7 : 2 = 3,5$.
  And if $a : b = c : e$ then $a = b \times c : e$.
A part of 100 parts is called one percent.

The measurement technology

A clock measures **time**: Per day 2 hours (h) per hour 60 minutes (min) and per minute 60 seconds (s).

On a tape measure, the **distance** of one meter (m) can be divided into 10 decimeters, 100 centimeters (cm) or 1000 millimeters (mm), and theoretically into one million micro, one billion nano and one billion picometers. 10 is called deca and 100 hecto. 1000 meters is one kilometer (km). Mega is a million, giga a billion and tera a trillion of something.

An **area** that is one meter long by one meter wide is one square meter (m^2).

A **space** that is ten centimeters long, wide and high (multiplied) is one liter (l) or 0.001 cubic meters (m^3).

We move at a **speed** of about four kilometers per hour (km/h) while hiking.

A circle has an **angle**sum of 360 degrees.

The **weight** of one liter of water at sea level is 1000 grams (g) or one kilogram (kg).

The **force** of one joule (J) acts when we lift 100 grams against the gravity of the earth by one meter.

The air **pressure** at sea level is about 1 bar.

Water boils at sea level at a **temperature** of about 100 degrees Celsius, and it freezes at zero degrees.

Below **pH** 7, a liquid is acidic, above that alkaline.

One meter away from a candle, it is about 1 lux, outside on a bright sunny day about 100,000 lux **bright**.

At **radioactive radiation** exposure from space, a person reaches about one millisievert (mSv) per year.

The **frequency** 1 hertz (Hz) is one impulse per second.

With **electric current**, which is flowing electrons, the strength of the charge separation is given as voltage in volts (V) and the quantity of the electron current flow in amperes (A). The electrical power one watt (W) is one volt multiplied with one ampere or one joule per second.

The communication and information technology

Language is a communication technique. With the vocal cords, we generate sound waves in the air that our ear perceives. If sound waves are converted into electrical impulses or radiation impulses, they can be conducted through metal conductors or fiber optic cables or "sparked" electromagnetically and converted back at the receiver. This is how the **telephon** and **radio** work. **Writing** are signs for sounds, syllables or words.

A **computer** processes bits: Power on or power off, as bytes, that's eight bits.

The propulsion technology

With **combustion engines**, gas or atomized liquid is brought to explosion-like combustion and consequently to expansion. This pushes a piston away, which moves a mechanism. In the **electric motor**, an electric current generates a magnetic field that causes a magnet in the core of the engine to rotate. In the dynamo or **generator**, conversely, the rotary motion leads to the generation of electricity.

If you connect a motor to the wheels of a vehicle via a gearbox, you have a **car** or a **train.** If you move an upward-pointing inclined surface in the air, it is pushed upwards by the air pressure on the lower or front side. This is how airplanes fly. **Ships** will swimm when buoyancy caused by the water displaced by the hull is greater than the downforce caused by the weight of the ship. Propellers, turbines, or ship's screws shovel air or water backward and in return, move the aircraft or ship forwards. A jet or rocket engine works by repulsion of mass during combustion.

Other techniques

When clay is fired, it becomes solid, and ceramic is produced. If iron ore is heated with coal, iron is obtained. Glass is obtained by melting quartz sand. Cement is obtained by heating and crushing certain rocks. If cement, sea sand, and water are mixed with steel rods, they are hardened into reinforced concrete. If chemically long organic molecules are produced, plastics can be created. If you weave or knit natural or artificial fibers, you get fabrics. If you extract the bacterial poison from certain fungi, you have antibiotics. If you extract the active ingredient from the willow bark, you have a painkiller. Vaccination brings weakened germs into the body where the immune system can learn to defend itself. X-ray use the body's different transparency for the x-rays, and ultrasound uses the various reflections of sound waves for imaging procedures. In light bulbs, electric current is used to bring energy into a system, such as a spiral-shaped metal fiber, which mainly causes electrons to jump back and forth. During this a part of the energy supplied is radiated in the form of light, as in the case of the sun or flames.

The task at the end of the chapter

Task 8 **My probable future?**

From technology back to us: What will happen next in your life? Concentrate on a rough assessment: What will await you professionally and privately?

Think of the last task: Which of that gives you meaning? Will you contribute to a good life?

8. *My probable future:*

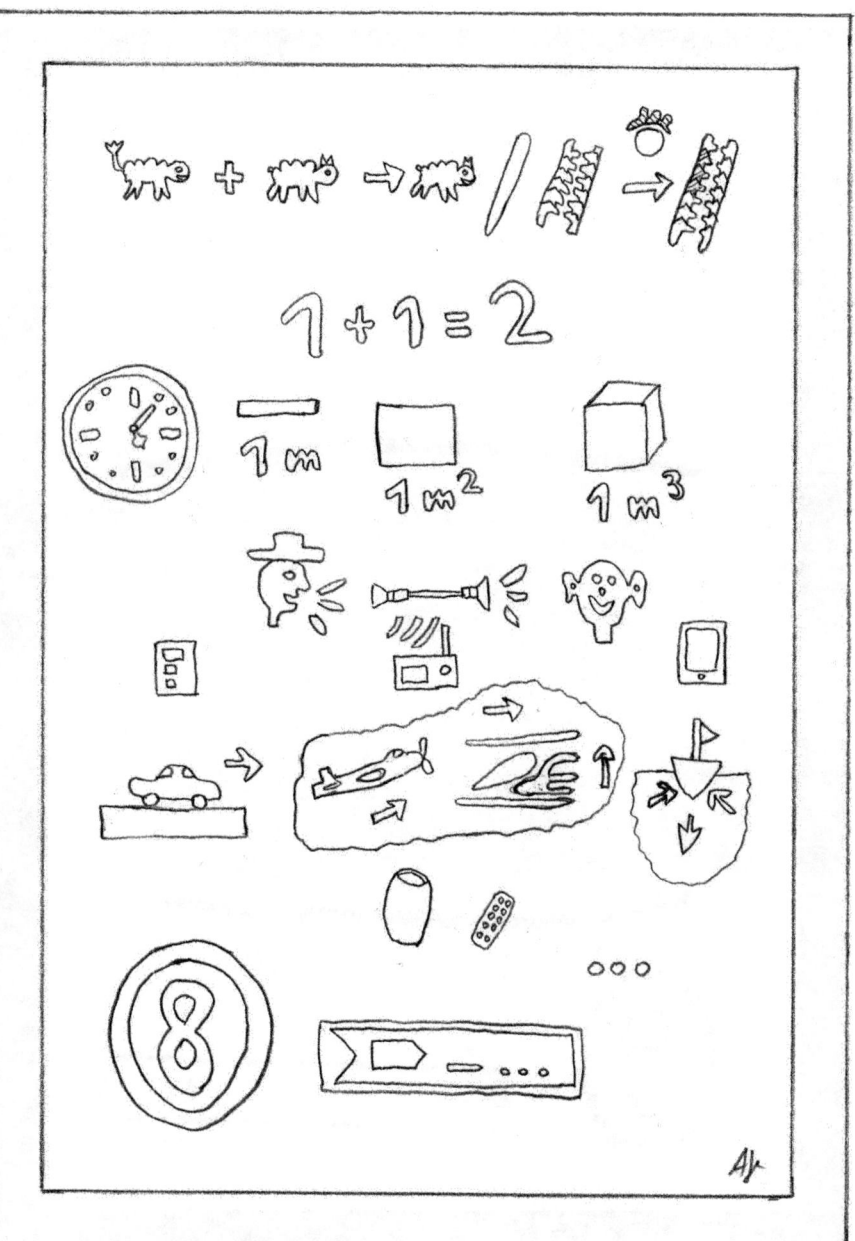

9. Chapter: Environment

The last chapter was about technology. Its use even changes the outer image of our earth. If up to now it was about general topics, in the following chapters, we will still stick to basics. But we will become more precise in content and tasks. This text is about the global living space, and the task is about the living space at your home.

Let us imagine that we are flying towards our habitat, the earth. From a distance, our planet looks like a predominantly blue sphere. The clouds look like white veils, and from time to time, we see the land, perhaps in green, yellow, brown, red, grey, or white.

The seas and the continents

Let us begin our mental flight over the Earth, where the story of us humans began: in Africa. Looking north, the Mediterranean Sea separates the continent from Europe, and in the northeast, it is connected to the largest continent, Asia, by a narrow landmass. South of Asia lies the Indian Ocean, even further south, above the South Pole, Antarctica and in between, in the southeast, Oceania. Further east, we cross the largest ocean, the Pacific, to America. North and South America are connected by a narrow land bridge, and between them lies the Gulf of Mexico. Further east we cross the Atlantic Ocean back to Africa.

The mountains, plains, and valleys

We continue our flight in thought. On the earth's surface, we now notice two mountain ranges. One from west to east, which seems to begin with the Alps in Central Europe and ends in Central Asia in the most extensive mountain range of the world, the Himalaya. There is the highest mountain, Mount Everest, which is over 8,800 meters high. Another mountain range in America stretches from south to north along the west coast of the continent. In the south, these are the Andes, in the north, the Rocky Mountains. In Africa, the south and east are more mountainous.

We find the lowest point on land east of the Mediterranean Sea at the Dead Sea, with over 400 meters below sea level. The deepest place underwater is with about 11,000 meters, the Mariana trench in the western Pacific.

Climate and vegetation

If the temperature on land is above the growth limit of five degrees Celsius, and if it is not too hot and it rains enough, then life can thrive well regularly. Also, brooks, rivers, and lakes are often formed, and many creatures live in and around them.

Now let's fly mentally through the different climate zones. We start at the equator, which is about 40,075 kilometers long. Here it is warm, because here, per surface area, most rays of the sun reach the ground. Heated air rises up, air from north and south flows as trade wind and brings clouds, which are pushed upwards, cool down and then rain down. In a warm and humid climate, there is rainforest on about two percent of the earth's surface, in which about 50 percent of the species living on land live. The Amazon rainforest in northern South America is the largest. There is also a tropical rainforest in the Congo Basin in central Africa and southern Asia. We find the rainiest areas mainly south of the Himalayas, during the rainy season, during the summer monsoon.

North and south of the tropics, there are often hot and dry deserts. It is often the trade wind that blows the clouds away towards the equator. In extreme cases, the temperature can reach between 50 and 70 degrees Celsius. The largest dry desert is the Sahara, which covers almost all of North Africa. Also, in Middle Asia, Oceania, or America, we can find larger deserts.

Further north and further south on the earth, there are moderate climate zones. The wind blows in the west wind belt mostly from the western direction, and it often rains the whole year through again and again. Also, there are significant differences in summer and winter temperatures, especially in the inner-continental region.

New ice forms above the North and South Poles, especially in winter, which floats at the North Pole on the Arctic Ocean and covers the Antarctic kilometer-thick at the South Pole all year round. There the temperature can drop to -90 degrees Celsius; along the fish-rich coasts, life on land is possible to a limited extent.

Quite a lot of different things, what you can see there, on a mental flight over the earth, I think.

Human life

Again and again, we will see other humans and their traces. People now live almost everywhere on earth; on the coast or in the inland, in the lowlands or in the mountains. Some of them live in the countryside: if we fly over it mentally, we will probably see farms or villages and not only occasionally agricultural fields or forests. Most people live more and more in big cities. Imagine flying over a city and seeing a city center with office buildings, department stores, restaurants, leisure facilities, and public places. Next to it we also see parks and more expensive residential areas. In the suburbs, we can mostly see industrial areas and cheaper residential buildings.

And we see how also people have shaped the earth between cities and villages with roads, rails, bridges, walls, and waterways.

If we pay attention to the appearance of us humans during our sightseeing flight, then the average is slightly different. For example, a black African has dark skin and often full lips. In the southeast of Asia, people often have smooth black hair and a flatter face. In northern Europe, on the other hand, people tend to be light-skinned, prone to sunburn, often have pronounced facial features and sometimes blond hair. America is characterized by a common mixture of predominantly European whites, African blacks, and indigenous peoples.

If we look deeper, we can see that the individual countries and regions also differ from each other in the state system, in language, culture, and mentality, in economic performance and in general technical and industrial development.

And now? What impression did you have of our mental flight over our habitat Earth?

I think: Although the individual habitats and cultures may be very different, we all live in one habitat, on one Earth. Significant dangers from outside or those that we cause also threaten us all.

Humans, the most intelligent form of life we know, are part of the only surviving human species, Homo sapiens. Our ancestors probably all come from Africa. Our common ancestors come from the sea, and we living beings are all shaped by our genes. And that is, like everything that is around us and with us and within us, energy in various forms that probably comes from the source at the place of the Big Bang. That feels connecting to me. We are all parts of one universe.

The task at the end of the chapter

Briefly describe the part of the universe you live in:

Task 9 **My local environment (and home)?**
(Location, climate, nature, urban offers,
typical people, ...?)

9.   My local environment (and home):

Location:

Climate:

Nature:

Urban offers:

Typical people:

Other:

71

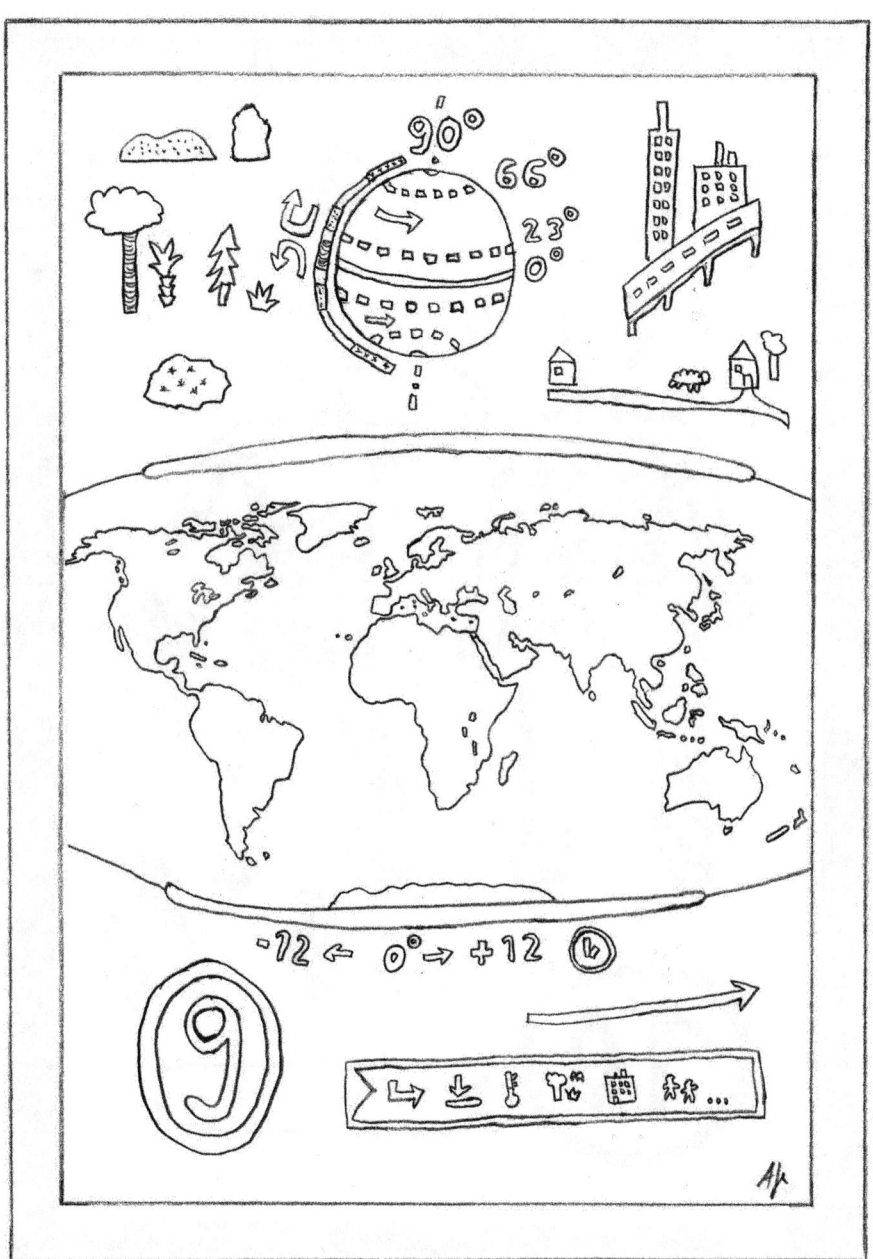

72

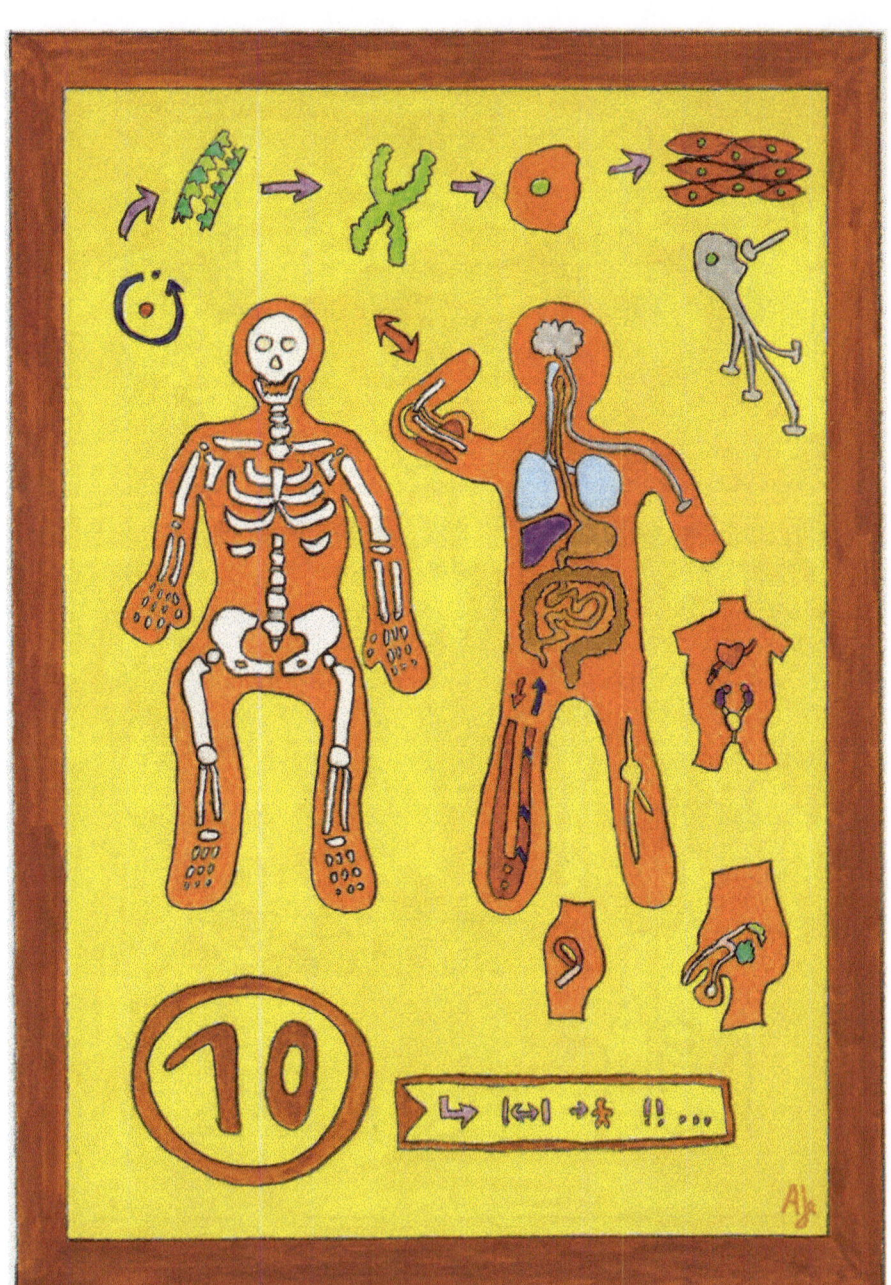

10. Chapter: Human

In the last chapters, we received an impression of our habitat and its origin. We learned that we humans are a part of it: we all consist of the building materials of the universe and are similar to other living beings. We interact with our environment and contribute to shaping it. Let us now take a closer look at humans.

Humans in general

We, humans, are biologically the most mentally developed land mammals. Our genes are about 98 percent identical to those of some monkey species.

The individual human being is shaped by inherited genes and by the environment in which he or she lived and lives. Some of our characteristics, such as eye color, are genetically determined, others, such as language, we acquired through our environment. Others, such as intelligence, are shaped by genes and the environment.

We perceive ourselves as one being, with body and mind. Let us first look at our body.

Our structure on a small scale

Primarily, an adult human being is made up of approximately 100 trillion cells. Each nucleus contains 46 chromosomes. 44 are the same for men and women. In the case of women, two X chromosomes are added, in the case of men one X chromosome and one Y chromosome.

The chromosomes contain on our double spiral DNA with approximately three billion base pairs, our nearly 30,000 genes with our genetic information. It is there twice: once from the father and once from the mother.

At heredity, the information of the two genes mix differently, and some characteristics seem to be dominant, recessive, or intermediate. Children are, therefore, never completely identical to their parents.

And, of course, our cells, meaning us, consist of atoms and molecules; we are made of approximately 70 percent water; protein, and fat are also typical building materials.

Our protection, our stability, and mobility

The skin protects our body externally. Hair that grows about one centimeter per month, continually renewing cornea, durable dermis and sebum as a protective film as well as sweat glands for cooling, are elements of the skin.

On the inside, our bones give us stability. Muscles consist of cells that can contract. They are usually attached to the bones via tendons and can, therefore, move our limbs. Joints often have cartilage, which protects the bones during motion.

Infectious agents such as viruses, bacteria, or small parasites in our body are mainly fought by the white blood cells that eat them, for example. Coagulants in the blood cause wound closure.

Our energy supply

By breathing, we absorb air into our lungs via the nose or mouth and the windpipe. Oxygen is absorbed by the red blood cells in the small air sacs of the lungs, and carbon dioxide is released.

By eating, we absorb nutrients into the blood, via our mouth, esophagus, and stomach, and especially in the small intestine. Water is extracted from the indigestible rest into the colon. It is finally excreted via the rectum, together with intestinal bacteria and dead intestinal cells.

Our heart pumps our blood, in adults about five to six liters, via veins through the body. When resting as an adult, it beats about 60 to 80 times per minute, at medium intensity about 120 to 130 times per minute and at maximum strength over 180 beats per minute. Infants have a resting pulse of about 130, children 100, and seniors 90. In arteries, in adults, it is pressed into the body at a pressure of about 120 and flows back to the heart at about 80 in the veins. The valves in the veins prevent the blood from flowing back into the heart.

Lymphatic vessels, which mainly transport more voluminous building materials into larger veins, supplement the system.

The liver is responsible for converting various molecules in the blood, for example, fat into sugar, the kidneys for flushing out waste products via the urinary bladder, and, above all, the bone marrow and partly the spleen and thymus for new blood.

Our cells regularly extract our vital energy from the exothermic reaction of sugar with oxygen to carbon dioxide and water. Some cells can also burn fat molecules or, although rarely, react without oxygen. In this way, they also maintain our body temperature at around 37 degrees Celsius.

Our reproduction

Our reproductive organs serve to procreate new life, to bring it into the world, and to feed it.

Our perception

Through our eyes, we can see a part of the electromagnetic radiation, visible light, and with it different colors and distances. Through our ears, we can hear sound waves in the air as different loud and high tones. Our sense of balance is created by the archways in our ears. Through our nose, we can smell different molecules in the air as scents. Through our tongue we perceive sugar as sweet, acid as sour, bitter, salty and umami. Only together with the smell does the full taste of our food emerge. Besides pain, our skin can also sense temperature and touch. We can probably also feel electromagnetic "energies" and thus sometimes feel whether someone is looking at us from behind, a person with whom we feel very connected is nearby or someone develops strong feelings.

Our control

Our information processing and control is mainly achieved with the help of nerve cells and hormones. We also use radiation energy for this.

Our central nervous system consists of the brain and spinal cord. Our brain probably forms our mind, and in it, different parts are responsible for different things. It is connected to the peripheral nervous system in the body via the spinal cord. The sympathetic part is mainly active during tension, the parasympathetic part during rest. We can control the animal part of the nervous system deliberately, but not the vegetative part. Nerve cells are connected to each other via many nerve tracts that end with synapses on other cells. On the nerve tracts impulses and thus information is passed on.

Hormones are chemicals that are secreted into the blood by glands and that often can cause a variety of different reactions in the body. They often also create feelings in our minds.

The task at the end of the chapter

Task 10 **My body?**
  (Measurements (height, weight, dress sizes...),
  appearance, special features...)

Also, think briefly how it was and how it will be, and feel how you relate to it. It's the only one you have!

10. My body:

My measurements (height, weight, dress sizes...):

My appearance and special features:

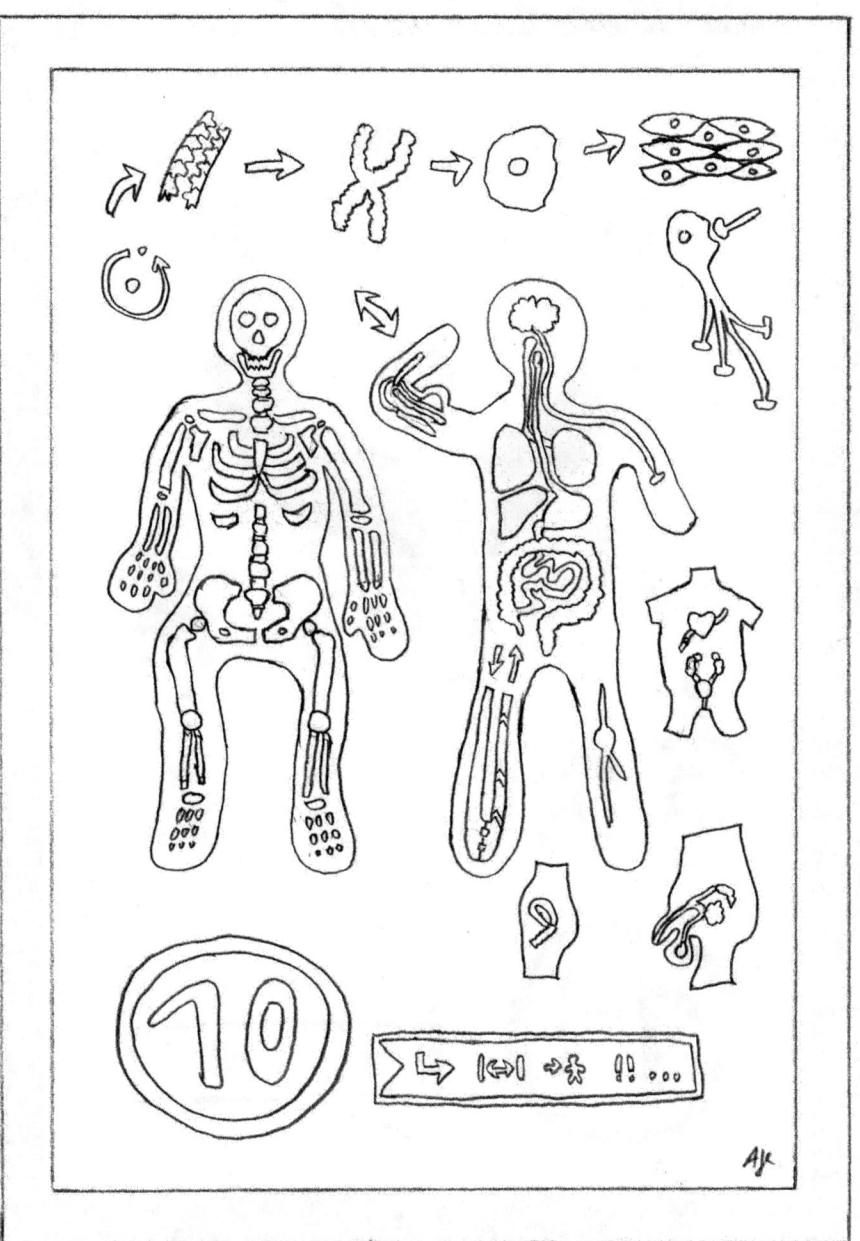

11. Chapter: Mind

In the last chapter, we mainly looked at the human body and alreay got an impression of how our body creates control. Somehow, this also creates what it is all about now: our mind.

The influence of the body

For instance, in our **brain**, part of our left cerebral hemisphere is responsible for controlling our right arm. Another part is specialized in image recognition and another in speech understanding. The cerebellum is probably mainly responsible for movement coordination. The brain stem, which every vertebrate has, controls above all the vital functions. The midbrain is primarily responsible for the transmission of signals from the sensory organs and for feelings.

For instance, **hormones** can be released via the pituitary gland. Endorphins, for example, make us less sensitive to pain and happier. The adrenaline from the adrenal cortex increases cardiovascular activity in stressful situations and prepares us for flight or battle. When testosterone is used, some cells behave as males.

Each individual **cell** is also capable of communication, control, and memory.

Together our spirit probably arises from this.

The mental self-awareness

Let us try to look at how we perceive our mind, its parts and its function.

In our **awareness**, or in our mind in the narrower sense, when we are not asleep or unconscious, our **I** (sometimes ego), like a boss with his big company, will experience some things consciously:

In the **perception** of the environment, we may see, hear, feel, smell, or taste something.
   Maybe we will **remember**, as an example, facts we have heard or read, or episodes we have experienced ourselves.

We might perceive a **feeling** or a mood with which perception or memory is linked, perhaps joy, interest, or peace. Or we think logically with our **minds**.

We may also **control** a movement of our body, the speaking of a word, or something else.

Or we listen to our **inner voice**: the part that explains, analyzes, assesses or warns us about something: I call it the inner critic. Or another part that perhaps tells us how we are, what we like, what we want, what astonishes us: we could call that part the inner child. If we give one side a serious, warm, and wise voice, the other a childlike one, we can distinguish them better. When we set our inner voice to "loud," we speak as if automatically.

The automatic comes from the unconscious part of our mind, that could be called our unconscious, our **soul** or our **inner self**. This part within us consists of a multitude of mechanisms that want to help us to live well:

It can not only control our voice, but also trance states, motion sequences, digestion, or cardiovascular activity as well as other things, independently.

It probably has two inner clocks. An independent one and one that follows the external, such as light or the amount of experience.

It transforms the signals of the sensory organs so that we can perhaps perceive them as colors, sounds, smells, or tastes.

It selects what comes into our consciousness so that we are not overwhelmed.

Appropriate memories, ideas, or feelings should help us to correctly evaluate what we are experiencing, to develop a will and to motivate to helpful reactions.

Sometimes our soul can steer us like an automat, or we are even forced to do something or to refrain from doing something, for example, if we pinch our eyelids reflexively or our muscles block when we no longer have strength. This should protect us from damage.

For our "inner compass", to recognize what is true, right, useful, or helpful for life, we use innate and learned things.

Instincts and reflexes, the ability to feel and some needs, which motivates us, for instance, in the life-preserving instinct, the herd instinct, the play instinct, and as an adult the sexual and brood care instinct, are probably innate.

Mainly learned in the conditioning and socialization process in childhood, adolescence and beyond, are above all attitudes, also conscience evaluations, typical behavior, habits, some goals or needs and experience, and factual knowledge.

Let us now try to perceive our **body** in our mind, from the toes to the very top.

We will also regularly perceive the things that are briefly connected to the body, such as clothing, jewelry, or tools, as part of us.

We often perceive external influences on our bodies clearly. Our body also belongs to us. And when someone holds our hand, they often touch us as a whole.

And there is something else that belongs to us. It is, so to speak, **our outer self**, the part of our environment that undoubtedly belongs to us. Think about what we own or what we have in possession.

People will also belong to us: Maybe we have a life partner, children, parents, friends or close acquaintances or we are part of one or more groups that belong to us, and we belong to them.

In our minds, we are aware of who or what belongs to us, and we will probably also **feel connected**. And what belongs to us, we often evaluate better than it is objectively seen.

And of course, there are also things which are not so closely connected with our spirit, whatever that may be.

Dealing with our spirit

I believe that in the course of the evolution of humans and in the course of our own lives, a spirit has developed that wants to take care of our life and species preservation as best as possible. Therefore it is good to trust it regularly.

Sometimes, however, needs, attitudes, or qualities that might have been appropriate in the Stone Age or in our childhood are no longer helpful.

We can guide our inner being a little by doing certain things, concentrating on certain sensations, thinking specific thoughts, or remembering or imagining certain things.

The tasks at the end of the chapter

In our minds, let us become aware of two important parts of ourselves:

Task 11.1 **My strengths?**

Task 11.2 **My weaknesses?**

(What can I do / what about me is very good, good, neutral, bad, very bad?)

What do others say about you?
How did you experience yourself - also in comparison with others - in certain situations? Where were you better, where worse? What did you do well or very well, what did you not do so well?

11.1 My strengths:

11.2 My weaknesses:

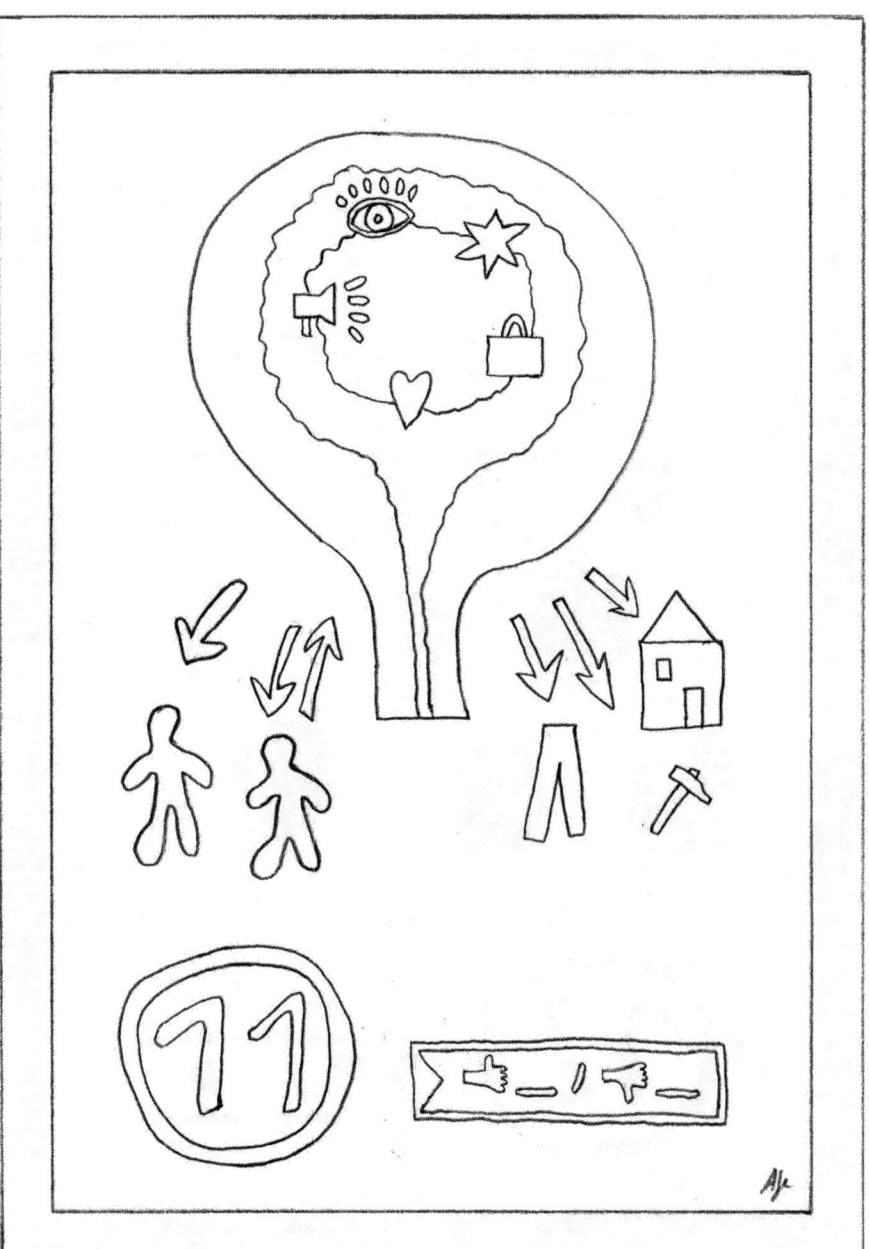

12. Chapter: Feelings

In the last chapter, we learned that we can perceive our feelings as a part of our mind. And now we will take a closer look at this significant part.

Feelings in general

Feelings are part of our mind. Almost always, our perception is backed by some weak or strong feelings.

If we receive a **stimulus** from our perception or from our thoughts, then this helps us to **evaluate** it quickly and to **motivate** ourselves **appropriately**.

Feelings are usually short-lived, then disappear again or are replaced by other feelings. If a feeling remains for a long time, we are in a **mood**.

When a feeling or mood is strong, we can almost only perceive or remember what matches it.

Feelings aren't self-explanatory. If we want to understand them, we have to think with our minds about their reasons. Often this is automatic, and often the cause of the emotion is also obvious.

Feelings can be flawed. If, for example, our psyche shifts a feeling, then it is possible that the anger that should have been directed at the boss at work, for example, now goes to the colleague who has nothing to do with it.

We **express** our feelings mainly through facial expressions, but also through gestures and the sound of our voice, and our cells can also feel some things electromagnetically or energetically. Not only can feelings cause emotions, but so can expression. Example: When we are happy, the corners of our mouths go up, when we pull up the corners of our mouths, this leads to happiness.

Good actors can simulate or suppress emotional expressions.

If we put ourselves in someone else's position, we can have **compassion**. In "rational empathy," we logically recognize how the other person is doing; in "emotional empathy," we feel the feelings that the other person presumably has within us. But we can also **delinerate** ourselves.

Being able to have, perceive, express, and read feelings in others is an almost wholly natural ability. Children are, therefore, particularly good at it. What we learn within limits is what triggers which feeling.

Regularly it is good to first pay close attention to our feelings and then deal with them well. With a trained mind, we should be able to do this automatically on a regular basis.

Some examples of feelings

Imagine someone taking something valuable from you that belongs to you, or lying to harm others. Then he does something terrible that you can influence. In the

91

first place, **anger**, passively defiance, helps you to recognize that. You may also remember other bad things on that occasion. And it motivates you to do something about it. Maybe you aggressively take back what was taken from you, or you rectify the lie. At the same time the other notices that he has done something that bothers you. He can then improve his behavior.

Now put yourself spiritually in the situation in which you are perhaps dressed very inappropriately among other people or you are dirty. This is poor behavior towards others that you can typically change. The **shame** you feel helps you to recognize this, to withdraw, and to improve the condition.

Imagine something threatening your health or your good life, maybe a physical or mental injury. The **pain** helps you to recognize where it is, what it is, and motivates you to retreat or to do something to improve or heal.

Another example: Maybe someone you loved has died. So something terrible has happened from your point of view, but you can't change it. You realize that you have to accept this. The **grief** helps you to recognize the loss, to process it, and to release bonds.

Imagine someone or something stronger than you is threatening you. A fright may shake you up. The **fear** helps you to recognize the danger and motivates you to escape or to rigidity. In extreme cases, you can react with panic or shock.

Imagine, for example, you see vomit, or you recognize malicious behavior that does not threaten you immediately. The **disgust** helps you to acknowledge that something could harm you and motivates you to stay away from it.

Imagine that someone has something that you would like to have and that, from your point of view, should instead belong to you or at least not to the other person. **Envy, jealousy,** or **resentment** let you see that.

Imagine you find an attainable goal that will improve your situation. The **will** to do so can make this visible to you and motivate action.

Thirst, hunger, chill, finding it too hot, curiosity, admiration, feeling of truthfulness, lust, tiredness, exhaustion, boredom, disappointment, remorse, helplessness, frustration, confusion, despair, despondency, loneliness, missing, closeness, feeling of solidarity, a feeling of home and **love** allow us to detect our needs and possibilities for drinking, eating, changing temperature, gaining new insights, mating, sleeping, relaxing, making a releasing change or let us feel a belonging or affection and motivate us accordingly. If we were able to satisfy our needs, we are regularly rewarded with a feeling of **joy**.

A feeling of **happiness** also follows joy when we recognize something good, perhaps something beautiful, fragrant, melodious, tasty, or something that feels pleasant. Something is missing, and now we receive it. We were lucky and receive something good unexpectedly. We managed a challenge, recognized something correctly, or

93

we proudly recognize that we have accomplished some-thing good, are good, or belong to something good. We are enthusiastic about something, satisfied with some-thing, or calm inside. We are relieved because something awful vanishes, or we realize that something will not harm us after all.

We can feel malicious joy when we realize that some-one else has suffered consequential harm. And if our op-ponent suffers damage, from our point of view, it may even be good.

We, of course, can remember something good or expect something good in anticipation.

The feeling of happiness motivates us to want some-thing good or to receive it again and again.

We will **laugh** regularly when something unusual and unexpected comes to us that we consider being logical and acceptable.

Sometimes we also have "in feeling" **behavioral patterns** or an **insight.** This can come from innate, instinctive, or mostly from learned, intuitive.

The tasks at the end of the chapter

After the last task, something important again:

Task 12.1 **My likes?**

Task 12.2 **My dislikes?**

(Love, like, neutral, not like, hate.)

12.1 My likes:

12.2 My dislikes:

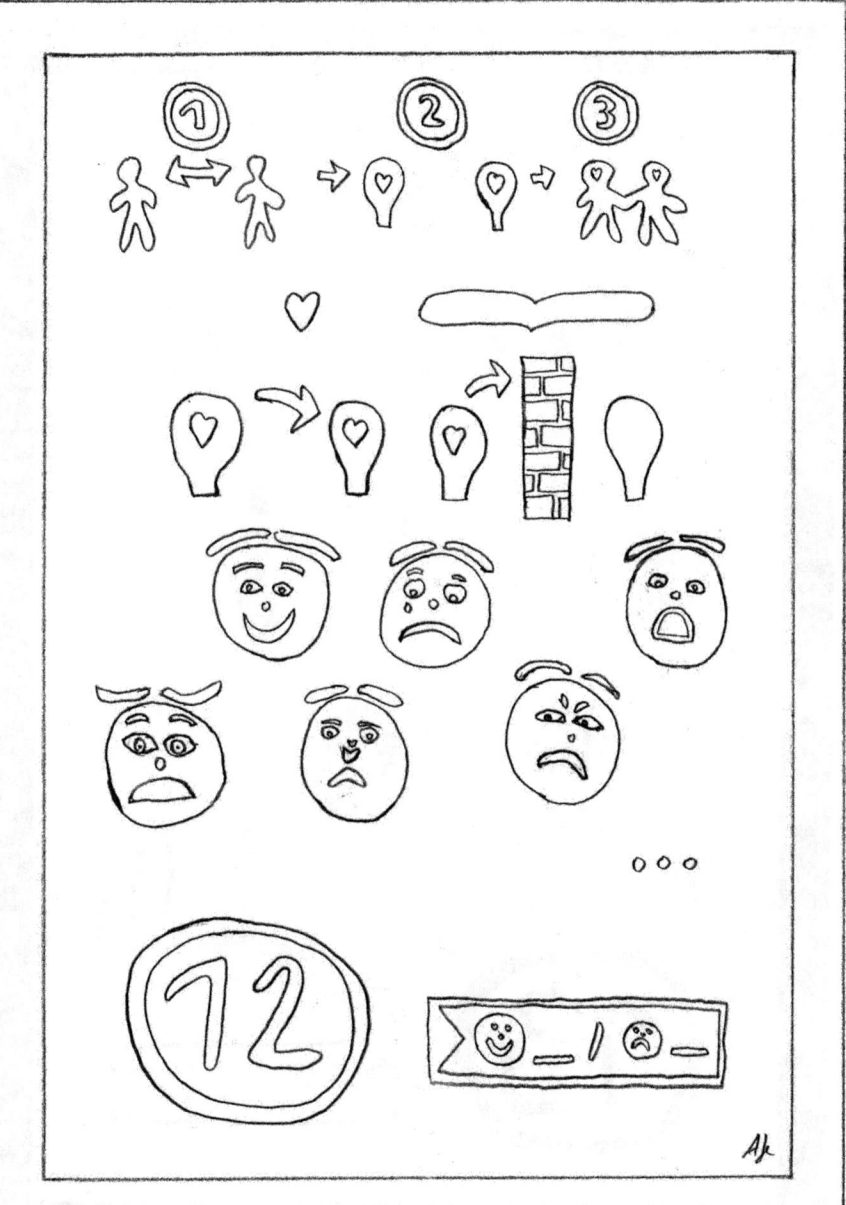

13. Chapter: Insight

We have already seen that feelings also help in recognizing. In general, it is now about possibilities of insight.

Insight in general

We can recognize something with our **feelings** and with our **minds**. What we already understood, learned, practiced, or repeated, will often be emotionally clear to us, will occur in time, or will happen automatically.

To recognize something well regularly means: to perceive it completely and correctly (**description**), to understand why it is (**analysis**), and to predict how it will change under certain conditions (**prognosis**).

One way to gain insight is **imitation**: We see what the others do or show us and simply copy it.

Thinking or feeling is another way. Maybe we want to recognize or be able to recognize something that nobody knows or can do yet. We consider fantasizing how it could be and then feel it.

Trying out or experimenting is, in the end, the way to check whether what others do or say or the result of thinking really works. If this is the case, it gives security and trust in truthfulness. And if we learn something from what we try out and what happens to us, we gain experience.

It is useful to regularly recognize what **is (the standpoint)**, what **should be (the goal)**, and, if necessary, how we can move from the actual to the desired **(the path)**.

Deciding

Let us assume that we want to know how we should **behave in concrete terms.** Often we will immediately have a decision in our minds for an action or omission. However, we can also make decisions as follows:

1. We phrase a **decision question,**
for example: "Should I eat some more?"

2. We **collect** sufficient **information** for this purpose: We clarify, for example: "What else is there to eat?" Or: "Am I already full?" Decision criteria can help you to recognize quickly and thoroughly.

Then we **arrange** the information: what are the arguments in favor, against and neutral? Example:

(+) To continue eating would still taste good.

(-) I've already eaten enough, and I'm already full.

(0) Eating more is neither unhealthy nor necessary.

Then we **evaluate**. We think, for example: "Over-eating can become unpleasant; later, if I am hungry again, I will enjoy it more to eat." Consequently, the second argument is given more importance.

3. We then briefly examine whether the question is now **ready for a decision**. Do we have all the necessary information? And is the time for the decision neither too late nor too early, because perhaps essential facts will change again before implementing it?

4. The **decision** is often the determination of what is better. In the example, we decide against continuing to

eat. As already mentioned, we can **think** with our mind, and also **feel** what is better. And both will influence each other.

Another possibility is to question a part of our **unconscious.** Example: Press with index finger and thumb of one hand against index finger and thumb of the other. A "Yes" or "Good" keeps the pressure intense, a "No" or "Bad" relaxes the muscle tension. Test this. If it works, ask if there is a willingness to make a decision. If so, ask the question and see what happens.

Alternatively, we can stand up: Tilting forwards means "yes," tilting backward means "no" and swaying "don't know." Or a pendulum: Up-down or forwards-back is "yes," left-right is "no," and circling is "neutral."

If it remains unclear or if reason, feeling, and the unconscious contradict each other, we can still decide or wait until the circumstances do this for us.

The search

To find, here's what we could do:

Unless it's clear what we're looking for: 1. Set **criteria,** how what we are looking to find is supposed to be. What should it have at least? What should it not have under any circumstances? What would be acceptable? What would be the optimum?

2. Going on a **search**. If you look at a lot or even almost everything before making a decision, you will regularly get the best. Those who make quick decisions as soon as something fits, are not only faster but often also more satisfied. The middle path seems optimal.

3. With any luck, we'll **find** something suitable.

Selecting

If we are faced with many alternatives and want to identify the best one, the following can help:

1. Make a **preselection** either by eliminating all those that certainly won't do or by selecting a few possible ones.

2. We **choose** the best alternative: Either we give out **grades or points** and choose the one with the best grade or the most points. Or we compare two with each other in the **knockout process** and separate the worse one until only one is left.

The lists

If we want to fully recognize what we are thinking about, or what we want or need to do, we can collect, organize, and evaluate on a list. What is on the list cannot be forgotten, and we can flexibly do what is urgent, important, or quickly done.

Recognizing the goals

Maybe **good life** in itself should be **the ultimate goal.** How and with what the individual can and wants to contribute will be different.

Achievable and suitable **long-term goals** (visions) give our actions a direction. Realistic **short term goals** bring us bit by bit closer to our long-term goal or goals.

Planning

If we want to identify a more complex path to a goal, planning usually helps. This could work:

1. We define our **target**.

2. We look at who must or should do what, when, where, and how (and why). The **plan** should be realistic and not too demanding or underemanding for anyone.

3. As we implement the plan, we respond to **changes** until the goal is achieved.

By the way: Even if it sounds trivial: A watch, an appointment calendar, something to look up for factual knowledge, and a place for notes are useful items for this.

The tasks at the end of the chapter

Task 8 was about your probable future. Now it is about your concrete goals: What exactly do you want to achieve or experience before you die?

Task 13.1 **My goals for life?**

Task 13.2 **My wishes?**

So: What would you consider to be good if it came to be?

Use this chapter for both and look at the last two tasks: What you like or even love and can do will probably make your life valuable.

13.1 My goals:

13.2 My wishes:

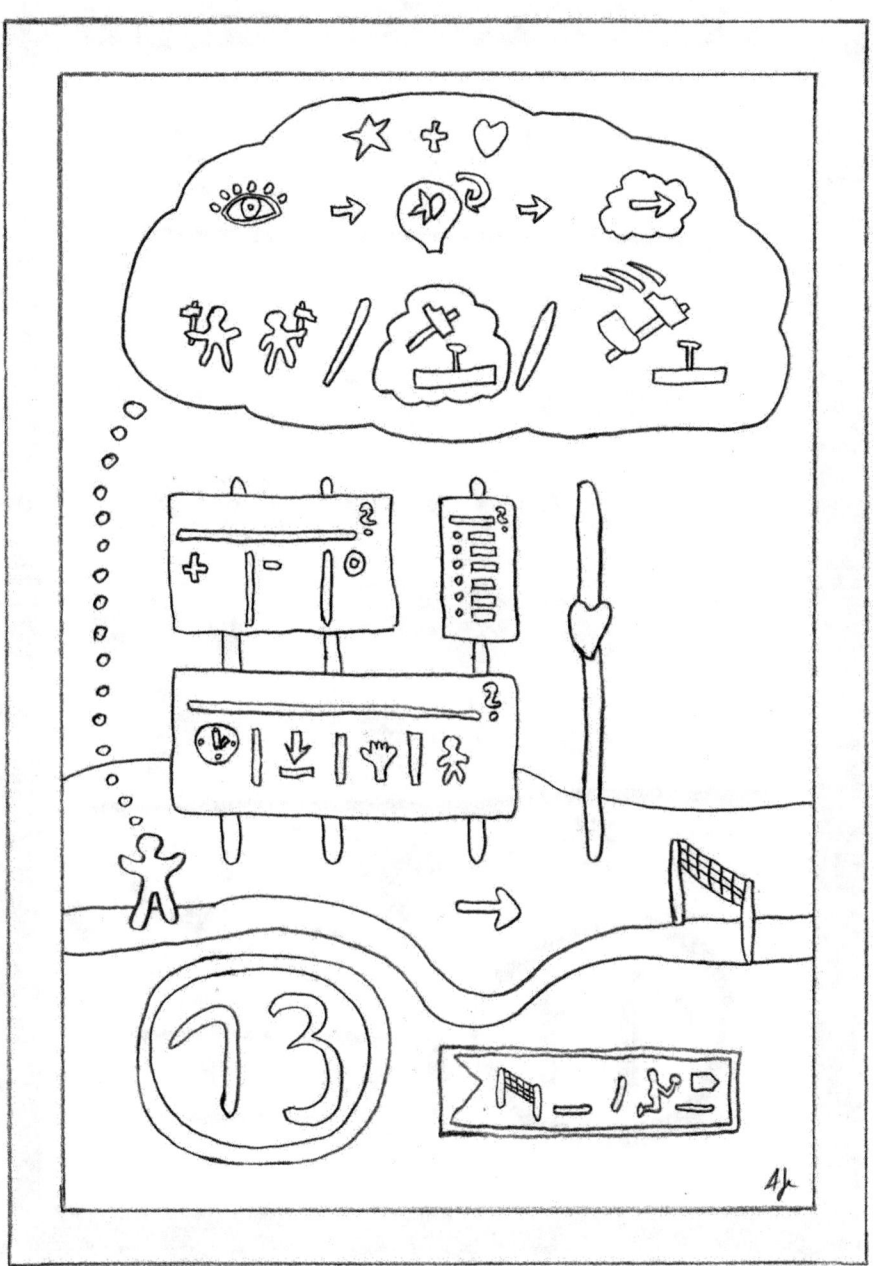

14. Chapter: Problems and chances

Despite careful decision-making and planning, problems can arise. And on our way, opportunities can open up that bring us closer to our goals and dreams. Therefore we take a closer look at problems and chances.

Instinctive problem solving

Spiritually put yourself in the place of a Stone Age problem: You are threatened by someone else. Your alternatives:

Attack: You realize that you are stronger. You fight and win. The threat is gone.

Escape: You realize that you are weaker. You flee and escape. Or you pretend to be dead and escape from the other person's perception.

Surrender: You realize that the other is mentally or physically superior to you and that you can not or don´t want to flee. You surrender. The other can now command you. You become valuable for him, and he actually has no reason to threaten you anymore. If you help him, he may even reward you.

Admittedly, all these things can go wrong. You lose in the attack, are caught on the run, or "the other" is a vicious sadist or a hungry animal that will more or less destroy you or eat you in more or less pleasurable agony.

The schematic problem solution

We can solve unknown and complex problems, crises, perhaps even catastrophes step by step. Let us try to think through the following ten steps; they can be helpful on the way to a solution.

First step: **Identify something as a possible problem**

We recognize that something prevents or could prevent us from continuing on well. Example: Somebody feels severe pain in their stomach.

Second step: **Accepting**

Problems for which we are responsible, we accept. In principle, we are responsible for ourselves, for the welfare of our children who are not adults and for what we have taken responsibility for. In the example, the person takes their pain seriously.

Third step: **Stabilize**

To prepare, we check whether the framework situation fits: Are the essentials adequately safe? When, where, and with whom or what can the problem be easily solved? If necessary, wait patiently. In the example case, the person takes the time required, perhaps tells the employer or family member about it, takes an insurance card or money, leaves the apartment safely behind, and goes to the doctor or hospital.

Fourth step: **Examine**

We take a closer look at the problem area. In the example, the person is examined by a doctor.

Fifth step: **Describe**

We note what is essential for the problem area. In the example, the facts or findings of the doctor could be: Abdominal pain in the lower right corner, moderate pain from pressing, stronger in letting go, a slight increase in the inflammatory value of the blood.

Sixth step: **Naming the problem**

We will then identify the problem or problems as accurately as possible or determine that there is no problem. If the problem is a conflict or quarrel, we name the contradiction of the parties. In the example, the doctor's diagnosis might be appendicitis.

Seventh step: **Recognizing the solution**

There are several ways to solve problems.

1. We could identify the **cause** and **eliminate** it.

We ask ourselves why the problem occurred, what drives it, and how we can fix it. Sometimes there are several causes and one trigger, sometimes there are many causes that become a problem at the weakest point. In a dispute, one could agree, give in on one side or find a compromise. In the example, the doctor says that he does not know what caused the inflammation, but it caused the pain. The appendix could be surgically removed and with it, the inflammation.

2. We could **ease** the **consequences** of the problem.

The adverse circumstance may not be gone, but it is no longer so unpleasant for us. In a conflict, we could either avoid it or let a higher hierarchical judge or the majority involved decide. In consolation, we turn our attention back to the good. In the example the doctor says that there are medicines, hypnosis or acupuncture for pain.

3. We might be able to **accept** the circumstance.
We then change our mindset. For example, we accept a difference of opinion in a dispute. What cannot be changed, we can often accept well. In the example, one could simply endure the situation.

Eighth step: **Decide and plan.**
   We decide on one or more solutions and how we intend to proceed. We solve huge problems bit by bit or step by step. In the example case, it is decided that the patient goes to the hospital for observation or stays there. Since the inflammation value is low, it is possible that the inflammation disappears by itself.

Ninth step: **Implement.**
   We implement what has been decided. If new problems arise, of course, we solve them too. In the example case, the patient waits in the hospital, and the pain and infection level goes down on their own.

Tenth step: **Conclusion.**
   We check at the end whether the problem is solved, ask ourselves whether we want to learn something, and then end it. In the example, the patient's abdomen no longer hurts, and the inflammatory value in the blood is healthy again. If necessary he pays his bill and takes his things with him and goes home satisfied.

The intuitive problem solution

If we already know a problem and its solution, we will, of course, not at first go through the ten steps but recognize the solution with the problem. Example: Someone has, as often, caught a cold. He allows himself a week's rest and is healthy again.

Seizing the opportunities

Perhaps we can **recognize** in a problem or suddenly also a **chance** for something to be good or to let it become something good.

We could briefly **think about the risks** and **decide** whether to seize the opportunity or not.

If so, perhaps we **plan** the process and **prepare ourselves well enough**.

Then we simply **try**.

The tasks at the end of the chapter

Task 14.1 **My frequent feelings and thoughts?**

What are the feelings you often feel in yourself, what thoughts do you usually have? They could indicate the following:

Task 14.2 **My problems and chances?**

Do you have bigger problems? Which ones? What do you see as your most significant opportunities? Are there important decisions to be made?

14.1 My frequent feelings and thoughts:

14.2 My problems and chances:

15. Chapter: Commandments and Values

If we thought about each problem and each chance individually, how we solve it, or if we take it, that would be a time-consuming task. Rules with commandments and prohibitions and values help us not to let problems arise and to recognize chances more easily.

The Commandments

When it comes to important and frequent matters, ethical rules help us to behave well. We then only have to follow them and don't have to decide new independently.

I once wrote down ten commandments that I think would be beneficial if we all followed them in our lives. Remember: If everyone follows the commandments for himself, everyone follows them!

1. Commandment: **Good life shall be.**
It is about preserving life and our life-foundation as best as possible. It is the first and most important command-ment that every species has to follow appropriately, re-gardless of whether it is aware of it or not; otherwise, it will die out in the long run. <u>In the end, it is always about surviving well.</u>
So it's about **survival** and **quality of life**.
Good enough is enough.
With **alternatives**, we choose the better one, because it makes life better and safer.
In each case, it depends on the <u>overall view</u>.
Other good rules help to fulfill the first commandment.
It can justify an **exception** to other rules.

Three questions can help us to recognize whether something, seen as a whole, is good for life:
1. Is it good for me and my environment?
2. Is it good now and for the future?
3. Is it balanced? Not too early and not too late, not too much and not too little.

This book wants to help fulfill the first commandment.

Remember that we living beings often fulfill this commandment evolutionarily by supporting ourselves and those who belong to us and by exploiting or fighting others. This might have helped the "better" lives to survive, but it is often harmful. Therefore:

2. Commandment: **I let other people what they have;** especially: Their life.
Their health and physical integrity.
Their children, life partners, parents, and communities.
Their things, animals, plants, money, rights, inventions.
Their sexual freedom of choice.
Their freedom of movement.
Their freedom of education, opinion, and work.
Their recreation possibility, private and intimate area.
Their time.
Their human dignity and honor.
   This commandment is the basis for peace and this regular basis for a flourishing life.

3. Commandment: **I strive for a good community.**
Especially with my children, parents, and partners. Only by working together can our life really succeed.

4. Commandment: **I protect nature in a sensible way.**
It is the basis of our life.

5. Commandment: **I am basically mindful and willing to learn.** If I recognize myself and my environment better, I know what is really good for life. I pay particular attention to the good, it is a pleasure and leads the way to the good life.

6. Commandment: **I am adequately emotional.**
With love and joy, is mostly adequate. Only when we're open to feelings, they will motivate us to improve what is rather bad and allows us to feel and enjoy what is good.

7. Commandment: **I'm honest and reliable.**
This is important for identifying what is really good and for mutual trust.

8. Commandment: **I accept my "fate."**
Fate number 1:
There are things that nobody can change.
Fate number 2:
Everything has its two sides: good and bad.
(You can't have everything. And sometimes you have to sacrifice something to get something better.)
Fate number 3:
One part I can change. For that I am responsible.
Fate number 4:
Whether there is a coincidence that is a question of belief.
   The following questions can help: "Do I have to? Can I? Is it useful? Is it fun? What do I really want?"
   This commandment makes regularly realistically more relaxed.

9. Commandment: **I set priorities.**

First things, first! In case of doubt: The urgent, i.e., the bad or not shiftable. The most important. Everything that can be done quickly. The starded. The temporal first.

Then concentrate: It takes as long as it takes. One thing at a time. And if it makes sense: Setting limits, omitting unimportant things, or leaving them to others.

Priorities help to act responsibly without overtaxing us because nobody can do everything immediately.

10. Commandment: **I follow the norms that apply to me.**

Others can then adapt to my behavior. And I am not threatened by any punishments. If the rules are ethical, it makes it easier for us to live together.

Through **principles,** we give us rules only for ourselves. Typical behaviors are, in fact, principles, too. A **motto** can be something like a guiding principle.

We should only deviate from a good rule if we are very sure that this is **exceptionally** good.

The values

If we wanted to regulate every detail, there would be so many rules that nobody could remember them. For questions of detail or rare occurrences, the value orientation can help. **Values** are the general moral goals to follow in our specific behavior.

The behavior towards values is called **virtue**. So the virtue honesty belongs to the value truth.

Values or virtues can **collide**. Example: It is basically good to endure and leave other people and things as they are. This is based on tolerance. But if someone steals out of greed, you can't tolerate that. Values such as security or trust, which now collide with tolerance, weigh more heavily here.

Valuable can be: Hope, gratitude, tolerance, consideration, acceptance, peace, freedom, happiness, health, nature, community, kindness, family, love, recognition, justice, politeness, beauty, security, trust, order, orientation, success, wisdom, truth, prosperity, benevolence and life.

The list is not complete, of course, and each person evaluates a littel differently what is of real value to him, or to life from his point of view.

Nevertheless: The presence of a value is regularly good and, therefore, recognized in something, cause for happiness.

The tasks at the end of the chapter

Task 15.1 **My principles?**

Everyone has their own rules, to which they typically adhere, even if they are not always aware of it. Observe yourself: what do you do, or not do regularly? Do you have a motto?

Task 15.2 **My values?**

Which values are, or what is particularly important to you?

15.1 My principles:

15.2 My values:

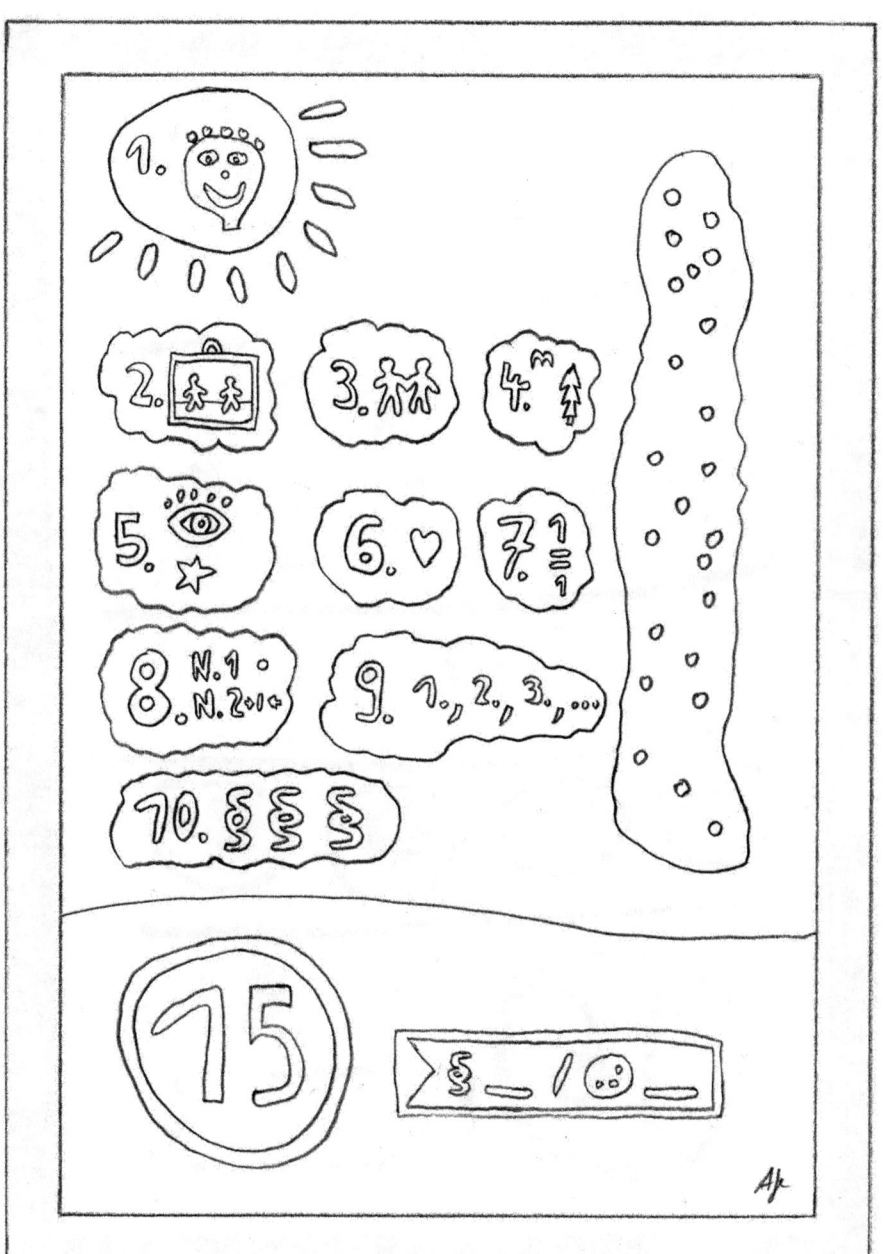

16. Chapter: Language

Whether it's about teaching rules and values, such as in the last chapter, or anything else we do, in almost everything, there's something involved that is the subject of this chapter: The language.

The language in general

Our language is a means of communication. From letters or sounds, we form words that stand for specific contents. We put the words together in sentences, and these, in turn, into texts. Often we simultaneously express rational core statements, feelings, self-revelation, relationships and request.

By **emphasizing** what is spoken, we can reinforce, weaken, and even change the content of the sentence or part of a sentence.

Body language

Especially with the **facial expressions** on our faces, we can express our feelings.

A few exercises: Pull the corners of your mouth upwards and open the eye area: That's happiness. Try pulling the corners of your mouth downwards, narrowing the eye area, and lowering your gaze: That's grief. Tears can increase sadness and joy in expression. Push the lower jaw forward and fix your eyes slightly in the front field of vision: That is anger. Pull up the upper lip and wrinkle your nose: You express disgust.

We can also communicate with the **gestures** of our bodies.

Further examples: You let your head hang, and your body is slumped down: You seem depressed and exhausted. You are upright and hold your head high: You seem powerful and awake.

A person's **appearance**, clothing, and surroundings also have a content expression.

Giving speeches

If we want to speak well alone in front of others, we need to pay attention to comprehensibility, short sentences, the lowering of the voice at the end of the sentence, as well as sufficiently slow speaking and making sufficient breaks.

Having conversations

When talking to others, we should formally and typically make sure that we **listen** to the speaker, **let him finish**, and **stick to the topic**.

We can **listen actively** by reacting with facial expressions and gestures. Or by repeating it in our own words, or by saying what we perceived beyond the content, for example, feelings or requests. We can ask comprehension questions, W questions, circular questions that is how others see it, hypothetical questions in the sense of: what would be if, and with caution, also provocative questions.

Contents of texts

Texts should be essentially **correct, complete** (Who? When? Where? What and how? Why?) and **useful.**

For entertaining texts, the benefit is the pleasure. By the way, factual texts can also be enjoyable. And entertaining texts may also convey knowledge.

We can be convincing if we **clame** something clearly, give conclusive **reasons** and, if possible, **prove** it by providing a few examples.

Noticing errors in speech and texts

1. Contents can be **false or incomplete.**

Behind this may be malice: Anyone who misjudges reality will have a hard time dealing with it. It may be selfish: For example, if you don't know about a product's flaws or believe in non-existent advantages, chances are you'll buy it. Often there is peer pressure behind it: It's better to say the wrong thing than being excluded from the group. Goodwill can be another motive: As an exception, the lie, concealment, or a speculative explanation can be more pleasant and even better than lack of clarity, truth or completeness, at least for a short time.

A story marked as invented, such as a novel or a fairy tale, can be good if the message is correct.

A theory can make predictions easier, even if, or precisely because, for the sake of simplicity, it does not fully or accurately portray the truth.

2. We can make **mistakes in perception**.

These can be optical illusions. Maybe we also misunderstand something. Some psychotic people see, smell, hear, or feel what is not present in the sure belief that it is real.

Or we pay special attention to certain things and not to others. Selective perception then leads to errors in estimating frequency. And what we do not pay attention to, we do not notice, although it is there.

3. We can make **memory errors**.

We humans only remember the core area of what we perceive and what is essential for reconstruction. Often this is the start, the highs, and lows, possibly also because they were filled with strong feelings, the standard case, strange exceptions, and the end. We can also forget things. And sometimes, we suppress unpleasant memories or insights.

When our brain reconstructs a memory, it occasionally makes mistakes. Nevertheless, we can judge the memory itself to be correct and will then reproduce it unintentionally incorrect.

4. We can make **interpretation mistakes.**

Perhaps what was said was meant ironically. Maybe we are denying or disregarding something or we are imagining something that was not there.

When we have to assess the unknown, we often fall back on the known: We project what we have in us or what we know from ourselves onto others, we transfer what we know from other people or from other situations to the new situation, although the new situation may be different. Or perhaps we have prejudices or our own beliefs that we would like to protect.

Our beliefs

From the many right and wrong texts and from our own experiences, we will remember right or wrong beliefs such as **sayings**, spiritual **attitudes,** or further individual insights.

Many sayings will contain something true, but will not wholly strike the truth.

We are strongly guided by our beliefs, so we should pay close attention to them.

The task at the end of the chapter

Task 16 **My beliefs?**

What insights have you gained?
What are your inner attitudes?
Every one of us has this, even if we are not always aware of it.
Try to find and name a few to sharpen your awareness.

Then think about which of them is more true and helpful,
which is more wrong or obstructive? For the latter: what would
be right or helpful instead?

16. My beliefs:

17. Chapter: Personality

The beliefs, principles, values, and other things we looked at in the last chapters interact with our personality, which we now look at more closely.

Personality in general

From my point of view, personality is what constitutes the essence of the individual, and this results from his or her **formative attitudes** and **behaviors.**

Genetic **predisposition** has a very great influence on personality. **Our own history** of development has another big impact. Our **present situation** also has a slight effect on us.

Personality is developed primarily in early childhood, becomes more stable in the course of childhood, still changes in adolescence, and remains relatively stable in adulthood. In old age, some people become a bit stubborn and whimsical.

Particularly formative: Parents or educators, the sibling role, the general living conditions in the area, group affiliations, important experiences, and our body.

With a stable personality, we and others can recognize who and what fits us well in the long run.

Attention: In different **roles,** we can be different or the same. So someone can be aggressive in the part of the sports boxer, peaceful and loving in the part of the father, or also aggressive there.

Personality traits

There are many personality traits. In the following, I will describe a few of them. While you are reading or listening to them, for exercise, please think about people or animals in which you can observe very clearly what is explained. So, the traits:

1. You perfer to be the dominant, assertive **boss**, who has power and control; or better the submissive **helper**, the employee, who likes to hand over responsibility?
2. More trusting in the **intellect** and using it actively; or is the **feeling** more formative?
3. More the **extroverted**, open-minded, talkative and sociable type who pays attention to his environment; or rather the **introverted**, observant type who concentrates on himself and likes to do things alone?
4. More **use-** and benefit-oriented, reasonable, maybe wise, creative, interested, correct, organized, controlled, responsible; or more **fun-** and experience-oriented, sensual, spontaneous, relaxed, and letting things flow.
5. Rather **calm**, quiet, slow, and steady; or rather **lively**, full of energy, active, athletic, spirited, and with delight variable?
6. **Nice,** "good," friendly, tolerant, altruistic, compassionate; or rather the **bad** one, "evil," aggressive, selfish, and ruthless?
7. Rather concentrated on the **positive**, often stable, balanced, basically satisfied and optimistic; or rather seeing the **negative,** and more often dissatisfied, pessimistic, occasionally extreme or nervous, rather careful or anxious?

In an evaluation, we tend to believe about ourselves that we are more responsive to situations, while others typically behave according to their personality. Advantage: We feel free to act as appropriate. And we allow ourselves to predict the behavior of others, which will often be correct. In fact, everyone is influenced in their behavior by their personality but remains relatively free to react on a one-off basis.

Also, from my point of view, every personality has all the components. Typically, however, we will indeed have tendencies and rarely be completely balanced. And these proportions are basically not better or worse. It is more the case that both sides have their advantages and disadvantages. For example, some characteristics fit some situations, people, or professions better than others. And different personalities in a group can contribute to the balance and quality of the whole group.

Dysfunctional personality

In extreme cases, personalities can disrupt your own life or that of others to an unacceptable extent. The line between being normal and dysfunctional is blurred. And even here, extremes can have extreme advantages. Dysfunctions in personality are usually caused by childhood. The perception of the child is very important. Children often view and interpret their environment in their own way. And different children can react differently to the same circumstances. Sometimes a child copies what he or she perceives and becomes the same. Or it makes transmission errors. And if it tries to be desperately different or to protect itself somehow, it can be disturbed the other way round.

In most cases, such dysfunctions can be prevented by a single person who is sufficiently loving, kind, honest, and helpful for the child.

Let's look at **examples of dysfunction** and consider that in reality, it can be different or combined:

Perhaps a child is treated maliciously and badly and copies what he has experienced or wants to give back to the world the bad that he has received. Or it could have fun being "evil" and playing "pranks" unhindered, not being taught how to handle it well or having alternatives. As an adult, it is a **malicious person** who repeatedly and deliberately harms others and finds fun and motivation in it. Most of them will try to do this in a way that makes you think it is well-meant or the others are to blame. Malicious people often accept self-harm, rarely their death. A person who is happy to win in a fair competition is not malicious. Malicious joy or the pleasure of an opponent's misfortune is normal; survival only works if you can take away from others or protect yourself and your own if necessary aggressively. And those who like to take action against bad things are even good.

Another example of a child is treated ruthlessly, neglect, random beatings, or "abuse" are common. It may learn that it cannot expect anything from the community, does not want to help it, becomes **antisocial**, criminal, and may even end up in prison.

Another child is treated without love or with contempt, on the one hand, on the other hand, the family wants to appear honorable on the outside, and in a certain way, even exaggerates in spoiling the child. In order not to feel the apparent worthlessness and to meet the demands, the child perceives himself in his imagination to be grand. His environment appears to him "black" or "white." It becomes selfish because it has learned that it will not receive love and recognition at all or will always be rewarded. It becomes **narcissistic**.

Some also become **schizoid, borderliner, histrionic, compulsively perfectionist, asthenic,** or **anxious.** Or someone is **traumatized** by intense, sometimes even individual negative experiences.

This often results in bonding disorders, fears, a lot of brooding, sleep problems, depression, addiction, in extreme cases psychoses, schizophrenia or mania or physical consequences, and often end up in an environment that suits the disorder and maintains it.

The task at the end of the chapter

Task 17 **My personality?**

Go through the chapter again and try to estimate yourself. You could write the personality extremes at the ends of a line and put a 0 in the middle. Then mark how much your personality goes in each direction. 0 would be: not at all, entirely outside: 100 % matching. Chances are, you'll find more such pairs of terms easily. Try to describe your personality further.

17. My personality:

1. Boss---------------------------0---------------------------helper.

2. Intellect----------------------0--------------------------feeling.

3. Extrovert---------------------0-----------------------introvert.

4. Useful-------------------------0---------------------------------fun.

5. Calm--------------------------0--------------------------lively.

6. Nice---------------------------0----------------------------bad.

7. Positive----------------------0------------------------negative.

18. Chapter: God and symbols

Having looked at our whole personality in the last chapter, we are now looking at the whole of the world in one symbol. We will also think about the highest, about God. With this, and with the question of how the world sees us, our public image, we will conclude the more general view of ourselves and of the world.

A symbol for the whole

First of all, I would like to present a symbol which, from my point of view, stands for everything and for all essential things.

We often use **symbols**. Logos often stand for a company or a group; trademarks for a particular type of product; flags, coats of arms or hymns for states; name, signature or sign for a person; and some things like titles, jewelry or a vehicle can stand for the status of the owner.
 In art or literature, images or other things can stand for something, perhaps the fox for a foxy being.

As I said, I will attempt to use a symbol that stands for everything:

Let's imagine a small **heart** as the first element in the middle of the symbol. It stands for **feelings**, especially for love and for the life force that motivates us living beings. Around it, there is a small **star**, a symbol for the **mind**, which can recognize with **logic** the world and what life needs in its own way. Around both is a small

circle, which gives these mental powers a **body**, like an ordinary home in which they can be and work.

Imagine that the small circle with the star and the heart would be the handle in the middle of a square window, which in turn consists of **four square window panes.** Through the window, the second larger element, we look into everything that is and will be. The window on the **lower right** stands for the **viewer** in the **present**, that means for you and for everything that belongs very close to you. The pane next to it at the **bottom left** stands for your **environment in the present,** and so for the rest of the universe. The window panes above stand for the future. On the **top right,** your **future**, on the **top left** the **future** of the **environment.**

Remember: Just as body and mind cannot be separated precisely, the border between us and our environment, and even that of time is blurred.

It would be nice if life, figuratively speaking, could flourish in all four window panes. It would also be wonderful if that could be our common goal.

Thirdly, let us imagine that, above the **four** sides of the window, there are **shutters** in the shape of a semicircle. The whole thing looks a little like the blossom of a flower with four semi-circular petals. Also, the four semicircles stand for something, let's say forces that perhaps work from the outside, maybe even from within ourselves into the world. The **semicircle above** stands for **one side**, for order energy or for heaven, the one **below** for the **other side**, for chaos energy or for hell. Everything consists of one side and the other. Both need balance, and they only exist mixed. Let's look at the semi-circular shutters on the left and right. The **left** stands for the power towards **less**, which sometimes, like a good angel, protects from too much from one side and sometimes, like your weaker self, prevents more of the good and leads to a deficit. The semicircle on the **right** stands for the power of **more**, which sometimes, again like a good angel, inspires to more of essential and beautiful, to one side that is important for balance at the moment, or sometimes, like a demon, to more of what is rather inadequate for life, to excess.

Again, there is no absolute little or much, because little of one will be much for something else. And what is good for one person can be bad for another. And sometimes bad things have to be, so that good things can happen, or bad things use good things for its own purposes.

The symbol also contains many symbols used by others. And all this can be a beautiful symbol for people who together orient themselves through this book.

It is like a "memo" for all the essential things about us and in the world and for a life as flourishing as possible: We use feeling, mind, and body above all for ourselves and our future, but we also think of others and their future and do not exaggerate.

It can also be a symbol for God:

God

There were and are many ideas of one God or of many Gods. In religious studies, one thinks that God, no matter which religion, stands for the highest authority over which there is nothing.

Who or what would God be if there was only one? For me, this is relatively clear: **God is the totality of everything that really exists.** Because higher, greater or more than everything can not exist. All power together is his omnipotence. Everyone is a part of him, everyone a child of God. What we do to the world, we do to him, and what it gives us, he gives us.

We can imagine parts of him symbolically as gods, angels, or similar beings. Example: Goddess Moneta could stand for the money.

And maybe there really are beings or worlds on the other side; then these are also parts of the one highest God, and whoever worships them worships a part of everything.

For some people, it can be helpful if they imagine God symbolically as a person.

If we want to talk to God, we could **pray**. We speak to him as we speak to a person. I'm sure a part of everything hears that: We and those who listen to us. When we speak to a person, we speak to their spirit. We continuously send and receive energetic information to and from outside without words. And both have an effect.

If we want to feel God's connection, we could **meditate**: let go of everything spiritually in peace until we feel our core-me and the link to everything.

Our perceptible public image

Some things of us also symbolize us. It is not uncommon for us to draw conclusions from specific things to the whole, for example, from the overall appearance or from particular things such as body, expression, charisma, clothing, what we say, or what belongs to us or appears to belong to us.

As an exception, it can be good to pretend, and as an exception, it can be good to have secrets.

Mostly, from my point of view, it is best if we appear to the outside the way we actually are. Then we attract what suits us. We don't risk anyone noticing the pretense and then rightly classifying ourselves as dishonest. Then praise is for the really good and blame for the really bad. And if someone loves us, he will love us and not the wrong image we show him of us!

The tasks at the end of the chapter

Task 18.1 **Who is God to me?**

You may also leave that open. Perhaps my idea of God is also yours? Or perhaps what you see as God is part of what I see as God?

Task 18.2 **My symbols and my public image?**

Which symbols do you use? Is the above one part of it?
What's your public image? In which points is this really you and where is it different? Ask other people about it.

18.1 Who is God for me?

18.2 My symbols and my public image:

19. Chapter: Nature conservation

Those who have understood the last chapter know that service for our environment and for ourselves is also worship. With this chapter, we begin to look at one area of life after another and to think in our tasks about how it is with us and what we want to do ourselves. We start with the area of nature conservation.

Nature is our basis for life; without it we cannot survive, if we seriously damage it, we are seriously damaging ourselves, if we help it sustainably, we improve our own basis for life.

Now life has probably developed in such a way that each and every species has tried to survive better and improve, also at the expense of the others. As a result, life has developed surprisingly well. Until the Stone Age, this also worked quite well for us humans.

With the age of civilization, especially since industrialization, technology gives us so many possibilities that we destroy nature and ourselves if we continue like this.

We need the clarity that we, as part of nature, must use it and protect ourselves from it to live, but that nature conservation also helps us and that it is necessary for the survival of our descendants.

Moreover, we humans, the most intelligent beings on earth, may and should also use our technical possibilities to harm nature as little as possible and even to help it. And perhaps nature even needs us one day to survive.

Let us now look at what we humans should do:

1. Avoid environmental pollution

We should **not emit** any **pollutants** into the air, water, or soil.

Radioactive radiation can cause damage. Above all, it damages the genetic material and can cause cancer.

Exhaust gases can cause damage. Examples: Soot and fine dust are harmful to the lungs and body; sulfur and nitrogen oxides damage plants through acid rain; extremely excessive release of greenhouse gases such as carbon dioxide or methane can warm the climate; chloro-fluorocarbons destroy the ozone layer; burning with little oxygen can produce toxic carbon monoxide; burning, especially of plastics at too low temperatures, can produce toxic dioxins. Air filters or catalytic converters can help to reduce harmful exhaust gases!

Wastewater or chemicals released into the environment can also cause damage. Examples: Residues of pharmaceuticals, pesticides, and other toxic substances, as well as excessive fragrances, can be harmful. And too much feces or fertilizers can over-fertilize waters and even cause them to tip over. Wastewater treatment plants can help where wastewater is produced.

Toxins can get into the soil, especially from unsecured landfills, industrial and military facilities, or polluting agriculture. From there, they might be released into groundwater and, via the food chain, into our food.

Too much light in the night sky and too much noise can irritate nature.

2. Sustainable management

We should try to extract only as much from nature, for example, food, wood, or other raw materials, as it grows back or is newly created.

And we should try not to produce any waste and, if it does accumulate, to recycle it completely. Biowaste can be composted, other materials recycled or, if necessary, used for heating.

3. Preserving and improving the environment

First of all, let us become familiar with what a good living space often looks like:

A high-quality habitat in the sea is not too warm, even so, that sufficient oxygen can be bound, not too salty and does not have too much or too little nutrients, is free of garbage and pollutants, has enough light, and is not excessively disturbed.

A high-quality habitat on land is one in which the individual species are not overly disturbed in their lives. It is not too cold and not too hot, and there is sufficient rainfall. The air ist healthy, enough light is present. A diverse area, with streams, lakes, perhaps coast, hills, mountains, forests, hedges, and meadows, offers space to many different, complementing creatures.

We should first try to **destroy as little environment as possible**, as we do for example through land sealing such as house and road building or through monoculture agriculture. Tunnels, bridges, skyscrapers, inner-city green spaces, even on roofs and the preservation of contagious natural areas and not too many people in the world as a whole are helpful.

If, for example, we turn healthy nature into a desert landscape in open-cast mining, we should **renature** it.

If possible, we should **not** dispose of any **garbage** in nature, at least not waste that rots badly or not at all.

We should try to give nature enough **nature reserves** on land and in the water so that it can recover and maintain there.

And we are invited to sustainably **improve** the **environment** following the local situation, on land, for example by creating small lakes, hedges, hills, loose stone walls, wild meadows, by watering, planting single trees or entire near-natural forests. Sometimes the targeted help for some living beings or interventions in the species population and sometimes also the discharge or withdrawal of certain substances is helpful.

What can we do ourselves?

1. If we have **domestic** or **farm animals or plants**, we can **keep them** mainly in a way that is **species-appropriate** and, if that is not possible, we should refrain from keeping them. We may even be able to keep them in such a way that they feel better with us than in the wild.

2. Each of us can also **behave in a nature-friendly way.** We can buy sustainable and environmentally friendly produced products, produce little waste, if necessary, dispose of it well, do not waste water, use energy not excessively and as sustainable as possible, discharge little household chemistry into wastewater, avoid harmful exhaust fumes, noise and unnecessary night sky lighting, as far as possible make our own house and garden nature-friendly and behave respectfully in nature, especially not poaching or disturbing rare species.

3. And we can **support environmentally friendly politics** and ecologically friendly **business enterprises** and **communities**, for whom at least environmental protection is also very important, and we can protest adequately against environmental sins.

Furthermore, we do not forget that we, too, are part of nature. Good, if we are such a part that must not feel shame for ruthless exploitation, but one that can be proud of a sustainable way of dealing with nature, of protecting, and maybe even of improving it, and who enjoys valuable nature.

The tasks at the end of the chapter

Task 19. 1 **My pets and plants?**

Task 19.2 **My contribution to nature conservation?**

What can you do, what do you want to do and what will you do in each case?

19.1 My pets and domestic plants:

19.2 My contribution to nature conservation:

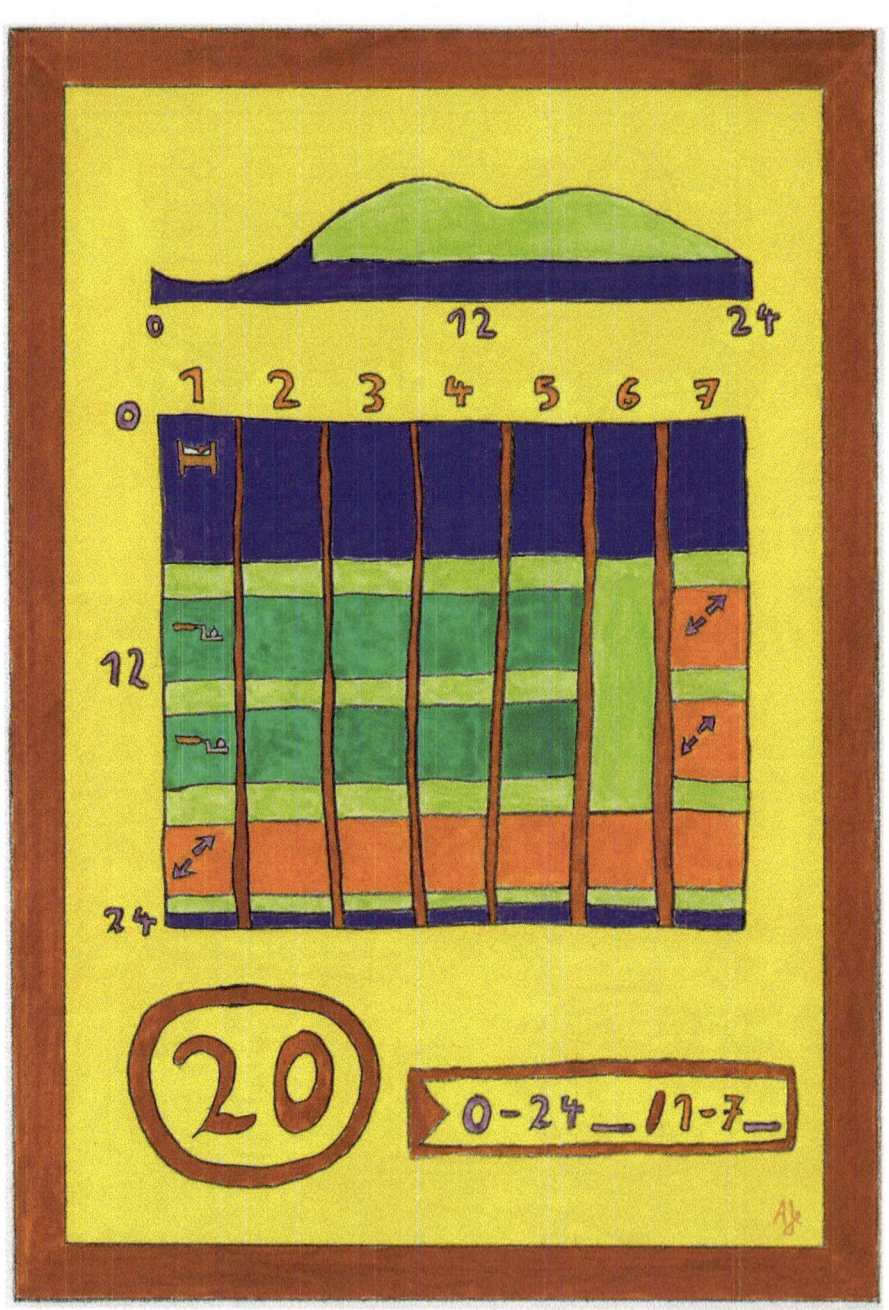

20. Chapter: Time management

After we dealt with the basis of our life in the last chapter, we now look at how our life typically works. In the following chapters, we can come back here and see when we can find time for something new.

The presumed daily routine in the Stone Age

Let us first put ourselves in one of our adult ancestors during the Stone Age. At that time, much of his time was determined by local circumstances. Probably it was like this or similar:

The Stone Age man lives in his small group in Africa, somewhere around the equator and at the border of the jungle and savannah where there is grass, some trees, and a few animals. Temperatures are almost always above 20 degrees Celsius all year round, at least during the day.

At about 6:00 a.m. (06:00 o´clock), the sun rises in the east, as it does all year round, and it suddenly becomes light. For the Stone Age man, it is still nice and cozy warm in his sleeping place. Outside it is still relatively fresh, hazy, and damp from the night. He hears a child crying; an early riser takes care of it.

At 08:00 at the latest, it is drier, the haze has gone away, the noise level at the camp is now high, and the Stone Age man enjoys getting up. He sets himself up for the day, perhaps eats something, and looks for his hunting, fishing, or gathering group.

Maybe around 09:00, he leaves the camp with others. A few from the group stay there and take care of the work in and around the camp and of the small children.

He goes his way with the group, and around 10:00 the group is highly concentrated and efficient in hunting and collecting fast animals or on tall trees.

At 12:00, the sun is at its peak. It's getting very hot. The work is finished, and a meal is prepared from a part of what was hunted and collected. After the meal, the sun is scorching. The effort of the morning and the sumptuous meal make people tired. Together the group lies down in the shade of a tree and rests extensively.

At about 3 p.m. (15:00 o´clock), the group drags the hunting- and collecting goods back to the camp. Once there, they use the time before sunset to process the food, perhaps to cook and to eat something together.

At about 18:00, the sun goes down in the west. This is also the case all year round. It is dark now, but still quite warm and dry. At the camp, the time is used to comfortably tell how the day was, the day at the camp, or the day in the hunting or gathering group, or stories are told to each other; maybe visitors do the same. And there is also no need for light to cuddle. The little children are put to bed early, then the adults are alone.

Around midnight the Stone Age man falls asleep at his sleeping place. He doesn't have to be afraid of dangers at night; a few nocturnal people are still awake and watch out until the early risers take over.

When the weather is awful or there is enough food in stock, the group spends a day together without much work.

The daily routine in civilization time

Let us now put ourselves in the position of a civilized adult man.

He may live in an apartment or in a house, alone, in a flat-sharing community, or with his partner or family and has a job.

At 07:00, his alarm clock rings. He stretches himself and slowly gets up. He enjoys his breakfast, maybe with his roommates, perhaps with his family. If he hasn't done it yet, he goes to the bathroom, freshens up for the day, and says goodbye. He sets off for his workplace.

Around 09:00, he starts to work concentrated. He divides up his work and his breaks so that they fit in well with what he has to do, or does it the way it should be done. He does not work longer than six hours without a break. In mental work, he takes a break of about 15 minutes after about 90 minutes, at the latest after two hours.

During a lunch break, he has enough time to have lunch with colleagues and then allows himself a short recovery period. If he works sitting down, he may take a walk; if he works physically, he may lie down briefly.

Then he continues working until 17:00 in the afternoon.

He uses the way home for something that is a balance to work, perhaps for exercise or to sit while driving. Afterward, there will be dinner, maybe again with the roommates. They talk about the day and inform each other about the coming one. If not yet done, the civilized person also looks at the news from the world, from his close environment and his friends in the media, and takes a look at his date book and his task list.

He spends the evening with a pleasant leisure activity that he deserves. Maybe he plays with his children, does something with his partner or with friends. Perhaps he visits between 20:00 and 21:30 or 22:00 an event, a discussion group, music, sports or gymnastics group, or something similar. Or he uses the media, communicates with people who are further away from home or reads, hears or looks at what interests him, does some housework, or pursues his hobby.

After 22:30, he doesn't do any things that make him wake up, goes to the bathroom, and prepares himself for his sleep, which he starts at midnight at the latest.

Monday, Tuesday, Wednesday, Thursday, and Friday are regular, Saturday, and Sunday, there is no work. Perhaps one day is used primarily for housework, the other for leisure. Maybe an assembly will be attended to as well.

Our actual daily and weekly schedule

Each of us has his own biorhythm and, therefore, times in the day when he is more efficient, ready to eat, sleep, or something similar.

For a typical person, it is probably the case that his performance increases in the course of the morning and reaches its peak of the day between 10:00 and 12:00. Then there is a slight dip in the early afternoon. In the late afternoon, it goes up again until the performance decreases towards the night and reaches its lowest point between 02:00 and 04:00.

There are also people who are most efficient earlier or only in the evening or at night.

It is usually good when we find a healthy compromise between our **biorhythm**, our preferences, and what our environment demands of us. There should be enough time for **health, work,** and **leisure**. With the repetition we can get used to a little bit, some variety brings a healthy balance to everyday life.

The tasks at the end of the chapter

Task 20.1 **My typical daily routine?**

Task 20.2 **My typical weekly schedule?**

How does it usually work for you?
What could you change?
What do you want, and what will you do?

20.1 *My typical daily routine:*

20.2 *My typical weekly schedule:*

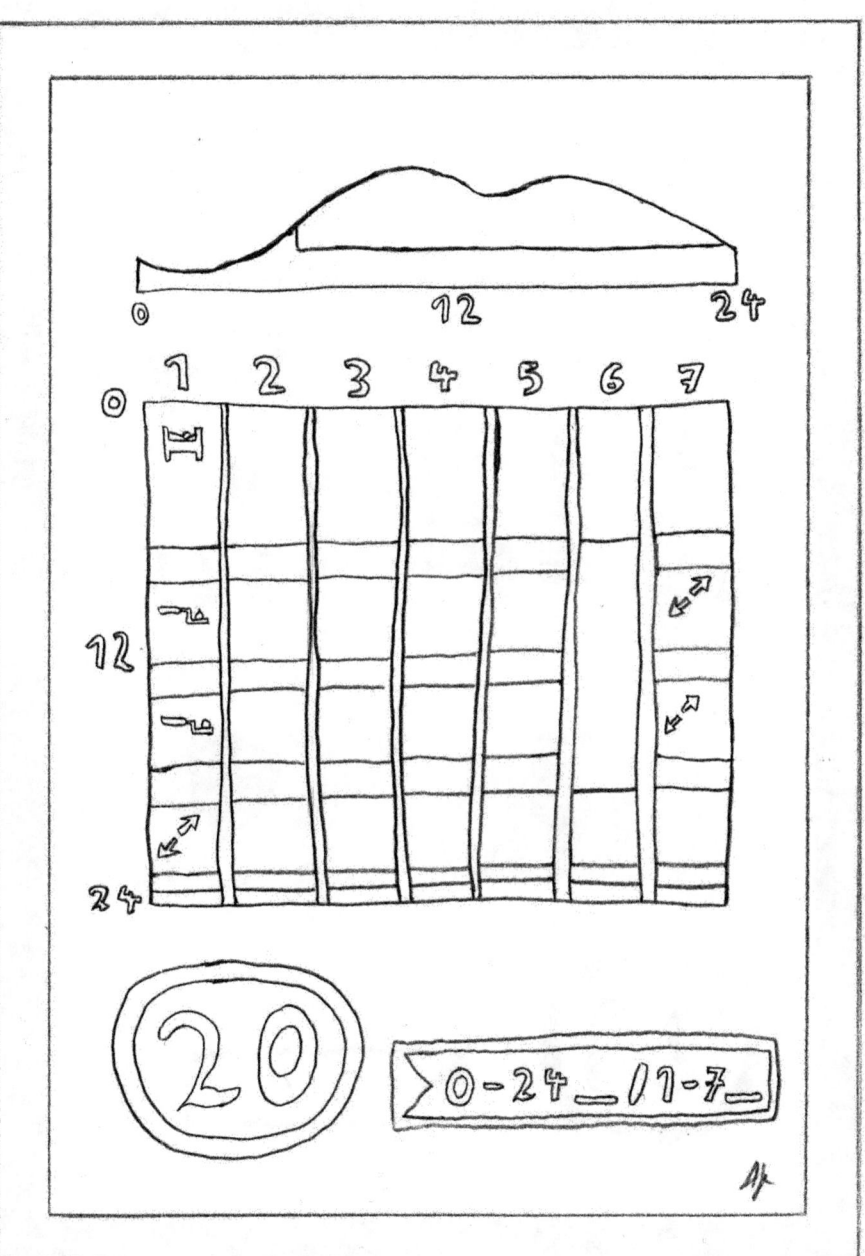

21. Chapter: Work

Now let's look at something where we often spend a lot of time during the day and the week: Our work.

The development of work in the course of life

For children, **playing** is, above all, a flowing mixture of leisure activities and learning. As an older child and teenager, we are preparing for our future work at **school.**

In a dual **training system**, in which trainees learn partly in a school and partly in a company, learning is practice-oriented. Also, training is provided where companies see a need and not where are too little jobs at the job market. And you recognize early on whether you really fit in with your job and your company.

In a university **course of study**, you can learn specialist knowledge in competence centers and be encouraged to think and work independently.

As a **working** adult, we typically distinguish between professional and private work.

The good framework conditions for work

Let us first think about our **working hours**. In terms of length, it will be impossible to do more than five hours of hard work a day and eight hours of medium work a day. We can do easy work, limited by the time we need to maintain our health. Easy work is often what is not too exhausting for body and mind, perhaps also because we can do it well, it is varied, and we like to do it. In case of doubt, full time 30 to 50 working hours per week might be good. In terms of working hours during the day, it would be good if they matched our biorhythm. And, of course, breaks appropriate to work are essential to remaining efficient.

At the **workplace,** it is best if it's different from where we spend our free time. Then our mind can adjust well. The workplace, working materials, and colleagues should be suitable for the work in question. This sounds trivial but is indispensable for good quality.

It is good if what we do **outside of work** fits in well with our work, especially if it maintains our health and offers the right balance.

Professional work

Most people specialize in a specific field of work in their profession. On the one hand, the individual can be faster and at the same time better than other people through specialization and practice, and some jobs, many people will not be able to do at all. Together with other specialized professionals, we make a compelling contribution to life. Also, not all activities give pleasure or even mental strength to everyone. In our job, we have the chance to make this our predominant activity which we can do with joy and for a long time.

We can work physically or mentally, highly qualified or semi-skilled, with or without management responsibility and as employees or self-employed in many different professions.

In most cases, it will be best if we focus on a single **main occupation.** However, we can also have several professions and **secondary occupations**.

Career choice is one of the most important decisions. When choosing a profession, we should keep four questions in mind:

1. What am I really good at? Our **competence** results from inborn talents and qualities and from learned knowledge and skills. We should pay particular attention to our talents because neither our competitors nor we can learn them. So: What have you learned in the course of your life? What can you do better than others? What activities can you do for a whole day without being overwhelmed or bored? Where could you do that? If you are thinking about a specific profession, ask yourself: Can you do what it demands? If not: Can you learn it or find an alternative?

2. What do I really want to do professionally? Only if our profession matches our **preference,** we will be able to perform well. So: What did you always like to do? What was and is essential to you? What do you want to contribute to? From which activities can you draw mental strength? In which professions is that possible? When you think of a particular job: Will it satisfy you - in the overall view of your life goals?

3. What do people really need? Only when something is in demand in the community, on the **job market**, or with potential customers does it make sense as a professional

job. So: Are you aware of the needs people have and for which they are willing to spend money on? What can you offer? Specifically, in a profession: Who needs how many? And: How much percent of people with this profession can really work in it?

4. Can and will I **afford** this profession? So: Is your health able to withstand the work? What will you earn? Is that enough for what you have in mind? Is the job sufficiently secure and permanent? Are there enough opportunities for further training or promotion for you? Can you or do you want to afford the travel time or a move? Do the working hours fit? Is the work permitted by law? Do you need and receive specialized training, equipment, or approval?

Consider the possibility of working without money, i.e., doing **voluntary work.** A job can bring other advantages besides money, for example: Recognition, companionship, variety, experience, or the feeling of being able to do something and being needed. And when others don't have to pay for it, work is often more "relaxed."

Before you make a final decision, you should 1. try to mentally visualize yourself in an **imaginative exercise** in your professional activity; and, if possible, 2. do a short **internship** in the imagined profession.

The **career path** often leads via training, admission, application, and familiarization to work in the occupation. Good performance, further training, flexibility, and hopefully gratitude, to be allowed to do something with pleasure, for which there is even a return, help to maintain the occupation well.

The private work

There will always be work that we cannot give to other workers or that we only can give away with difficulty: Shopping, tidying up, preparing meals, doing bank or tax matters, preparing a party, taking care of relatives, commissioning someone to do something for you and to control it and the like.

Or we want to do some of the work ourselves that we might also leave to others, either because we like doing it because it's important to us, or because we can't afford it any other way.

We should also have the strength and time to do this.

The tasks at the end of the chapter

Task 21.1 **My professional work?**

Which professions might suit you? Use this chapter and the answers from almost all previous tasks.

What do you do professionally, or on which way to it are you? How does this contribute to the quality of life for you and others? What can you do, what do you want and what will you do here?

Task 21.2 **My private work?**

What other work do you do?
What can you do, what do you want and what will you do?

21.1 My professional work:

21.2 My private work:

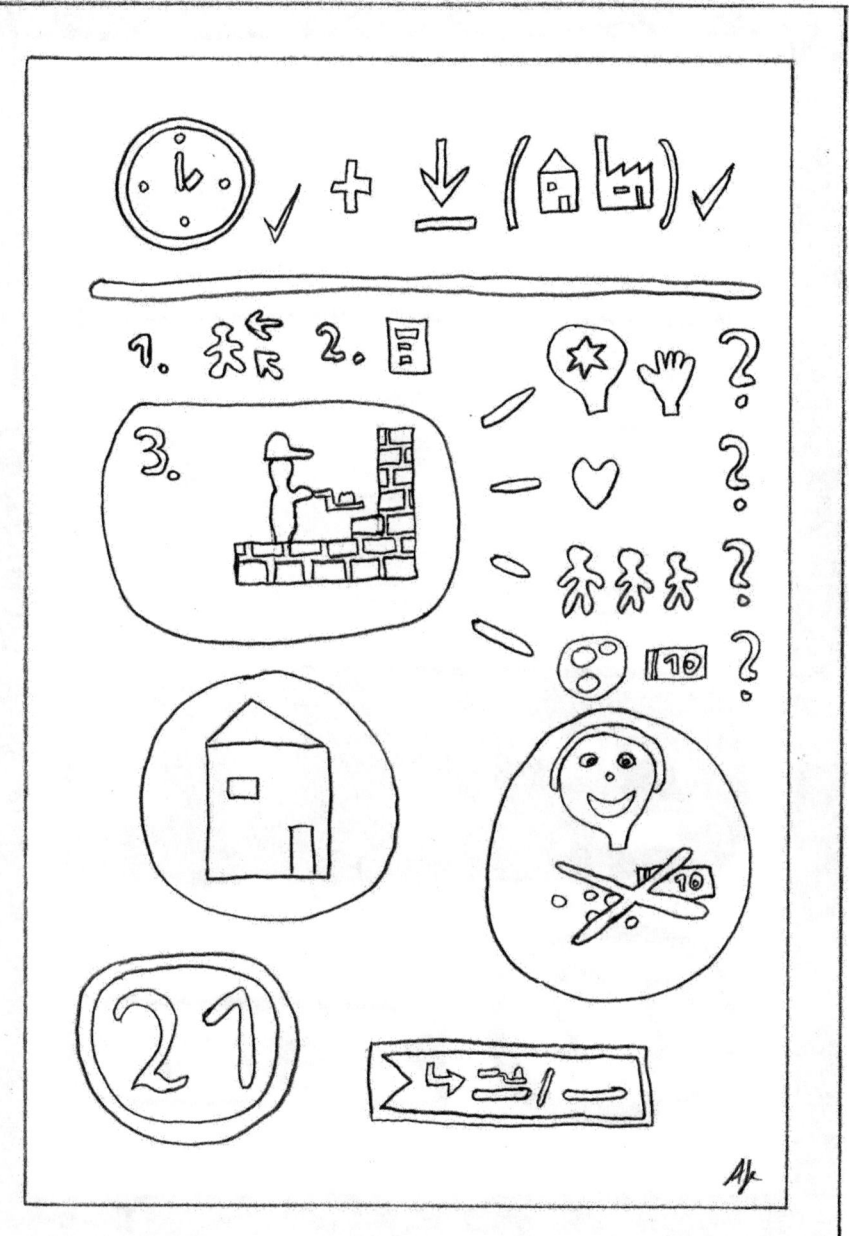

169

22. Chapter: Money

The last chapter focused on professional work. Typically, this is how we earn our money. In the following, we will look at what money actually is and how we can deal with it.

Money in general

Money is a **medium of exchange**. The real value of money coins and banknotes is regularly scarce. Money gets its value primarily from the fact that people believe in it. Not necessarily, but it is possible to use valuables like money, for example, gold coins. It is also possible for the state to tie the amount of paper and coin money to existing values such as gold stocks.

With money, one can easily **determine** and **compare** a **value**, for example, that of a loaf of bread. Since money, unlike bread, for instance, does not spoil, it can also be **stored** relatively well as a value.

Attention: There is the theory that if prices in an economy rise slightly on average, about two percent per year (relatively stable), then this **inflation rate** motivates people to spend their money or leave it in a bank for interest.

The general level of interest rates is influenced not only by the market but also by **central banks**. They set **base rates** for money transactions between them and commercial banks.

At a **commercial bank,** you get a **credit balance** on an account for the transfer of the money. In this case, you have a money claim against the bank in the amount booked. In this way, book money is created in addition to cash. The bank can, in turn, give money as a **loan** to companies, private individuals, or the state, thereby increasing their financial opportunities for action and investment.

If the **interest rate** on our account is above the inflation rate, the equivalent of our book money grows.

With the book money also the money supply within an economy grows. If people lose confidence in a currency, this can lead to a **high inflation** rate and, in the worst case, to a complete devaluation of money. States can and should then implement a new currency.

Companies, private individuals, banks, and states can become **insolvent**, i.e., illiqid or overindebted. If the assets are liquidated and distributed in insolvency proceedings, the creditors usually get almost nothing for their claims. In fact, this also leads to the destruction of money.

Insolvency insurance or, often with banks, state guarantees can keep the risk of loss low.

Our own financial budget

It is, of course, good when we keep an eye on our **income and expenses**.

My idea: We can look in our **wallet** or electronically on a card or a device and also on our **giro account** that there is always enough money available for current payments.

Also, we could build up **reserves** that are available quickly enough, for example, in a savings account. A general contingency reserve for at least one year and reserves for future, relatively probable major expenses such as renovations, training, new acquisitions, travel, and the like make sense. This keeps us solvent.

Those who can offer sufficient security - such as secure assets or income - can obtain money in the form of **loans**, which they often have to repay with interest.

Insurances

You regularly pay money to an insurance company so that it pays money to you in the case of an insured event. In this case, we do not need to set aside any reserves.

I think it makes sense to have a liability insurance that pays for the damage for which we are negligently responsible. If someone owns a property, it is important to have a building insurance policy that pays money for the restoration after a fire, as an example.

It is also good to think carefully to what extent health insurance, unemployment insurance, pension insurance, long-term care insurance, term life insurance, or other insurances make sense for you concerning your own assets and state benefits.

Capital accumulation

If someone can regularly save some money, it often makes sense to invest smaller amounts mainly in money at a trustworthy bank, and average amounts primarily in a home provided that you will live in it for longer.

It is recommended to invest one's capital, especially if it is large, in different investment forms to balance out their advantages and disadvantages. Examples:

Investment in **money**, for instance, as a deposit at a bank: advantage: little effort, relatively low risk of loss; disadvantage: low yield. Investing in other currencies has advantages and disadvantages in the case of exchange rate fluctuations.

Investment in **movable assets**: advantage: no insolvency or inflation risk; disadvantage: regularly no income and often high accompanying costs due to profit surcharges, taxes, or commissions. You usually have something immediately from everyday objects such as jewelry, expensive furniture, art, or vehicles, but the loss when reselling is often quite high. With valuables such as gold or precious stones, the chance and risk of fluctuations in value must be taken into account.

Real estate often generates a rental income of four to five percent per year. But rental is time-consuming, maintenance costs will destroy part of the income, and without tenants and in the event of non-payment, there ist no revenue.

Company holdings, in particular shares, have the risk of fluctuating value or a total loss due to insolvency. On the other hand, the highest returns can often be achieved by increase in value and profit distribution.

Does money make you happy?

Money can make you happy. Once our psyche has understood that you really can have valuable things for life for money, such as a loaf of bread, obtaining money as well as the later exchange will regularly make us happy.

Earning more money can also increase happiness. How much does a very inexpensive new car cost for you? I read that scientists say that the closer you get to half of this amount as income per month, the happier you become. Beyond, ecpacially responsibility and risk because of the people who want something from it, increase.

If our survival is adequately secured, however, genes, health, inner attitude, interpersonal relationships, and occupation are much more important for our happiness than our money.

The tasks at the end of the chapter

Task 22.1 **My total assets?**

What do you have in money, material assets, real estate, stocks,...?

Task 22.2 **My insurances?**

Task 22.3 **My financial budget?**

How do you manage your money: Cash, accounts, ...?
What is the ratio between income and expenditure?

What can you do, what do you want and what will you do?

22.1   My total assets:

22.2   My insurance:

22.3   My financial budget:

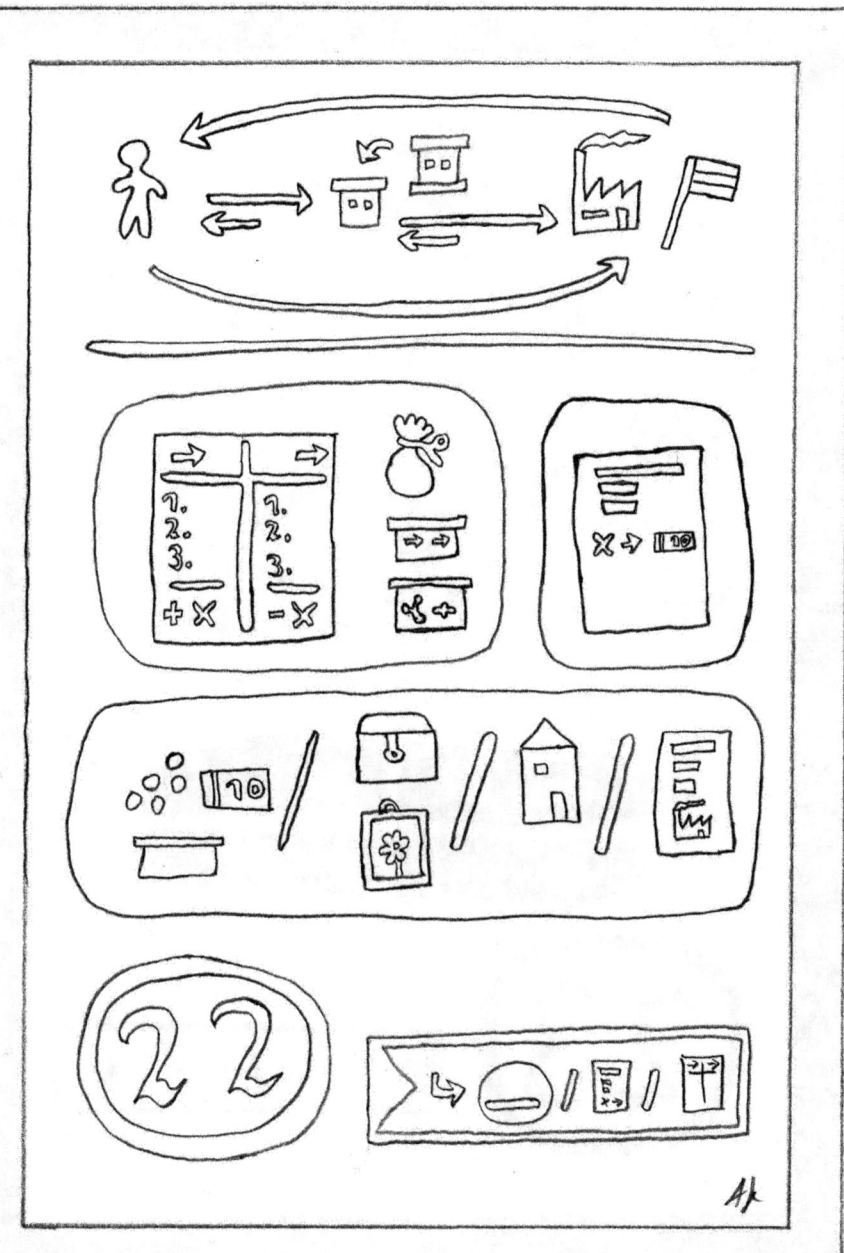

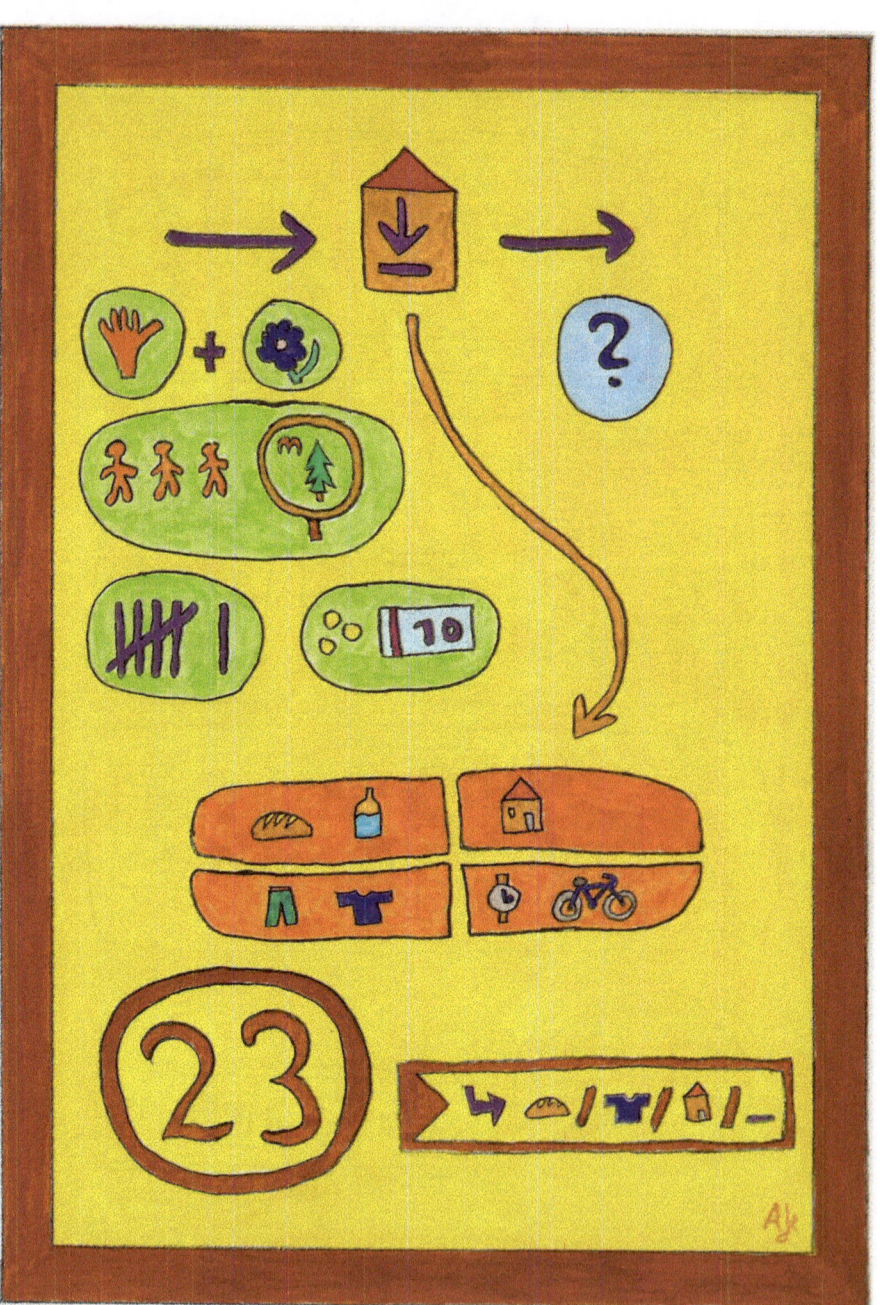

23. Chapter: Things

The previous chapter was about money, and this one is about something for which we can exchange money: things.

It is likely that here, as in other chapters, you already know many things or would rather do them differently. However, the handling of our things is important because they help us to live. So let's take a closer look:

The acquisition

When acquiring things, it is good to make sure that they are sufficiently **practical.** So do they serve the purpose well for which they are intended?

A very simple example: A plate is practical when the type and size fit, it is leak-proof, the material is scratch-resistant, not harmful to your health and easy to wash-up.

It is good if the purchased item is **beautiful**. For instance, do you like the plate?

It would be great if the products were manufactured, transported, and sold with **respect** to nature conservation and the employees. Admittedly, this is not always easy to judge.

The **optimum quantity** is also important. With plates, at least everyone in the household should have one, and a little more for security, for guests and to avoid having to wash everything at once, would also be good.

And of course, the item should be **good at the price.** Can you afford it? Is it worth what it costs? Is the price for the service reasonable?

Buying makes people happy, keeping only if we make ourselves aware that the things are still good. In the Prehistoric and Stone Ages, this was sensible, since what was acquired was usually food that was easily perishable or tasted good to others too. To buy, to enjoy, to eat, finish, that was often optimal at that time.

I find it better to have few but sufficient and good things than many low-quality ones. Because then one can be proud that nature and employees were taken into consideration, and one keeps the overview when joyfully using and looking at practical and beautiful things.

Storing

If we store things in a suitable **place, check, maintain,** and clean them properly and repair them if necessary and as well as possible, they will stay in good condition for a long time.

The elimination

I try to get rid of things when I am at least **almost entirely sure that** I will **never need or want them** again. So my things stay organized, and I have nothing that bothers me.

Whether and when to sell, give away or dispose of professionally, we could decide above all according to economic efficiency. Be careful when giving presents: not everyone wants to have what is garbage for us.

The foods

Let's start the consideration of individual groups of things with the most important ones: Foods. For drinks and food, we should pay particular attention to **storage**, because they are perishable.

Most living organisms, including bacteria and mold, no longer grow or hardly reproduce at temperatures below five degrees Celsius. In the refrigerator, therefore, many things stay fresh longer. This effect is even more pronounced in a freezer, for example, at minus 18 degrees Celsius.

Almost all living creatures die above 60 degrees Celsius because the life-essential protein denatures at this temperature. Foods can, therefore, sometimes last for many decades by preserving and hermetically sealing.

Dried foods last longer because bacteria or mold spores lack the water for their growth. Salting and sugaring a lot increase the effect. Airing often reduces the formation of molds.

Mechanical protection against animals such as flies, worms, ants, mice, or rats can also be useful, as well as protection against discoloring sunlight that destroys some vitamins or promotes plant growth.

Clothing

When it comes to clothing, it seems important to me to pay particular attention, that it is **clean** and **suitable**; suitable for the body size and the occasion to which we want to wear it, e.g., for work, sport, leisure or a festive occasion.

A closed wardrobe protects against moths, dust, and bleaching light. And if we don't have more than what fits in our wardrobe, we also have an optimal overview of our clothing.

The home

The most important thing for the value of an apartment or a house is its **location**. Can we reach our workplace easily? What are the people, shopping, and leisure facilities like in the immediate vicinity? How is the air, the noise, or the risk of flooding or similar? Maybe also: How is the apartment located inside the building?

Also important is the **condition of the building** (foundation, cellar, stability, insulation, roof), **size, equipment, furnishings,** and, of course, the **price,** including **aditional costs.**

I think a perfect apartment or a detached house has a slightly larger living room with a balcony, terrace, or garden. It has somewhat smaller rooms for a toilet, bathroom, perhaps with washing machine, kitchen, bedroom, children's or guest room and, if someone works at home, sufficient workrooms. It also has a storage room and garages or parking spaces of adequate size.

The other things

There are many other things, such as accessories such as wallets, keys, bags or glasses; telecommunications equipment such as mobile phones; work equipment such as computers or tools; transportation equipment such as cars or bicycles; leisure items such as instruments, sports equipment, games, books or cosmetics, and health items.

It's good if we deal with them in a way that gives us a lot of use and pleasure.

The tasks at the end of the chapter

Task 23.1 **My food?**

Task 23.2 **My clothes?**

Task 23.3 **My home?**

Task 23.4 **My other things?**

What do you mainly have in the mentioned areas?
How do you deal with it in general? Like in the text or otherwise?
What can you do, what do you want and what will you do in each case?

23.1 My foods:

23.2 My clothes:

23.3 My home:

23.4 My other things:

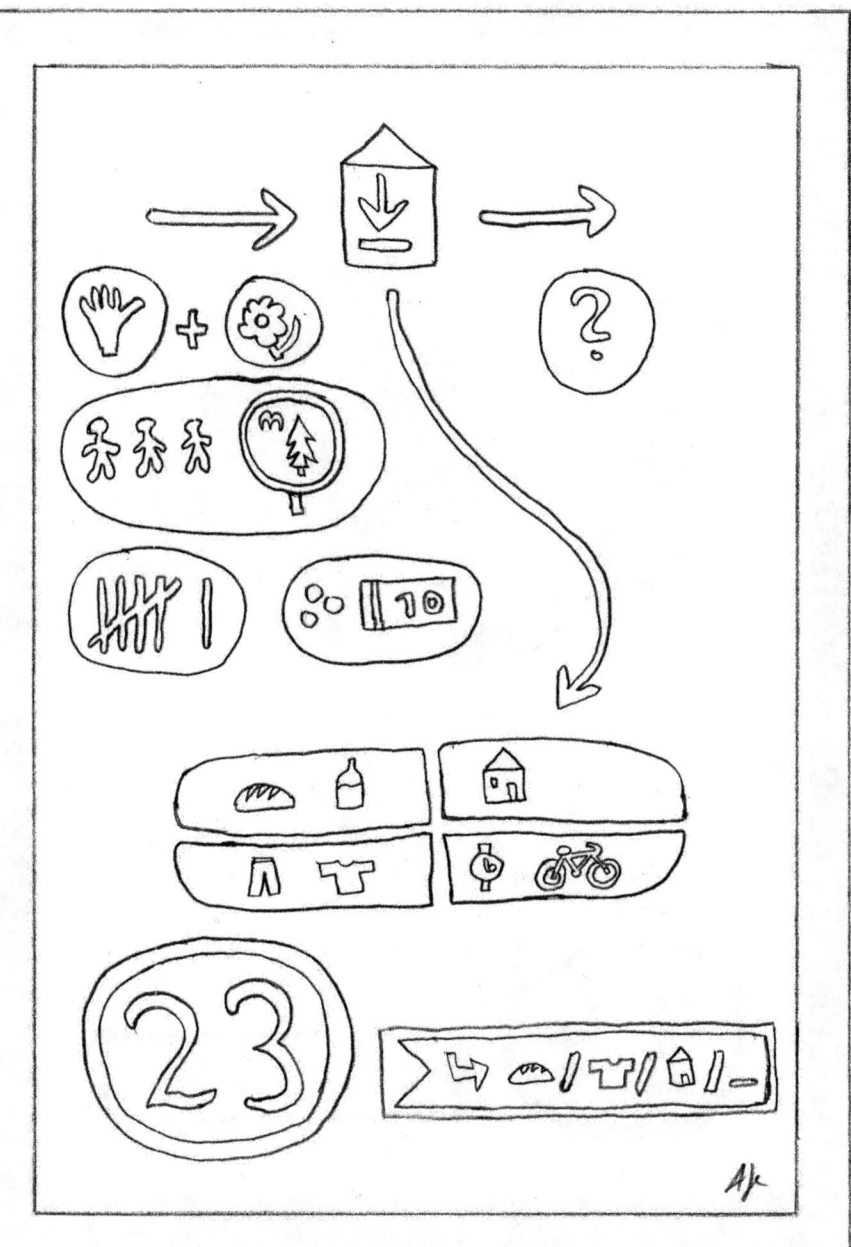

24. Chapter: Health, breathing, and drinking

We use many of the things, the last chapter was about, to maintain our health. In this chapter and the following, we will look at how well we can do this well. Sufficient health is indispensable for life, and since it is similar for everyone, it is worth it to treat this area more extensively.

Health in general

Health could be defined as the well-being of the body, the mind, and the, above all, social environment. Entirely healthy there is nothing about us that would still need healing. If we are not healthy, but capable of healing, then we are ill. If something is not curable, it is called a handicap. Probably no one is really 100 percent healthy. It is regularly sufficient to be healthy enough to be able to live well.

If we want to stay or become healthy, we should pay attention to ten things: To **1. Breathing, 2. Drinking, 3. Eating, 4. Sleeping, 5. Body moving, 6. Mind training, 7. Recovering, 8. Motivating, 9. Prevention and 10. Healing.**
If we also want to appear healthy, furthermore we pay attention to our **beauty.**

As a rule of thumb, it can be said that after three minutes without breathing, three days without drinking or three weeks without food, it can become life-threatening. This can be different in individual cases. Without sleep, we are no longer able to perform as we should; not sleeping for weeks or months will also become life-threatening. In other areas, life can likewise be endangered.

It is said, on average, about two-thirds of the age we reach depends on our lifestyle and environment, and one-third of our inherited genes. However, no way of life will give us eternal life. So we should neither over- nor underdo it here.

Let us now take a closer look at the ten health areas and begin with the first, breathing.

Breathing

In our lungs, we absorb oxygen from the air into our blood and release carbon dioxide into the air.

When we need little strength, we breathe through the nose and into the abdomen. If we exert a lot of effort, we can also breathe through the mouth and into the chest. Both works automatic or controlled.

Hyperventilation, i.e., breathing too much, causes unconsciousness.

It is good if we get **enough fresh air** to breathe. Inhabited closed rooms that are not automatically ventilated should be well ventilated at least once a day. For this open as many windows as possible until you get the impression that all the air in the room has been replaced. This is generally the case after about five minutes. Of course, rooms in which there are many people in a small space, or something else burdens the air more heavily should be ventilated more often. Even rooms that are usually hardly affected should be ventilated occasionally to prevent mold from forming.

It is good to make sure that we do not inhale any harmful substances, especially smoke. This is particularly important during pregnancy.

It is also good if we regularly go out into the fresh air and consider and hopefully notice that fresh air can also make us happy.

Drinking

Our body cleanses itself mainly by eliminating harmful substances from the blood through the kidneys and bladder, regularly up to six times a day through our urine.

By the way, nerve cells only work well with enough water, and too little can cause headaches.

Our body cools itself especially by sweating. At a maximum sweating performance, i.e., at maximum physical performance or at air temperatures above 60 degrees Celsius, this can amount to up to two liters per hour. Even when breathing, liquid evaporates continuously.

At room temperature and without significant physical exertion, our body probably needs 0.2 liters of water per ten kilograms of body weight per day. At 70 kilograms, that would be at least 1.4 liters per day.

This loss of fluid must be compensated. So if someone has around 70 kilograms, it would be a good idea to drink about **two liters** a day and more if necessary to be on the safe side. If you want to find out correctly, you should collect your urine for one day. If you pass out 1.0 to 1.5 liters, the drinking quantity is optimal. Too much drinking might also be not good, because the kidneys probably discharge useful minerals with the water.

We should drink our daily amount **throughout the day** and not drink too much before going to bed.

It is good to regularly drink healthy **water** without or, if you like and tolerate it, with carbonic acid and perhaps with or without lemon or something similar. Herbal or fruit tea or strongly diluted fruit juice spritzer (about 10 percent juice) is also good.

Drinks that may be contaminated with germs should be boiled before drinking. If necessary, put it in a transparent bottle and let it sit in the sun for several hours.

Occasionally we may enjoy a hot chocolate, a fruit juice, a lemonade, mixed drinks, or similar, but because of the high sugar content, we should not drink too much of it.

Due to the effect of **caffeine**, we should only drink a maximum of three cups (seven grams of arabica coffee powder each) per day. In the case of caffeine-containing tea, it may alternatively be about twice as many cups because of the lower amount of caffeine. At least five hours before you start sleeping, you should not drink any more of this so that the caffeine can be broken down by the body before sleep and that it does not prevent you from falling asleep.

With alcoholic beverages, it is probably good not to drink more than three centiliters of **alcohol** a day as a man because of health risks, effects, and nutrient content. Since women are usually a bit smaller, have a lower water content in the body, and their liver does not work as fast and therefore does not break down alcohol as quickly, women should drink a maximum of two centiliters of alcohol per day. Two centiliters are contained in about half a liter of beer, a quarter of a liter of wine, or a double schnapps.

Children should not consume caffeine or alcoholic beverages. Pregnant women should not drink alcohol and, at most, the specified amount of caffeine, as the infantile body cannot handle the substances well.

Of course, we should not drink anything poisonous. By the way, water that contains too much salt increases the thirst because the kidneys rinse out the excess salt with water.

And we can also enjoy our drinking gratefully and with pleasure.

The tasks at the end of the chapter

Task 24. 1 **My breathing?**

Task 24.2 **My drinking?**

How do you relate to each area?
What can you do, what do you want and what will you do in each case?

24.1 My breathing:

24.2 My drinking:

25. Chapter: Eating

After breathing and drinking as the first and second health area, now comes the third: Eating.

Why do we eat, and how does food work?

We gain our **energy** mainly by the reaction of carbon and hydrogen with oxygen to carbon dioxide and water. This happens in the cells that "burn" fat and, above all, glucose in the mitochondria. Sugars are molecules of carbon, hydrogen, and oxygen. The sugar comes from our food. This is chewed in the mouth and interspersed with saliva. The food is collected in the stomach and released into the intestines in portions. There the digested food components are absorbed into the bloodstream. The liver can convert many things into fat or glucose sugar. The components:

Sugar is found in various forms, can be broken down and absorbed in the intestine, and later transformed into glucose.

Starch consists of very long molecules, which are composed of many small sugar molecules. Our saliva, in particular, breaks down starch into sugar during digestion in the mouth, stomach, and intestines.

Fats are molecules with less oxygen content and therefore higher energy content than sugar. Larger fat molecules only enter the blood via the lymph.

Proteins are molecules primarily composed of amino acids, which in addition to carbon, oxygen, and hydrogen, also contain some nitrogen.

In total, there are about 40 so-called **essential food components**. These are components that the body needs sufficiently but cannot produce itself. These include a few amino acids and omega-3 and omega-6 fatty acids. We also need **minerals** such as calcium, chlorine, potassium, magnesium, sodium, phosphorus and sulfur; **vitamins** such as vitamins A, B1, B2, niacin, B5, B6, biotin, B12, C, D, E, K; **trace elements** such as iron, iodine, cobalt, copper, manganese, molybdenum, selenium, silicon and zinc, possibly also secondary plant substances and others.

Indigestible dietary **fibers** ensure that our intestines function well and can empty between three times a day and three times a week.

How much should we eat?

Excess energy is initially stored partially in glycogen, the "animal starch," in muscles, liver, and fascia and a lot in fat in fatty tissue.

Let's take a look at our own stomach. Too much abdominal fat is unhealthy. If we can pull it in in such a way that it disappears, that could be good.

To find out exactly, we take our **body weight** in kilograms, divide it by our body size in meters, and then divide it again by our body size in meters. What comes out is our body mass index or BMI. Between 20 and 25, everything usually is fine. A little less can be acceptable with young women, a little more with muscular men and in old age, but over 30 is regularly bad.

It sounds simple: Being too thin, we should eat food that is richer in energy and too fat we should eat food that is low in energy. Let us bear in mind that the same amount of fat in weight has about twice as much **energy** as starch or sugar and that these again have almost twice as much energy as protein products. Fruit and vegetables, if they do not contain a lot of sugar, starch, or protein, contain considerably less energy. Also, some drinks may contain energy-rich nutrients; pure water may not.

A few weight loss tips: Regularly weighing. To avoid the "yo-yo effect," lose a maximum of 500 grams per week. Above all, eat less sugar and starch and not too much fat. Sport, otherwise the body will lose too much muscle mass. Do not eat late in the day and no snack between meals, this can trigger hunger.

We often already feel **hunger** when we perceive good food or when our blood sugar level is too low. If we wait for a while, our body will have balanced this out of reserves. In any case, we feel full when our stomach is full. And this should not be before strong physical or mental exertion so that digestion and performance function.

What should we eat?

It would be good to eat at least four to five servings of fruit and vegetables, green salad, cabbage or similar per day. One serving is about a handful. It provides many vitamins, minerals, trace elements, secondary plant substances, and fiber.

One to three servings of **starch suppliers** provide easy to digest and relatively quick available energy. Bread, muesli, potatoes, rice, corn, pasta, or millet, for example, contain a lot of starch.

About one to two portions of **protein** a day could be just as good. Meat, fish, eggs, dairy products, some nuts, and legumes such as soya are protein sources. Muscles, immune defense, and other functions are well supplied with the most essential necessary building materials.

Also good is a portion of **fat** and a maximum of one **sugar**, each mixed with other food. Vegetable oils or butter consist almost exclusively of fat, nuts often only half. Aroma substances can dissolve in fat, and some vitamins can only be absorbed dissolved in fat. On the other hand, the conversion of a lot of fat can strain the liver and digestion takes a long time. A lot of sugar is found in honey, dried fruits, and sweets. Sugar is the easiest to digest and provides the fastest energy; on the other hand, intestinal fungi and bacteria that can cause abdominal pain and tooth decay, also like sugar.

Mostly, not always, "organic," fresh, and unprocessed foods are particularly healthy.

Of course, we do **not** eat **poisonous foods**. Mold is often poisonous, some bacterial waste can it be too; putrefactive bacteria are rather not. Burned things are unhealthy in larger quantities, and with heating probably over 250 degrees Celsius toxic substances can form. Salt is vital but harmful in large quantities. It is better to use fewer aroma substances, colorants, and flavor enhancers; they are usually not unhealthy, but they make even bad food appear good.

And of course, our food should **taste good,** too.

How often and when should we eat?

Breakfast, lunch, and dinner are good. Snacks between meals are useful for children and when there is high energy demand. Because the glycogen in the body only lasts about one day, I would eat it at least **daily.** Since a full stomach needs about two hours to empty, we could give it at least this time before the next meal and before sleeping.

How should we eat?

Hot cooking can destroy pathogens, make food tastier, and more digestible, but it can also destroy parts of healthy food. When we drink before we eat, it runs directly into the intestines via the "stomach street" and does not unnecessarily dilute the digestive juices. It is helpful if we take enough time to eat and chew thoroughly. It is wonderful if we do this in good company and **enjoy** appearance, smell, and taste.

The task at the end of the chapter

Task 25 **My eating?**

What does your stomach look like, or how high is your BMI?
When do you eat what and how much? How do you eat?
What can you do, what do you want and what will you do?

25. My eating:

What does your stomach look like, or how high is your BMI?

When do you eat what and how much? How do you eat?

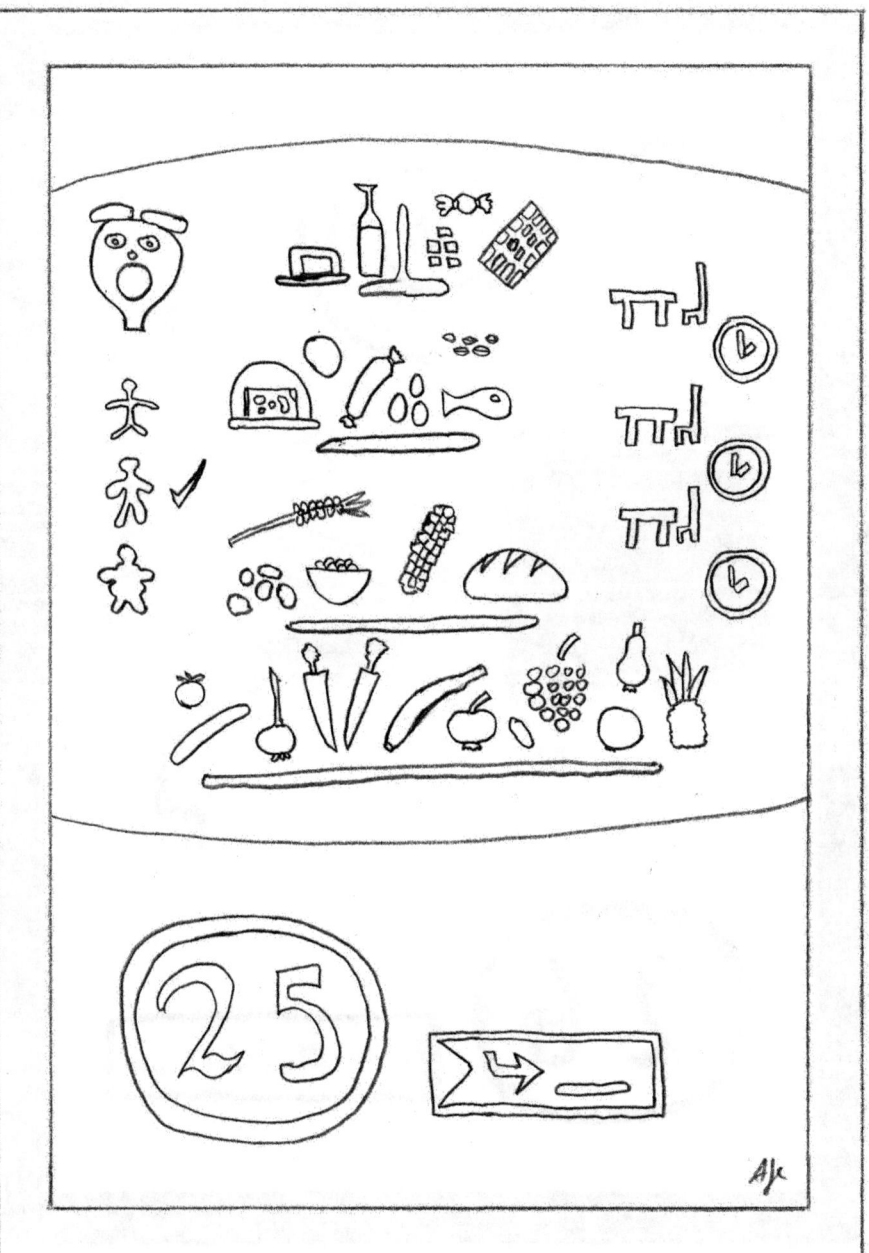

Chapter 26: Sleeping and dreaming

In this chapter, we continue with the fourth area of health, sleeping. On this occasion, we also take a closer look at dreaming.

Sleeping in general

In our sleep, we regularly do not consciously perceive ourselves anymore. Our body, including our brain, usually continues to work unconsciously. We can recover relatively well. And our unconscious can process experiences and thoughts independently of consciousness.

How much sleep do we need?

As adults, we should probably have **at least five** hours of good sleep regularly. Also, it is good if we allow ourselves some "luxury sleep." **Seven to eight hours** a day should be good usually, six to nine at any rate normal.

Only you can find out for yourself how much sleep is exactly the optimal amount for you. There are people who regularly need more or less than "normal." A child needs clearly more than an adult. An infant usually sleeps for about 16 hours a day. In old age, five to six hours of sleep are often enough instead of seven to eight.

We can catch up on missed sleep over the next few days. Sleeping in advance is also possible but only for a short time. For example, if we intentionally sleep a little longer this morning, we can easily do without some sleep tonight.

Those who sleep too little and those who sleep too much will typically become tired and weak.

When do we sleep?

For most people, the time **between 23:00 (11 p.m.) and 08:00 (8 a.m.)** should be ideal for sleeping. Anyway between midnight and 06:00 we should therefore think of a considerate night's sleep. Our personal optimal sleeping time can be at a different time. It makes sense that we regularly go to bed and get up at about the same time, then we can get used to our personal sleeping time.

A short nap at noon is also supposed to be healthy.

Where do we sleep?

Let's think about what **environment** is generally good for a restful sleep.

Our sleeping place should not be too hard or too soft to protect our joints.

Our pillow should only be high enough to allow our spine to remain straight when lying on our side.

Our blanket should be in a way that we are neither cold nor sweaty under it. We could wear socks against cold feet, comfortable sleeping clothes or nothing.

A bed not only makes it easier for us to get up, it also protects us from the dust, the coolness, and perhaps the creeping animals on the floor.

A quiet, dark, and not too warm or cold environment also helps to sleep.

A bedroom in which we are safe from dangerous animals, weather, and other dangers is also good.

Inner calm sleep

If the essentials in our lives are in order, our minds will calm down relatively easily, our muscles will relax, the pineal gland pours out the sleep hormone melatonin, and we fall asleep.

If this is not the case, in the long run, we should take it seriously and decide to think about our problems during the day or seek help.

The sleep ritual

A ritual helps many people to fall asleep. I have come up with one. So:

Shortly before going to bed, we remember that we ate enough, moved enough, didn't sleep too much, and managed to control essential things sufficiently.

We don't do anything anymore that is strenuous. Maybe we have something to drink, go to the bathroom and then to bed.

As a religious person, we could fold our hands and pray, in any case, we could say the following:

"The good life shall be. Amen."

We continue with: **"Today I am grateful for ..."** and above all, briefly go through the essentials of the past day. If something was bad, perhaps there is something good about it for which we can be grateful, maybe we have learned something from it.

With: **"For tomorrow I wish ..."** we start to say something about the next day.

And with: **"Especially important to me is ..."** we make ourselves aware of what seems particularly important and desirable to us at the moment beyond the days.

I cannot rule out the possibility that a God on the other side can hear this as well. I think it is probable that the energy of our thoughts, especially in a relaxed state during the night, can at least partly leave our mind and radiate into the mind of others. In any case, it helps us to come to rest and to adjust ourselves inwardly to dreaming at night and to the goal-oriented action the next day.

If we haven't already fallen asleep, we give a loved one a **goodnight kiss.** If no one else is there, we may also give ourselves one.

If we are together with our partner, also something more than a kiss will lead to better sleep.

Dreaming at night

Our sleep takes place in sleep phases, which become less deep in the course of sleep, but longer and last regularly about 1.5 hours each. During every stage of sleep, we dream, in some sleep phases, particularly intensely. The dream is probably a means by which our unconscious tries to process experiences, insights, wishes, fears, and other things.

If we wake up with fear from a dream, we had a **nightmare.**

We can **remember** nightmares, intense or regular dreams, best write them down and try to **interpret** them: What does this imagery mean? If possible, we could lead the dream to a **good end** in our mind.

The daydream

Even awake, we can dream. We can use this consciously:

Examples: If we face a test or another unknown situation, we can imagine it – and ourselves in it – spiritually and thus **learn** to deal with it without actually having to experience it.

We can also think of feelings, dreams, problems, desires, and the like and see which images our unconscious provides us in our daydreams and **recognize** from the interpretation what it wants to tell us.

The tasks at the end of the chapter

Task 26.1 *My sleeping?*

Where, with which ritual, how much and how well do you sleep?
What can you do, what do you want and what will you do here?

Task 26.2 *My dreaming?*

Do you remember strong or regular dreams?
What could your unconscious process in it?
If the dream was not a good one, how could it end well?

26.1 My sleeping:

26.2 My dreaming:

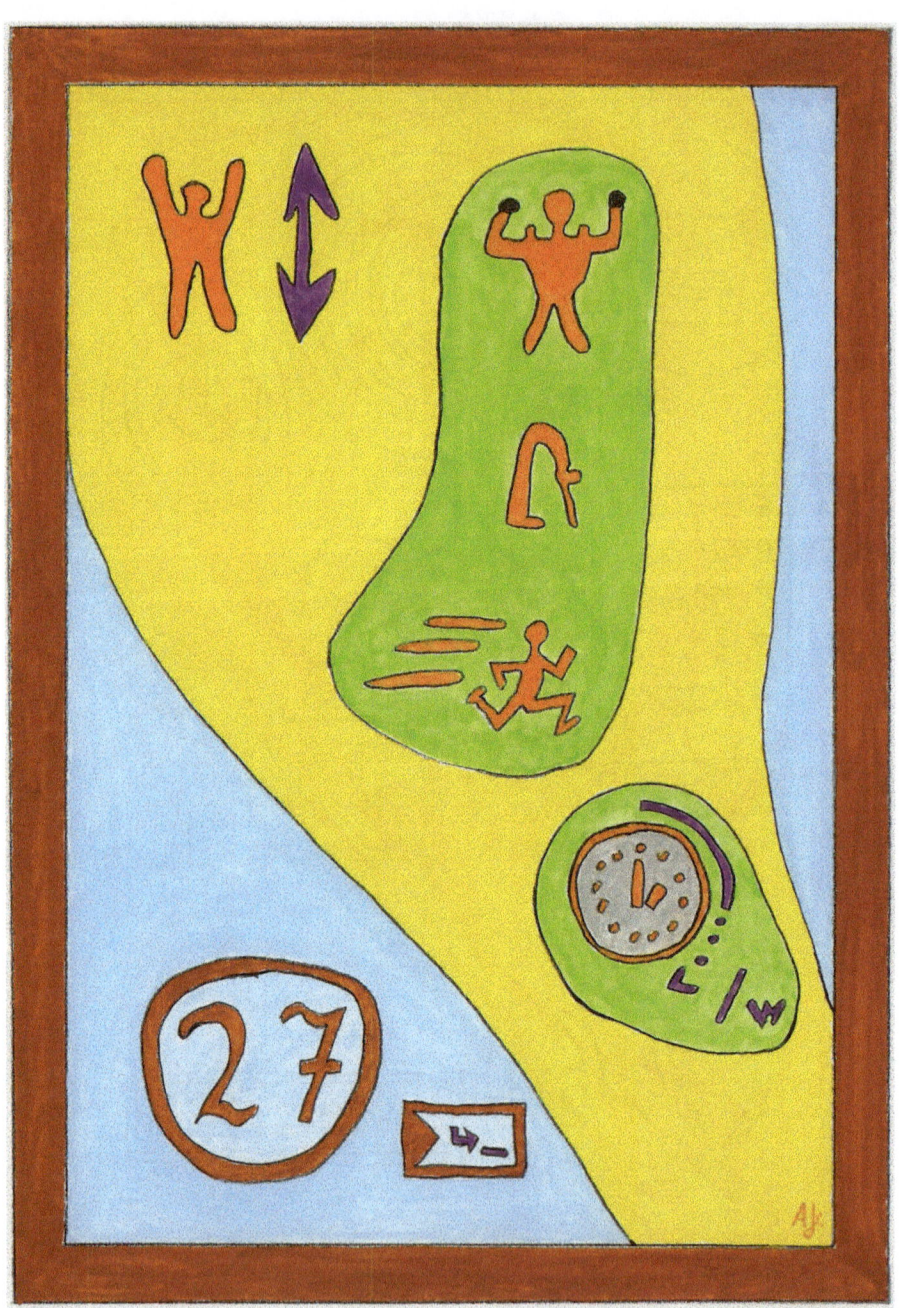

209

27. Chapter: Body moving

After sleeping and dreaming now to something more awake, the fifth health area: Exercise.

Physical activity in Prehistoric or Stone Age

It is easy to imagine how our ancestors exercised in pre-historic or stone age. **Every day** they had to walk **moderately** on their way to and from the collection and hunting places. They had to bend over and over again through thickets, push branches and twigs away by hand or climb over obstacles.

From time to time, great effort was necessary: hunting, climbing up a tree, fleeing from an attacking animal, or fighting with others.

Wherever possible, they did not move so that they coud recover and **not consume energy unnecessarly,** as food was probably in short supply.

Exercise as a civilized adult city dweller

A person living in a civilized environment can travel to work and back. At work, he hardly moves or only moves one-sided. At home, he can spend his free time on a comfortable sofa.

For many, that might feel okay. Only some movement people will feel an inner need to move.

Why move?

Our organism is adjusted to regular exercise. It trains the heart and circulatory system, helps the intestines to digest, is vital for well-functioning joints, stable bones, strong muscles, mobile connective tissue, and for our well-being.

Studies probably show that as adults, we should do something for **endurance, strength,** and **mobility** for **at least three hours** a week with moderate stress. For smaller children, at least three hours of exercise per day are probably good.

Too much and too strenuous can, as is so often the case, do more harm than good in this area.

Exercising purposefully

Following I suggest a good exercise. Feel free to do what is right for you.

To do this, we first use opportunities to exercise in our everyday lives, for example, on the way to work, shopping, or in our leisure time. Walking, cycling, swimming, table tennis, badminton, or volleyball are definitely suitable. Per day we should have at least half an hour **medium-intensive movement**.

If it seems necessary for us, because we may have one-sided stress or problem joints, we allow ourselves to be shown compensatory **physiotherapy exercises**, which we perform daily for three to 15 minutes.

Once or twice a week, we can do the following or a similar **body fitness program**:

1. Warm-up and train **endurance** and circulation at the same time, for example, jogging so that you can still talk or your pulse is between 120 and 130. Or for instance, on a cross-trainer, increase the performance during 15 to 20 minutes, hold the maximum performance, i.e., as much as possible, or pulse rate about 200 to 220 minus age, for a short time and then follow a short run-out phase.

Then train **strength**; in each case, about 15 repetitions at medium to slow speed with almost as much weight as possible. If we do more than 20 repetitions, we train more endurance, less repetition with more weight would increase the strength but could put a lot of strain on the joints.

Perhaps we wear weight cuffs around the ankle joints to make things more difficult. It is good if we do the exercises standing on a therapy spinning top because this trains the muscles between the vertebrae.

The posture while standing is upright, knees slightly flexed, abdomen and bottom firm, shoulders loosely straight, and the head slightly bent forward.

The following exercises could be functional:

2. Take dumbbells in both hands, do squats so that the back stays straight and the knees hardly get over the tips of the toes.

3. Stand on the ball of one foot and stretch the ankle joint. Switch.

4. Let your arms hang, circle your shoulders back and forth and pull them upwards.

5. Bend forearms upwards towards chest (biceps).

6. Bend raised arms backward (triceps).

7. Move the dumbbells up along the body to the chest and / or open the arms upwards like a bird. The little

fingers are furthest up and / or push the dumbbells up over the head.

8. Bend upper body slightly forward with a straight back, move dumbbells up to the side like a butterfly with hanging arms. Are you able to do the 15 repetitions, are your dumbbells too light?

9. Squats in a lunge. Switch.

10. Sit on a chair, place your forearms on your thighs, and lift your wrists.

11. Turn wrists 180 degrees and repeat.

12. Right knee and right hand on a chair. Move left stretched arm back up. Switch.

13. In the same position, but, if possible, with heavier dumbbell, pull it to the chest as if rowing.

14. Stand, bend one knee joint backward, switch.

15. Bend straight upper body to the right and left.

16. Do pull-ups, for example, on a door bar.

17. Get a training mat, go to the "all fours position," stretch one foot to the ceiling, and lower. Switch.

18. Pushups, i.e., put your hands on the floor with your body stretched out, move upper body up and down.

19. Lie on your stomach, pull in buttocks and stomach, shoulders back, head up in double chin, both palms forward, push right forward, pull left-back, then reverse movement.

20. Lying sideways, lift up the upper leg. Switch.

21. Stay on the side, make side prop. Switch.

22. Sitting, bend your legs, pull your knees outwards with your hands and move them inwards against pull.

23. Sit-ups: Lie on your back, bend your legs, move your head and upper body to the ceiling, looking upwards.

24. Just move one shoulder up. Switch.

25. Raise buttocks up and towards the head.

Then warm down and train your **flexibility** by stretching for about 15 seconds each:

26. Stretch both hands far up, maybe on a therapy spinning top, then stretch each side.

27. Stretch one elbow over your head and touch both hands on your back. Switch.

28. Hold the head with left hand on the right back side, stretch angled right arm down-back. Switch.

29. Press hand and head together: right, left, front, back, top, and while turning right and left.

30. Push slightly bent arms backward in three positions (first at right angles to the torso, and then two times further down).

31. Press all fingers back, one at a time.

32. Circle hips repeatedly to the right, then turn the upper body to the right and hold. Switch.

33. Stand, 2 x, vertebrae by vertebrae, hands to the floor.

34. Bend one leg, circle ankle, switch.

35. Stand, pull one foot up at the ankle joint. Switch.

36. Stretch achilles tendon in a lunge step.

37. Lie on stomach, raise straight arms and legs.

38. Sit on mat, touch toes, and stretch legs.

39. Candle: Lift legs up, rest body on shoulders.

40. Maybe do more, in any case, be happy that the holistic body fitness program was achieved. ☺

The task at the end of the chapter

Task 27 **My exercise?**

What do you do how often and for how long?
What can you do, what do you want and what will you do?

27. My exercise:

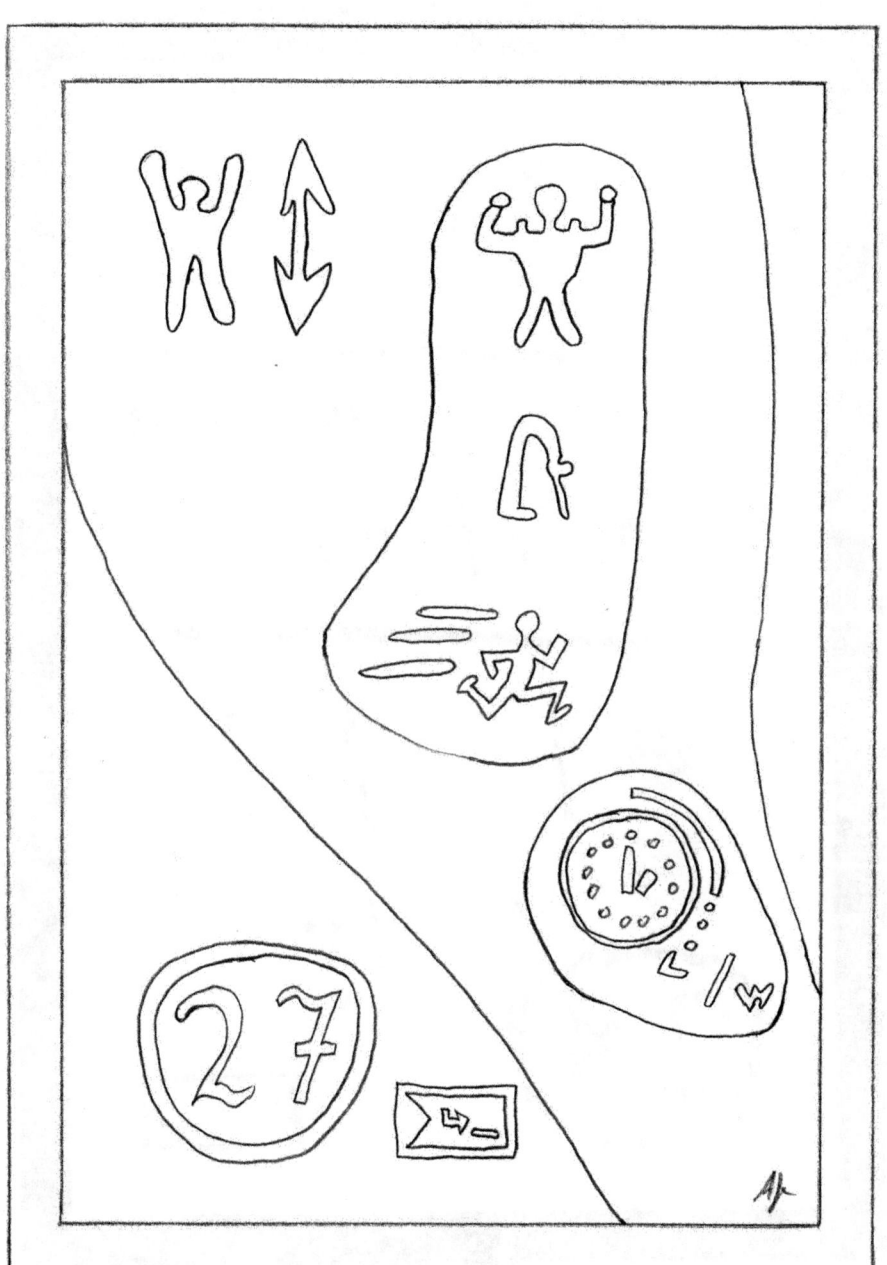

217

28. Chapter: Mind training

We already talked about the training of our body. Let us now look at my ideas and in the tasks at our ideas on how we can do this with our minds.

Training the mind at the opportunity

It is good when we use our minds when there is a good opportunity to do so. ☺

We pay appropriate attention to the **perception** of our senses. We see colors, shapes, structures, and movements. We hear noises and sounds. We feel the temperature and texture of something on our skin. We smell scents. We taste or perceive something. Some things we enjoy appropriately.

When **feelings** or moods such as joy, love, sadness, anger, hunger, or others appear in us, then we notice them and deal with them.
    Maybe we name the feeling briefly in mind.
    Maybe we express our feelings.
    Maybe we will find an explanation with the mind.
    Maybe we enjoy some feelings consciously.
    Maybe we can dissolve others by distancing ourselves inwardly, making a different assessment, thinking about something else, or doing something else.

We use our **mind**, again and again, to think about something and to understand it as much as possible. Attention: Anyone who, even unconsciously, ponders too much about seemingly unsolvable problems can mentally "go crazy," be distracted, mentally dazed, and burdened with further stress symptoms.

We train our **mind** by **learning, practicing,** and **repeating** knowledge and skills when we need them or want them.

Our memory works something like this: A part of our perception is only a very short time in our consciousness. In short-term memory we keep some things briefly, for example, a sentence during a dictation. In long-term memory, important things are stored permanently, and facts are stored elsewhere in the brain as episodes we experienced ourselves. This difference can be noticeable. During storage, new nerve tracts with links to other cells with matching contents are created in the brain. Often used nerve tracts become thicker and thus faster. Content that is no longer used is hardly reconnected and can be forgotten. Remembering is finding core content and reconstructing. With routine, we can do something very well, but we are often unaware of how exactly it works.

Memorizing and clarifying techniques, if required

The following technique can help you to remember facts:

1. Get the **facts** straight. For example, write the question on the front of a small card, the answer on the back. If possible, the answer has no more than seven units of meaning. If you note down to the question, how many units of meaning there are, it helps to be complete. For larger units, use paper or a file.

2. **Learn** the facts well: Make yourself aware that they are important facts. Try to understand them as much as possible. Try to associate them with familiar ones or use "mnemonic aids." Also, use this book; it contains something to all essentials. Then try to reproduce the facts by heart. It helps if one has heard or experienced the facts already once or tells someone.

3. **Repeat.** Super would be four times: after about a day, a week, a month, and a quarter of a year. If you find that you can't do something anymore, start all over again.

Techniques that can help us **clarify** our minds are, for example, **talking** to a suitable person or in a suitable group, talking to an imatined person or group, the **prayer**, **writing** a letter, diary, or working with this book. Using it, especially in a good discussion group, is helpful here.

Informing the mind

For our mind, to be able to steer us well, it needs sufficient knowledge and ability in its memory.

Basic knowledge and basic skills include what is essential and fundamental for us in one area.

Generally, for life, we typically learn most of it in our childhood in family, kindergarten, school, and in our private environment and perhaps accompanied by this book. And we can also use this book regularly to repeat and keep up to date.

In other, for the individual important areas, for example, the job, one will acquire basic knowledge and skills first in a similar way and then keep up-to-date by repetition and further training.

Detailed knowledge and skills are individual facts or skills that supplement the basic knowledge and that occur less frequently or are not so important in the application, but can be indispensable important.

Here it is sufficient if we know where we can read it, look up, ask questions, or learn it ourselves.

For us, **specialized knowledge** and skills are something that typically only specialists have to have, because it is not generally necessary for us, or the acquisition would be too time-consuming or too difficult.

Here it is enough if we can find out who can help us if necessary, and then use this or them when it makes sense.

Daily knowledge is what is only important for the moment. For example, how the weather will be or what task should be done right now.

We should inform ourselves regularly about the essential daily knowledge through news, mail, conversations, diary, task list, or notes, pass on important things to others, and remember what seems to be worth remembering.

Nobody needs **luxury knowledge,** but it can and is allowed to be fun to learn it and to show off. And you don't always know what you need and what you don't need.

If we have time, strength, and desire, we can also treat ourselves to it.

Our mind training

I think it is enough for a healthy mind if we follow the procedure as mentioned above.

Our mind is trained with almost every action we do, for example in sports, making music, handicrafts, reading or speaking.

Although learning new things and the knowledge and skills of old things make people happy, many people, especially adults, find learning exhausting, and only few people see it as something easy, which is done with great pleasure and dedication.

And there is a reason for this, because here also exists a too much. Too much at once can lead to fatigue syndrome, and there are indications that too much in total slows down the brain because it takes time to search through the many facts.

The task at the end of the chapter

Task 28 **My mind training?**

How do you like the ideas from this chapter?
What can you do, what do you want and what will you do?

28. My mind training:

29. Chapter: Recovering

After "exercise" and "mind training," now the seventh health area: "Recovering." This is about the safeguarding of our physical life force. The maintenance of our mental life force comes in the next chapter.

The effort

It may sound unbelievable, but if you want to be physically rested, you first have to make regular efforts so that your body and with it the nerve cells remain in training and smaller efforts can easily be coped with. Because what is not needed, our body will reduce over time. This applies to muscles and bones, as well as to the functioning of our nerve cells and our mind.

Exercise, thinking, and **feeling** are strenuous when we perform them very **strongly** or moderately, but for a **long** time. Examples of something strenuous are: Running, learning something difficult, or prolonged intense fear.

Also, our work, some leisure activities, our efforts to achieve and maintain some goals, to adjust to new things or to solve problems, are regularly exhausting, at least in the long run.

Efforts are necessary for a good life. As I said, they keep us fit, often make us happy, and often lead to recognition in the community.

But we should not overtax ourselves. Too much effort at the top or too long effort can harm us. In extreme cases, we can even die from excessive strain, i.e., from excessive dis-stress.

When we feel powerless, **exhausted**, or perhaps even blocked, our mind regularly notices that we need time to recover. Overexcited, we are perhaps still fighting against this insight.

Recovery

In recovery phases, our cells can replenish their nutrient reserves, break down waste, and repair possible damage. Our nerve cells can reconnect. Stress hormones in the blood can be broken down, and our hormone depots in the hormone glands can fill up again.

The **change** can have a relaxing effect. While we move other muscles, think, or feel something else, the previous one can recover.

Slight, pleasant activities often have a particularly relaxing effect. They hardly exhaust us but distract us from what could strain us. An example is the colouring of a given picture: We don't have to think much, and we don't have to do much.

Sleeping and **resting** also have a relaxing effect. When we sit down or lie down comfortably, our body regulates our performance down, and often our sense of time becomes somewhat faster. So we are motivated to rest long enough. In the Prehistoric and Stone Age, this resting mode probably helped us not to use energy senselessly when there was nothing essential to do.

Shorter **breaks** between strenuous activities, even the involuntary ones, help to hold out longer. **After-work-hours** and **holidays** at least also help to recover.

Recreation is good, and therefore regularly makes happy.
    During many or long periods of recreation, or when there is simply nothing to do, we can feel bored and actually feel lethargic or weak and lazy, because of the reduced performance.

Three relaxation techniques

Let's look at three techniques that, among other things, also serve relaxation.

Meditation: This is just an attempt only to be. Perceiving mindfully without much evaluation, thinking, or feeling. If you like, we can try this together as an example:
    We sit upright. If we want, we can put our hands open on our thighs. If this is not good for you, you can also try lying down, standing up, or walking gently.
If you want, close your eyes now.
You perceive how you breathe: In – out. In – out.
You sense yourself; all the way from the bottom to top.
You sense your surroundings:

Maybe nature, a candle, or a picture.
Or you repeat a short text meditatively.
If thoughts do come, you look at them briefly and let them go again.
Together we take our time.
At the end of the meditation, we bow deeply.

Meditation helps spiritual people to connect with the divine. Perhaps you, too, can feel especially deeply connected with everything that is really there. And maybe something good will come into us or back to order within us.

Autogenic training: This is an attempt to positively influence one's own perception. Feel invited to do the following exercise:
You lie flat on your back or sit comfortably.
You are completely calm.
It breathes you.
Your body becomes pleasantly heavy.
Your body becomes pleasantly warm.
Your forehead is pleasantly cool.
If you want, you can now imagine something beautiful. For example, flying over a beautiful landscape or seeing how you achieve a beautiful goal.
Allow yourself the time you need.
In the end, you extend and stretch yourself and come back awake and satisfied out of the relaxation.

We can also use autogenic training in a kind of "daydream" to practice new situations and to recognize things. In calm-mode, new settings are also particularly memorable. Our brain works in this phase with the frequency of about ten hertz, awake with 30, in sleep with three to seven hertz.

Snuggling: This is the shared, intimate rest, best with people we like very much. Tenderness can pleasantly accompany snuggling.

And also this not only relaxes, but moreover strengthens our spiritual bonds and makes us happy.

Our entire physical life force

Overall, the following should be good:

Regularly we do medium or slightly strenuous activities, and alternate these with others, as clearly as possible different, medium, or somewhat strenuous activities. Occasionally we also have strenuous activities, but not too strenuous.

We treat ourselves to regular relaxation sessions, for example, after lunch, when necessary, and if possible, before we feel completely exhausted.

The task at the end of the chapter

*Task 29 **My physical life force?***

29.1 *My effort?*
       What is exhausting for me in my everyday life?

29.2 *My recovery?*
       When and how do I regularly recover from it?

What can you do, what do you want and what will you do in each case?

29.1 My effort:

29.2 My recovery:

232

30. Chapter: Motivating

In the seventh health area, "motivating," the question is from where we draw our spiritual or mental strength to live. Why do we do what we do? What for are we alive?

Motivation in general

Why don't we just lie down somewhere, like a rock, and stay there? Well, if there had been a living creature that would have done this in the past, it would have died, had no offspring, and consequently would not have been able to pass this behavior on through its genes or through its role model. In the course of evolution, a multitude of mechanisms emerged that motivate us living beings to live successfully. Feelings, needs, instincts, and learned behavior patterns are some examples.

Motivation often begins with an **idea,** the belief to be able to achieve it and the will to obtain it. It continues with the **path** towards it, does not end with the adequate achievement of the **goal,** but continues with the adequate **securing** of the goal and culminates in the addition of **luxury.**

Sometimes the motivational impulse comes **from inside,** such as hunger with a low blood sugar level, the intrinsic motivation; sometimes, **from outside,** perhaps we see something tasty or someone forces us to do something, which we then call extrinsic motivation.

Too little motivation can make us frustrated or down-headed powerless, lead to brooding, anxiety, or physical or mental addiction as a substitute, or cause cancer and chronic disease; and **over-motivation** can overtax oneself and others.

The motivational tools

Let's look at four motivational tools.

1. The force. Violence is a means by which we can enforce something against someone's will. **Actively,** perhaps by carrying someone away from a place where they are not allowed to be, or by "chaining" them to a place where they are not supposed to leave. Or **passive,** for example, by locking away or hiding valuable things in a "safe" so that they are not taken away.

Examples of violence of our own body against us are, active: chemical reactions in us, a blockade of the muscles when they are exhausted, a compulsion to breathe when one has not breathed for a long time, or, passive: our skin as protection against disease-causing germs.

2. The pressure. By **rewarding,** we promote something by offering something pleasant, such as a friendly smile, a so-called "sugar bread," or permission to be in a good community; or we reward by taking away bad things.

Through **punishment**, we can counteract behavior by taking away good or giving bad things. A changed facial expression can achieve this without having to use a "whip."

3. Reason. In an appeal to reason, we can try to convince others of something. And as role models, we can motivate others to imitate us.

4. The habit. When an activity becomes a habit, it is usually automatic. We no longer feel the negative so severely when we are used to it, but we no longer feel the positive as well, unless we become aware of it again.

The areas of motivation

Let's take a closer look at the areas in which we typically find motivation and mental life force to live:

1. The life security experience. We often feel comfortable and want to stay in a life-friendly environment. In a life-threatening situation, we are motivated by the fear to bring us to safety, where we feel joyous relief. Internally we are also regularly driven spontaneously, for example, to breathe, drink, eat, sleep, recognize, relax, heal, and also to buy clothes, a home, and many other things that serve our lives. If we have enough, we regularly feel relatively calm, forcefully, and safe.

2. The community experience. Survival alone is not enough. Children are dependent on adults, adult people live work-sharing. We cannot conceive offspring alone. We are social beings. Those who belong to strong and helpful others in a sufficient and secure way will rightly feel secure and powerful. And we are also motivated to do this by feelings and needs such as loneliness, longing, joy in reunion and in being together with people we value, love, bond, security, as an adult often also joy in sexuality and caring for children, as well as by goals such as acceptance, recognition, honor, justice or harmony.

In relationships with **individuals**, such as children, parents, partners, and friends, we can experience strong values and bondings. Belonging to **groups** has the advantage that they can be maintained independently of the individual. Examples are here: Family, relatives, a circle of friends, a village or state community, economic enterprises, faith community, associations, or clubs.

3. The competence experience. To succeed in our life together, everyone needs to contribute appropriately. Maybe we have, know or can do something useful or learn or acquire it. To be as good as others, to be better, to perform, to be successful, to help oneself and others, to get praise, to be allowed to stay in communities, this typically motivates.

4. The experience of freedom. Independence protects against exploitation. **Freedom of choice** helps to attain the best. Often **power** provides unique motivation. If we have it, we can enforce what is life-friendly.

With enough freedom, we can realize ourselves, create a functional living space and belongings, develop a great deal of competence, and tap sources of mental life power and make use of them.

Subjective mental sources of strength

What gives us explicitly noticeable mental life force, what our **energy sources** or resources are, and what our energy thieves are, can be very different. The same things can give a lot of energy to some, even under eu-stress; they can be flowing, immersed, happy, and motivated; to others, the same things can be depressing. Even though this feels like coming from the outside, it is primarily our organism that causes it in us.

Also here, four areas in which we can find our power sources, but also our energy thieves: **1. Our past**, for example, our origins or previous experiences. **2. Behavior** at work or during leisure time. **3. Things,** such as objects, buildings, places, people, groups, animals, or plants. **4. Our probable future** in hope or fear.

It is also good if we make sure that we, and our inner voice treats ourselves propperly.

The task at the end of the chapter

Task 30 **My mental life force?**

Where do the four motivational tools work for me? Examples.
What do I have in each of the four areas of motivation?
Which concrete energy sources and thieves do I have?
Do I, and does my inner voice treat me well?
Do I have enough supporting mental power sources?

What can you do, what do you want and what will you do?

30. My mental life force:

Where do the four motivational tools work for me? Examples:

What do I have in each of the four areas of motivation?

Which concrete energy sources and thieves do I have?

Do I, and does my inner voice treat me well?

Do I have enough supporting mental power sources?

241

31. Chapter: Prevention

If we can implement the previous areas well, we are already making a substantial contribution to our health. Nevertheless, some things can still weaken us or make us ill. In the ninth area of health, we are therfore focusing on prevention.

Recognizing the dangers

First, let us be aware of ten things that can endanger our health:

1. When it is **cold**, our body first tries to warm itself with muscle tremors. An air temperature of under two to eight degrees Celsius, especially with wind or air draft, can let us catch a cold and in the long run, reduce our body temperature to below 28 degrees Celsius, which often leads to cardiac arrest. And frozen skin can die. **Heat** can also be harmful. From 40 degrees body temperature, the circulation can fail, and at 60 body protein degenerates. Fire and hot liquids, hot solids or hot gases can burn us.

2. **Noise** in excess (permanently starting at 85 decibels (dB) and once at 120 decibels) can damage the hearing.

3. Radioactive **radiation** in large quantities, such as some electromagnetic, electron, proton or helium nuclear radiation, can damage DNA in particular and often lead to cancer or miscarriages.
   Too much **sunlight** on the skin can result in sunburn and sunstroke. Not enough lets our body produce insufficient vitamin D through the skin. A light-skinned body

probably produces vitamin D in the first 20 to 30 minutes, at least if the shadows are shorter than the illuminated objects. On both sides, ten minutes of sun should be good.

Too **bright light** can damage our eyes.

4. The flow of **electric current** through our body can, because of the heat development and the influence on our nerve cells, damage from about 24 volts. Strong current flow through our body is fatal.

5. For us, some substances are **poison**, which leads to chemical or physical reactions in our body that damage us. Some poisons work immediately and quickly, others slowly and creepingly. Some are non-toxic in small quantities, sometimes even vital, but deadly in large amounts. Most toxins can be broken down by the body in the liver or discharged through the kidneys or other body fluids. Depending on the substance, it can do this at different speeds.

Radioactive substances in the body can act as toxins. Certain organic substances, usually specific proteins, also have a toxic effect. Some parts of plants or animals are poisonous. Some non-organic substances such as some acids or heavy metals are toxic. Solids can also injure, inflame, or clog.

Toxins enter our bodies mainly through food, respiration, or skin injuries. Also thin mucous membranes such as those in the eyes, nose, mouth, genitals, and anus are also endangered areas.

6. **Bacteria** and **viruses** are the smallest life forms beneath the organization of a eukaryotic cell. In blood, feces, or warm, humid areas, there are often a lot of them. UV radiation, alcohol, acidity, each in high doses, and temperatures above 60 degrees Celsius can kill them. They can enter our bodies like toxins and multiply significantly. Our body's defense fights against them. If this is weakened, because we have become hypothermic after sweating, for example, or if there are enough intruders, they can make us ill. Some **fungal** spores can also do this.

7. **Parasites** such as fleas, ticks, mosquitoes, worms or protozoa feed on our body and weaken it or make it ill, perhaps also because they transmit other disease-causing pathogens.

8. **Attacks** can harm us. Especially some snakes, spiders, jellyfish, and spiny fish use poison to defend themselves or to catch prey. Some predators, especially big cats, crocodiles, or bears, can hurt or kill us if they feel threatened or very hungry. Hippos, rhinos, and elephants like to defend themselves.

And some people are also dangerous if they feel threatened or if they want to ruthlessly gain their own advantage.

9. **Accidents** and **natural disasters** such as floods, storms, earthquakes, volcanic eruptions, or major fires can cause harm. We can drown. Impacts, bruises, abrasions, or cuts can lead to wounds, broken bones, blood loss, organ failure, or other external and internal injuries. Blood loss becomes dangerous from 20 percent, in adults one liter. And the body cannot heal everything.

10. **Excessive stress**, for example, due to heavy carrying, constant, heavier, regular motion, or immobility, can cause damage. A mentally stressful environment, which harms us permanently and without compensation, can also damage us.

Our prevention

In the following, I will formulate ten rules in the first-person form that we could follow as a preventive measure. Feel free to do it this way or in a similar or better way.

1. I generally pay attention to my health so that my **defense** works well.

2. I am **careful** with the dangerous or unknown. I avoid, if possible, places, things, living beings, or behaviors, which can be seriously dangerous. If necessary, I think of sufficient information, protective clothing, vaccination, and the like.
   3. I wash my hands, if possible, before handling unpacked food and after the end of unclean activities, such as going to the toilet or dirty work. In the morning and before going to bed, I brush my teeth with a toothbrush for about two minutes. For the latter, I also use floss. I wash my whole body on a daily or weekly basis, only applying lotion if necessary.

4. I do not sleep close to infectious persons or have insufficiently protected sex with them.

5. I regularly have my health risks checked enough by a specialist.

6. I refrain as much as possible from the consumption of substances, the practice of behaviors or the cultivation of beliefs with drug effects. I am aware that the effect of drugs can depend not only on the type but also on the quantity and the motivation behind it, i.e., the use as an unsuitable problem solver or simply as a source of fun or experience.

7. I try to avoid permanent or strong physical or mental overload or underload or pay attention to a balance. If possible, I lift less than 25 kg.

8. I look for a sufficiently safe place to live.

9. I keep my things adequately clean and safe.

10. I think about what will happen if something happens: **First aid**, contacting rescue services, people, and things that can help me or something similar.

The task at the end of the chapter

Task 31 **My prevention?**

Review the ten behavior rules suggested above for yourself. For each rule, think about what you want to do, how you want to do it, or what you want to do alternatively?

31. My prevention:

1. Strengthen your defense:

2. Be careful:

3. Sufficient hygiene:

4. No high risk of infection:

5. Preventive check-ups:

6. No real drugs:

7. No excessive load:

8. Safe dwelling:

9. Safe things:

10. Clarity on first aid:

Other:

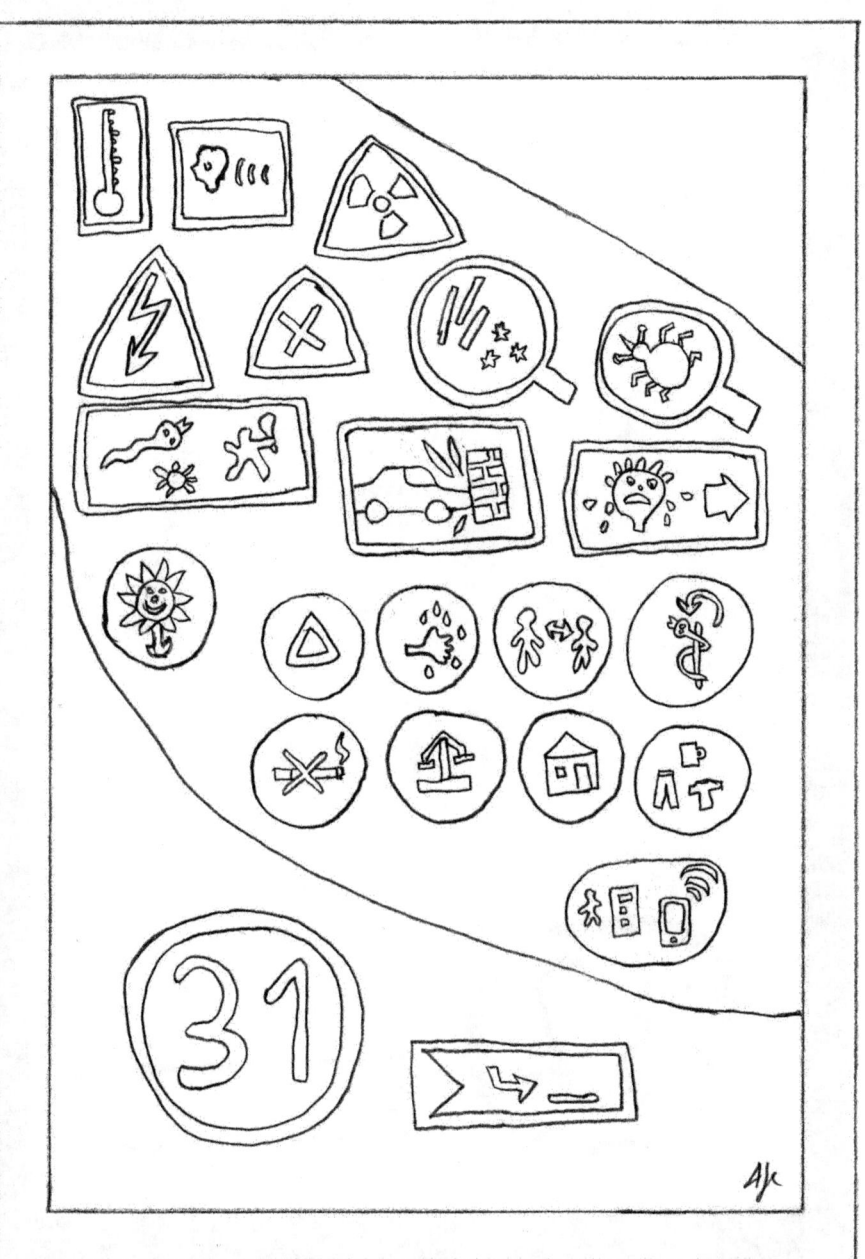

248

32. Chapter: Healing

We cannot prevent every risk through prevention. Once in a while, everybody gets sick. Then it is good when we heal again. Healing is problem-solving in the area of health, and sometimes this also has chances for development. We already looked at both in the chapter: Problem and chance. This tenth and last area of health wants to supplement that, and the things learned in the previous chapters.

Diseases and injuries often burden us with pain, weakness, or functional impairments, and some can be fatal.

For others, our disease can sometimes be contagious. And when we are no longer able to make our contribution to the community due to illness, and the community may even have to help us during this time, we are a short-term burden.

The better a person who is actuall fit, but currently ill, recovers, the faster he and the community will feel better again. This is why we are now taking a closer look at the causes of the illness, their consequences, and the cure.

The causes of disease and their effects

Most **physical** diseases or health problems have their causes in **physical** pathogens such as viruses, bacteria, fungi, parasites, in toxins, accidents, attacks, hypothermia, overheating, or other organic or physical imbalances. (Also see last chapter.)

Most **mental** disorders have their cause in a **mentally** stressful environment or event to which someone, mostly as a young child, was exposed without protection. People copied disturbed behaviors or attitudes, adapted to them, or transferred their experiences to the rest of the world. Later, perhaps in a different environment, the resulting errors (correctable with clarification), psychoses (patient obviously out of reality, but not recognizable by him), or neuroses (something in between), are then those that disturb our well-being. (See also chapter: Personality.)

Physical damage can sometimes have **mental** effects. If, for example, deposits form in the brain in old age, nerve cells can die as a result, and dementia develops.

Mental problems can sometimes lead to **physical** disorders. For example, if someone is constantly afraid, his organism will often release stress hormones and often work in the sympathetic nerve area to be prepared for danger. The result can be overload: Heart and circulation work too much, and there is a lack of supply: Defense, skin, digestive, and reproductive organs are neglected.

In **conversion**, problems are expressed physically. Examples: Stress can lead to headaches, anger to sore throat, relationship problems to heart pain, life problems to abdominal or back pain, and those who do not want to continue as before can get knee pain or even paralysis. Anyone who has a problem with their environment or with themselves could also develop allergies or autoimmune diseases in which the body's defense system, representative for the real problem, attacks, harmless pollen or itself.

251

And individual mental or physical disorders can, of course, have further **effects** on others, actually healthy parts of the organism, which then cause pain or malfunction.

And **different factors** can come together: Dis-stress, for example, caused by other people, inadequate living conditions and possibly intensified by weather and climate; consumption of addictive drugs, overweight, poor nutrition, lack of exercise, harmful treatment methods and other things can lead to heart attacks, strokes, diabetes, cancer, and other illnesses or subsequent symptoms.

Often a disease breaks out at that point in the body that is weakest at the moment.

The healing methods

We can leave the illness to the **self-healing** process. It then makes sense to regularly try to behave particularly healthy during this time and allow our body time to recover.

In the case of a normal "cold," for example, this method alone leads to healing after about a week. This is because, in infectious diseases, the primary non-specific immune defense initially reacts with many general measures, such as fever, nausea, diarrhea, feeling of illness, weakness, and pain, which will motivate the patient to rest. The specific immune defense often needs a week or more to recognize the disease-causing germs and release antibodies that attach to them. Marked like that, defense cells, such as white blood cells, recognize the pests and destroy them. In many diseases, the secondary immune defense remembers the germs and, if they reappear, combats them before they cause an infection.

Cancer cells can also be recognized as such and be destroyed. And wounds very often heal by themselves.

Sometimes **medication** can help us. It has an active ingredient that causes chemical reactions in our bodies. In the illness, the desired effect can have a helpful, sometimes life-saving function. Adverse drug reactions can damage us. Antibiotics, for example, fight bacteria; unfortunately, healthy ones too, however, not the resistant ones and harmful ones may develop new resistances.

Through physical or mental **therapy**, healing can be supported or made possible. Physiotherapy can improve mobility and muscle building. Psychotherapy can help to recognize mental disorders, deal with them well, and sometimes heal them. Acupuncture often helps against pain temporarily and can occasionally stimulate self-healing.

During an **operation**, surgery is performed on our body, for example, to cut out something harmful, to sew something torn, to reopen something clogged, or to splint something broken. Surgery is associated with the risk of failure, infection, thrombosis, or adverse effects from anesthesia and medication. In the Middle Ages, one of two operated persons must have died. When I write this and here it is about one of fifty.

Faith alone also has an effect. Those who believe that something helps will become calmer, enter the parasympathetic healing system, will concentrate on healing the organism, and can learn to perceive symptoms differently. **Placebos** often have success probabilities of around 40 percent. Attention: In the **nocebo** effect, a deterioration occurs simply because of the belief that it will get worse.

When **choosing** the method, it is, of course, important to use the one that fits to the real existing disease in type, quantity, and duration. Combined methods may also help good. It often makes sense to get help from the right specialist. The will to heal is also helpful and sometimes necessary.

The task at the end of the chapter

Task 32   *My diseases?*

What harmful diseases did you already have?
What diseases do you have now, permanently or frequently?
What has been done so far, and what has been helpful?
Are there any warning signs that appear before the illness?
What can you do, what do you want and what will you do here?

32. My diseases?

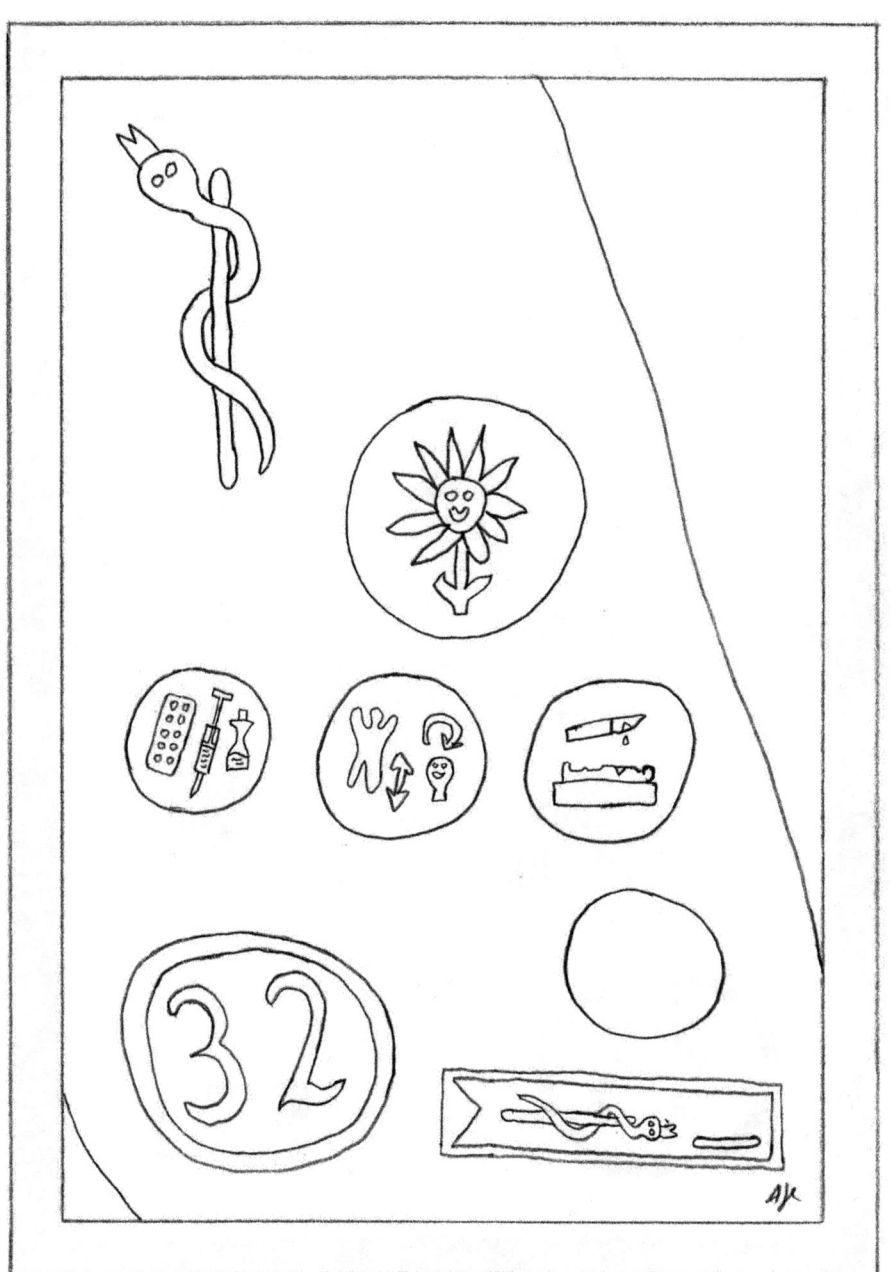

257

33. Chapter: Beauty

In the last chapters, we focused in great detail on health. Now we are also dealing with how things can look healthy on the outside and feel healthy and pleasant on the inside: It is about beauty.

Beauty

Our feeling regularly tells us whether we perceive something as beautiful or not. And when does it do that? Perhaps beauty is something similar to what is **outwardly good.** Here are a few thoughts:

At first, we seem to find things outwardly beautiful **that fit in well with this world:** The energetic and balanced or symmetric, which also contains a mixture or diversity.

Imagine, for example, a beautiful flower or a sunset: intense colors, symmetrical blossoms or round sun, symmetry relaxation by leaves on the stem, or by a few clouds or birds in the sky around the sun.

Also, healthy and **life-friendly** things appear to be beautiful. We often find the sight of harmonious, biodiverse nature, with mountains and waters, in which one **fits well with the other** or blends in well, and therefore has a particular order, beautiful. Also, beautiful things about people are often healthy or beneficial for offspring.

It was and is often good for life to be up to date with good evolutionary or technical development. Something **modern,** i.e., currently up to date, is not necessarily good for that reason alone.

In addition to the objective, there is also a **subjective beauty.** We have a partly innate taste, and also learned that certain things seem to be particularly good for us. Regularly we find **average,** i.e., **accustomed and proven,** as beautiful. And if we **like** someone, they often seem more attractive to us because we consider them to be good for us.

With **all our senses,** we can perceive externally good things: beautiful sounds like music, or taste, smell, surface texture, temperature, and energetic moods.

The pleasant

We probably perceive in feeling and mood as pleasant what seems to us to be good or life-friendly. That is often, but not always, the same as the outwardly beautiful or the really good.

What we can do

Following, I will present ten ideas for beauty treatment, once again in the first person form. Let's try to think and feel if this fits for us or what we find better instead:

1. I see that my **body** is neither very fat nor too thin, that my fingernails, toenails, teeth, hair, and skin are sufficiently clean and groomed, that I walk upright instead of humpbacked and that I don't smell too bad. Smelling like myself is fine.

2. I make sure that the **clothes** I wear are clean, tidy and comfortable. It suits my size and the occasion. Style, shape, and color suit me and the other dresses. I keep in mind that optical breaks tend to shorten. In dark colours things appear rather smaller, in bright colours rather biger. Dark looks warmer and nobler, bright friendlier.

3. I regularly pay attention to a mindful and life-friendly attitude of mind, which I **express** appropriately. I am cultivated in behavior and language, not artificial and altogether like myself, in other words authentic.

4. I make sure that my objective **environment**, especially my home, is sufficiently beautiful and pleasant.

The air is clean, and often pleasant at medium humidity, i.e., 30 to 70 percent. Where heating is used, water bowls or hygroscopic carpets can help. At 21 to 23 degrees, our body doesn't need to warm up or cool down. The temperature is often pleasant with 20 to 23 degrees Celsius when clothed; higher when not clothed and resting, lower when clothed and exercising heavily. For working, it should be bright but not garish; in the evening slightly muted, at night dark.

5. I take care that there are **people** for me who are, if possible, as pleasant as I am. I feel connected with them in an appreciative way, and I also show this.

6. I take time again and again to open up and consciously **pay attention to the good**, the beautiful, and the pleasant. I recognize it, rejoice and enjoy it. I seek the good, accept it, feel connected with it, promote or maintain it.

I can appreciate the good at any age: a certain light-heartedness in childhood, the freedom to try out during the youth, being especially valuable as an adult, and more calm and serenity in old age.

I recognize the bad when it shows itself to me. Perhaps I can accept it as an insignificant part of something good overall. Maybe I can reject it or use it to turn it into something good. Maybe I also recognize that sometimes ugliness or displeasure is needed as a sacrifice to get the good. Im happy when the bad it's over. And I can use the comparison with the bad to make the good or the better appear even better to me.

7. I strive for **realistic claims** and helpful attitudes. Satisfied too early and I lag behind my possibilities, too late, and I miss pleasant pleasure.

I keep in mind that there is also justice in the, however limited, possibility of lowering claims and changing attitudes. And something more valuable than the feeling that I am very happy to live, no one else can have.

8. I try to **combine** the **useful with** the **pleasant.** If, for example, I like to take care of my family, my work, or my health, my life will be easy and seem beautiful, enjoyable, and good to me, and rightly so.

9. I also accept **the beautiful and the pleasant as a value in their own right** that contributes to a good life.

I can also appreciate leisure time and, in addition to the great fortune, for example, in partnership, family, work, and safety for health; even the small fortune, such as the sight of a beautiful flower, a sunset, or a pleasant scent.

Above all, I can **enjoy the moment.** And I can also be grateful for the beautiful memories and look forward to the good things to come.

10. I use **this book** because it helps me to have sufficient and sustainable good things which hopefully carry my hopefully beautiful life securely.

The task at the end of the chapter

Task 33 **My beauty?**

Go through the ten points again one after the other. What can you do, what do you want and what will you do in each case?

It would also be good if we would write the answers to the questions nicely in the empty books and colour the pictures at the end of the chapters nicely or have them coloured beautifully and this gladly with a signature at the bottom right next to mine. ☺

33. My beauty:

1. Beautiful body:

2. Beautiful clothes:

3. Beautiful expression:

4. Beautiful surroundings:

5. Pleasant fellow human beings:

6. Pay attention to the good:

7. Have realistic expectations:

8. Combine the useful with the pleasant:

9. Appreciate the beautiful and enjoyable as value of its own:

10. Use this book for sufficient really good things:

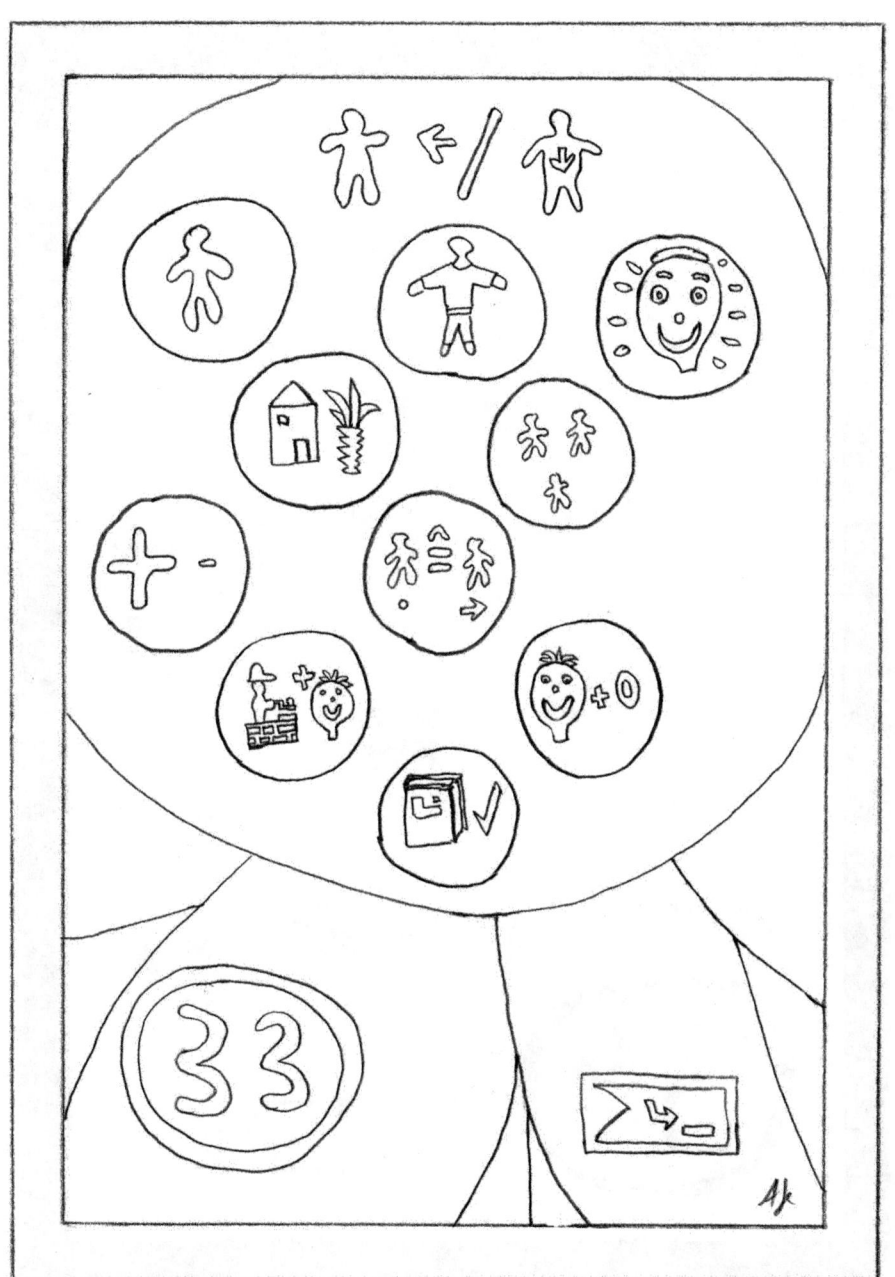

34. Chapter: Leisure

Most people find their free time pleasant because it allows them to do what is pleasurable for them.

Those who have gone through the chapters of this book week after week for themselves, with a partner, in a discussion group or in an assembly, and started in the week in which January 8 falls, are now, in the 34th chapter, also in the 34th week. This should be at the end of August. In the northern hemisphere, many will already be back from their summer holidays and will be able to talk about their leisure activities.

So let's take a closer look at our leisure time.

Leisure in general

When the work is done, and enough is done to maintain health, then we have leisure time. If we do a leisure activity regularly and gladly, that is our hobby.

I believe that the main benefit of leisure time is **safety** for survival. Anyone who has a lot of free time also has time available in it, which can be used, for example, in the event of illness, relocation, children, additional expenditure for food purchases due to drought, for defense, or to respond to natural disasters. If our ancestors had a lot of free time, they could survive crises well and pass on their joy of free time to us.

Furthermore, in our free time, we can find a **balance** and **reward** for what we do in our work and for our health.

Ten ideas for leisure activities

Below are ten ideas that you might already be doing or could newly do in your free time. Simply feel for a moment how the described things affect on you:

1. You could do **sports**, for example, table tennis, badminton, volleyball, boccia or football: Exercise, compete with others, achieve something together in a team, help each other, join in, rejoice or comfort each other.

In Prehistoric, Stone, and Civilization Age, there was always something important to fight for. Many are very motivated to do so. You can live this out in sport.

With board **games** and card games, you could have a similar effect.

2. **Music** and **dance** might be something, too. You could sing, play an instrument like a guitar, dance, or just listen or watch.

3. You could have **entertaining conversations**, for example, at a meeting for dinner, an afternoon coffee, an evening drink, at a party, celebration or festivity, at the edge of a parade or any other event. Casual topics of conversation could be leisure activities, feelings, travel, news, individual experiences, or the weather.

4. In fiction **literature, theater, film, television, radio,** or the **internet,** you could experience the stories of others in a spirit of compassion. In **role-plays,** you can feel yourself a little bit in it.

5. If you like to do something that serves your health or if it gives you life energy, it may also be a little **luxury in the area of health**. Luxury exercise: Walking, hiking, swimming, cycling, cross-country skiing, sledding, for example. Luxury food: You treat yourself to something that tastes particularly good and allow yourself a little more time to enjoy it. Luxury knowledge: New findings from non-fiction books, newspapers, and magazines, knowledge films, lectures, or intellectual conversations could be exciting. Luxury sleep or luxury relaxation: Meditate, rest, snuggle or something similar, or luxury beauty care, just because it feels good.

6. How about a little **"Stone Age work:"** Hunting, fishing, and collecting? Perhaps no longer necessarily venison, herbs, and berries, but maybe special books like this book, works of art or clothes? Or an agricultural or forestry activity? Taking care of plants, fruit or horticulture, making wood, keeping rabbits, dogs, or horses? You might as well do something handcrafted: Making jewelry, painting or sculpting, knitting clothes, model building, making you or other people beautiful, cooking, or baking?

Not everyone can do what he likes to do as a profession. In your free time, you can do that, even without pressure.

7. How about celebrating a unique success or something special with a **celebration?** In weekly assemblies after this book, we could celebrate the theme of each chapter: This week the leisure time. Important things can be remembered or kept, and a celebration can be rewarding.

8. Or **cultivate social contacts?** Partying, meeting relatives or friends, or visiting a discussion group, also for companionship?

9. Or you could **travel**, go on excursions or **visit** something? Let yourself be impressed by the beauty and uniqueness of the world and nature, marvel at architecture and technology, or get to know the art and culture of other people.

10. Maybe you can think of **something else?** Within certain limits, you are as free here as nowhere else.

Four criteria for good leisure activities

The following criteria or questions can help to find and have good leisure activities:

1. **Freedom.** Is the individual activity sufficiently free to do for me? If you have to do it, on the one hand, it's probably working or life support, not really free time. And if, on the other hand, you can't or can only rarely do it, you can only dream about it.

2. **Consideration.** Does the individual occupation take sufficient care? Consider especially nature, your fellow human beings, the laws and customs, your work, your wealth, and your health. You don't have to do leisure activities, that's why you can and should afford yourself the consideration. With a ruthless activity, you have a vice.

Consideration for work is often given to things that are different: If it's better, it's rewarding; if it's worse, you can look forward to work again; and other things have a balancing effect. Some things can also complement or support the work.

3. **Will.** Do I really want to do that? Because it gives me energy? It is fun? It will offer anything else? You don't have to, just stop the activity if you don't want it.

4. **Selection.** Do I have enough possibilities for leisure activities to choose from? Maybe something for inside and outside? Something for the summer and something for the winter? Something you can do alone and something you can do with others? Something quieter and something more invigorating? Something that gives energy and something with which excess energy can be reduced? Something more physical and something more mental?

With enough choices we can find a suitable leisure activity, we won't get bored, and many things can be combined well.

The task at the end of the chapter

Task 34 **My leisure activities?**

Make a list of the leisure activities you regularly do or want to do. Use the ten idea points.
Then check the list with the four criteria.
What can you do, what do you want and what will you do here?

34. My leisure activities?

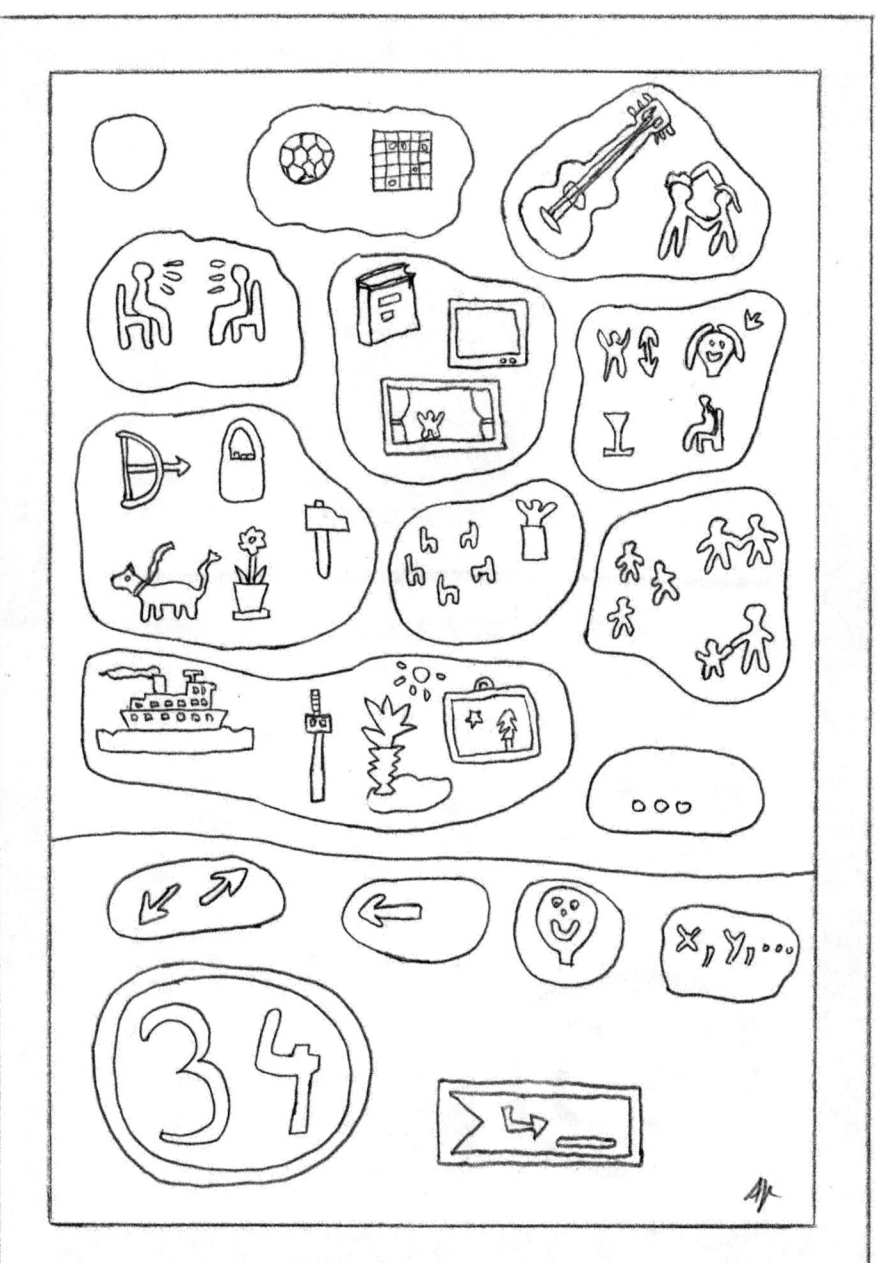

273

35. Chapter: Family and relatives

Leisure time, the topic of the last chapter is often spent with our family, relatives, or other communities. And communities are the focus of this and the following chapters.

The family

Let's start with a few thoughts on the family. They also help us to understand other communities.

The family is the most original community into which we are born regularly and which we often start anew when we start our own family.

Let's look at the **members.** The family regularly begins to develop when a man and a woman decide to be together permanently as **life partners.** The **nuclear family** consists of the parents and their children. It often has a common family name and a family seat, usually the family residence. In the **extended family,** many other members can also live in the same household, for example, grandparents, other relatives, friends, domestic employees, and animals.

Hostels, shared flats, or other communities where we feel at home can become something like a **substitute family.**

The family is not a closed space, it has **external relations.** The individual family members will have relationships with relatives, friends, and acquaintances. In the circle of relatives, the circle of friends, the state, the school, the business in which one works, a religious community, or an association, the family as a whole or individual family members might be members.

Communities have, at least, in fact, a **community constitution** that regulates the essentials. In families, this is usually clear. In other communities such as the state, business enterprises, or associations, it often makes sense to record this in writing. Essential are name, seat, goal or purpose, members, organs, contributions and financing, substantial rights, the external relations, beginning and ending as well as further, especially for the respective community substantial things.

Rudimentary rules in every community, also with animals, are: 1. Don't collide, 2. stick with it, 3. pay attention to the close environment and 4. to the leadership.

The **community leadership** can, in the family, be the "head of the family". Often this is either the father or the mother, there may also be several in common, and it does not have to be the same in every situation. It is not uncommon for the led ones to influence the boss in such a way that they actually decide. And as a **deputy,** someone can also take care of an area or a matter, for the whole community.

The **aim** of the family is to serve each other and to serve life by sharing tasks and, if possible, to produce offspring so that the next generation can become a good one.

The **contribution** of the adults will be primarily to provide the family with money, things, work, knowledge, and appropriate feelings. The main task of the children will be to become competent adults in the long run.

The **benefits** of the family are many. You get help from the others, you can feel secure, belonging and also valuable with your contribution, and a lot makes especially much joy together with and for those who you appreciate and maybe also love.

In the community, you will always have to react to changes, and **clarify what exactly is to be done.** At the latest when differences of opinion become **disputes,** this is a problem (Chapter 14) that should be solved, at least in the long term. There are four ways to do this:

1. The **consensus principle:** There is an agreement. Perhaps because it becomes clear who is right in whole or in part, or because a compromise is achieved.

2. The **majority principle**: You vote and follows the will of the majority that concerns it.

3. The **hierarchy principle**: It is decided by the one who is more powerful in the decision-making area. This can be a person or a group.

4. The **judge principle:** The decision is made by an independent third party, which is as competent as possible.

All four ways have advantages and disadvantages, which can outweigh depending on the individual case. It is often important to do one method of clarification. Otherwise, **war** can break out in which it is not only about the individual situation, but about fighting a whole person or group, and this usually costs both sides unnecessarily much strength. By the way, bullying is an attempt to displace others. If someone certainly does not fit into the community, he should leave it and, for example, change to a "substitute family".

Although **individual case decisions** are again and again in demand in the community, **rules** and **rituals** for important or frequently occurring matters give security and structure to a family community. Perhaps there are everyday meals, a particular way of bringing the small children to bed or a weekly family discussion group. Some things are done by the family, or within it by the family leaders **themselves**, but they can also **be helped**.

It ist important to appropriately recognize and observe **feelings** such as belonging, solidarity, sense of togetherness, identification, cohesion, love, sometimes partisanship, the need for honor, recognition, or justice, but also the herd instinct or peer pressure.

Family and other communities also shape our thinking, behavior, and personality.

It is good when the individual is clear about why he belongs, what the essential rules are, what his contribution and benefits are, and how he takes care of both. It is also good if he receives and can give both community and adequate freedom.

The relatives

Let us look at relatives as another community. It is often a loose community to which one belongs as family and as an individual. It consists of genetically related, adopted, or married people. In one line there are children, grandchildren and great-grandchildren or parents, grandparents and great-grandparents. In sidelines, sisters and brothers, nieces and nephews, aunts and uncles, bases and cousins, great aunts and great uncles, and so on.

It might regularly be good if we meet with relatives occasionally, for example for family celebrations, and if we appropriately maintain contacts to some relatives like to friends and to others like to acquaintances.

The tasks at the end of the chapter

Task 35.1 **My family?**

Who belongs to your family? How are they essentially?
What distinguishing features and rituals do you have?
What is your contribution, and what is your benefit?

Task 35.2 **My relatives?**

Draw your family tree by using letter abbreviations or symbols for yourself and your essential family members and relatives. Connect them as they belong together (two rings between partners) or descend from each other (lines extending from the rings). Persons of one generation side by side, dead people in brackets, circle your family, partnership, or, if necessary, only yourself.
  Briefly think about each essential relative and how you deal with them.

35.1 My family:

35.2 My relatives:

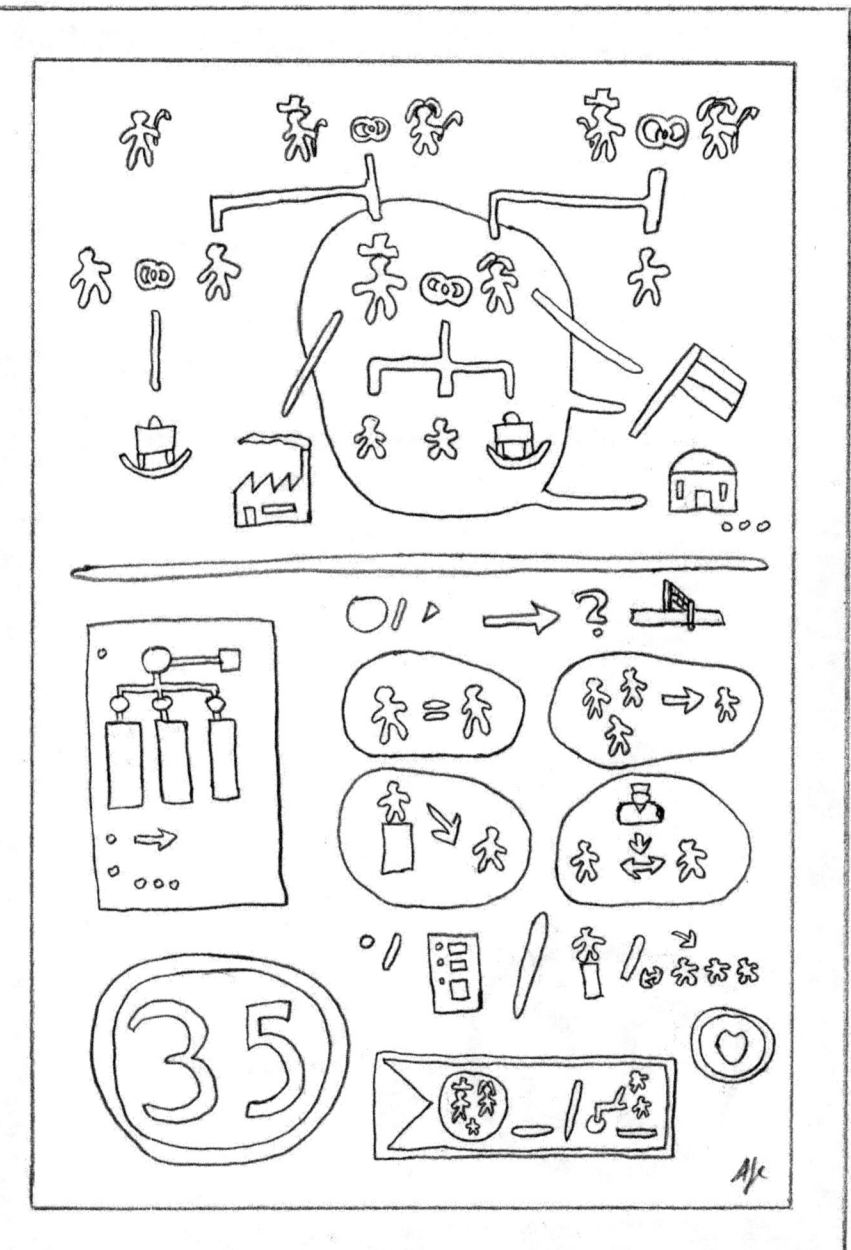

280

281

36. Chapter: State

As individuals, we not only regularly live in the community of family and relatives, but we are also almost always a member of at least one state.

The state in general

The "roots" of today's states reach deep. Already in the Stone Age, families and relatives lived in groups or clans. We can assume that a chief took over leadership and representation and sub-groups took over tasks that individual members could not or scarcely do alone.

Over time, states arose from this through propagation, mergers, conquests, and conscious organizing. A state has one **state-territory,** one **state-people,** and one **state-authority.** One becomes a citizen regularly by descent of members of the country, in some countries also by birth within the national territory, or by naturalization.

A flag and a national anthem are typically symbolic of a state. Often there is also one or more national languages.

The essential **goal** of the state is to create or maintain conditions in which life in the country can develop as well as possible. For this, it will also be necessary to pay attention to the neighboring countries and the living space as a whole. No one can live in isolation.

The tasks of the state

In my opinion, a good state has four tasks and one auxiliary task which it should take good care of. It does not have to take over the individual tasks itself, it can be helped, for example, by commercial enterprises or by other states.

1. **Security**, above all through peace and sufficient reliability, is one of the most essential tasks of the state.

States regularly try to ensure this **externally** through friendly contacts, international treaties, partnerships, and the military.

Internal security usually requires the state to ensure and enforce law and order through legislation, the police, and the judiciary.

2. Ensuring a well-functioning **infrastructure** is also essential. The following should be kept in mind:

Childcare, education, training, and science. When children go to good nurseries, kindergartens and certainly to schools and can receive an excellent education later, they benefit themselves, the parents and the community as a whole, because well raised, educated and trained people can make a valuable contribution to the community. Science helps with new and old knowledge.

Transportation infrastructure. Are there enough roads, sea routes, railways, airports, and the like?

Communication. Does the post office, telephone, Internet, print media, radio, television, and the same work?

Security of supplies. Can the citizens, especially with the help of the economy, sufficiently supply themselves with the goods and services they need? (In particular, food, clothing, housing, medical treatment, water, energy and money as means of payment). Can they dispose of waste and sewage properly?

3. The state also has a **compensation function.** The evolutionary principle, according to which the more able to survive prevails at the expense of the weaker, becomes problematic with the possibilities of modern humans. The modern state must ensure that nature and habitat are adequately protected. And, also because of internal security, it should provide adequate support for weaker people. And those who can achieve more should also give more to the state and feel accordingly valuable. However, those who achieve a lot should also be rewarded appropriately. It seems normal and acceptable, that social classes such as a leading elite, an often university-educated or wealthy upper class, a well-educated middle class, unskilled workers, or even the homeless are created, as long as the classes are adequately permeable.

4. It is also good if the state makes adequate efforts to maintain **cultural heritage.**

5. To be able to finance all this, the state must take care of the **state budget** as an auxilary task. **Duties** to the country can be **taxes**, i.e., those without concrete return. They can be added to the price or to a specific product as turnover tax. They can be levied as income tax on wages, capital gains, gifts, or inheritances. Property taxes burden the holding of individual assets or the assets as a whole. **Contributions** are paid for the possibility of use, such as that of a library, **fees** for concrete consideration, such as issuing an identity card. A state can also have **economic**

income if, for example, it offers electricity or water. And a state can also finance itself through **debt.** In my view, it should only do this in exceptional cases and only if it can pay off its debts again.

The state structure

Modern states are first structured **horizontally**. Typically there is the area of **government and administration**. The government represents the state externally, gives the policy guidelines to the inside, and heads the administration. In principle, the administration takes care of most of the government's tasks.

Then there is the area of **legislation and government control.** This area is often shaped by an elected parliament or a council, which has to agree on important changes or might be able to push them through themselves. Largely free media are usually very valuable for state control and for informing citizens.

Finally, there is the area of **jurisdiction,** which resolves disputes based on the applicable law and thereby shapes the law itself.

Vertically, statehood is usually subdivided into parts responsible for specific areas. Each part should perform the tasks that it can solve best. Here, too, mutual control can and should take place.

It is good if there is a specific **"world state"** that, within the United Nations, for example, deals with matters that affect everyone on earth, such as environmental protection and nature conservation, world peace, and a minimum of good economic and human conditions.

It is also important to have a functioning **municipal area** in which communities or cities take care of their own affairs, of the individual, and of local nature.

In between, there are the nations, mostly the actual states, alliances between them, administrative districts in them, and the like.

The task at the end of the chapter

Task 36 **My state?**

Which state or states do you belong to?
Which symbols (flag, anthem, ...) stand for it?
What is its state-territory - what belongs to it?
Who is part of its state-people - who belongs to it?
How is the state-authority of the country organized: What are the main sub-areas and institutions, and how do they work?

What is your contribution to the state and your benefit from the state?

What can you do, what do you want and what will you do here?

36.   My state:

Name:

Symbols:

State-territory:

State-people:

State-authority:

My contribution:

My benefits:

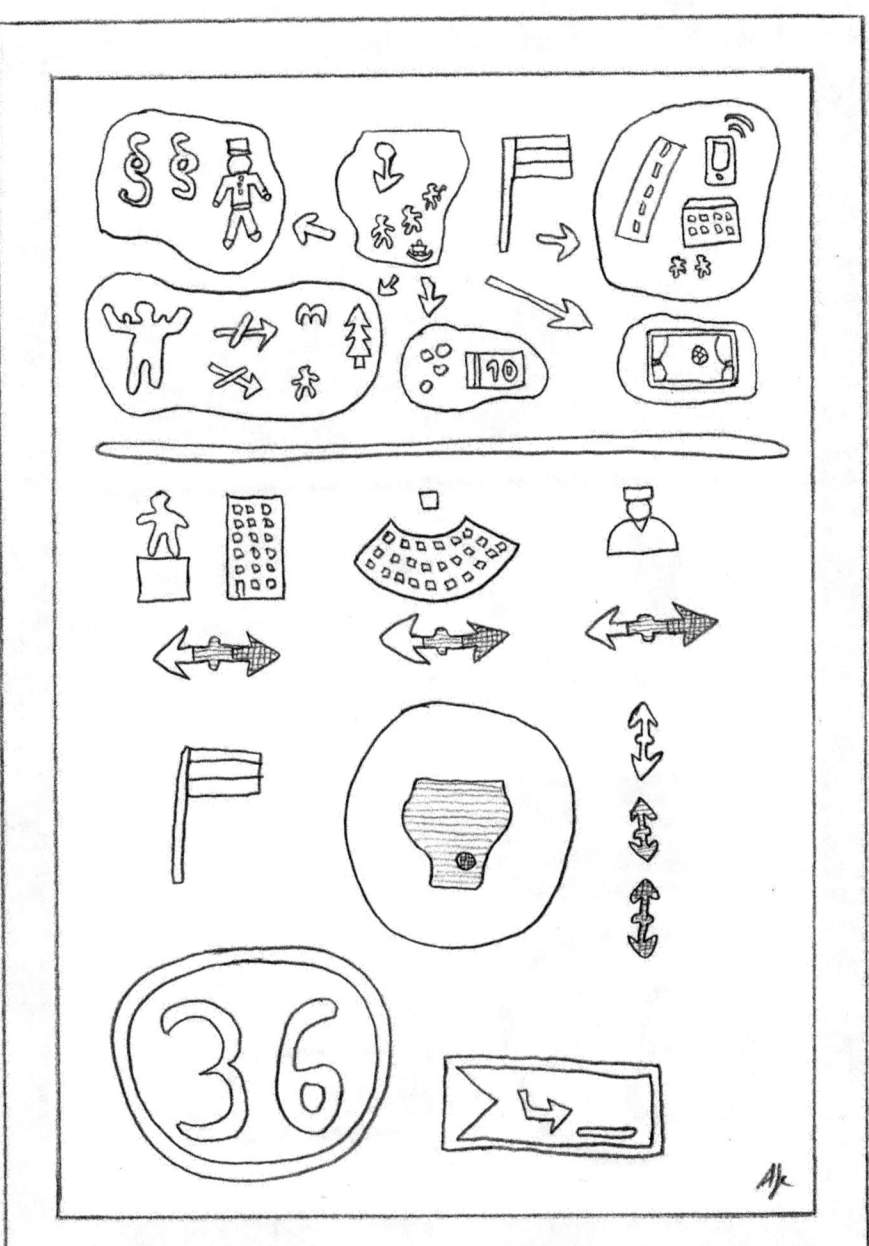

37. Chapter: Economy

In the last chapter, it was mentioned that the state can be helped in its tasks by the economy. Of course, families and individuals can also benefit from a functioning economy. And this is what we will deal with in the following.

The economy **aims** to provide people with the **products,** i.e., goods and services they need. And that regularly in exchange **for money.**

The economic participants

There are mainly four economic operators:

1. The entrepreneurs or **enterprises** are the traders who offer their goods. They are regularly active in agriculture and forestry, industry and crafts, or trade and services.

2. **Consumers** are regularly private individuals who consume products. For example, you buy food and eat it.

3. The **state** can also offer and demand products and intervene in the economy via legislation, taxes, and subventions.

4. **Employees** offer their labor and ask for jobs. Companies or entrepreneurs, as potential employers, often offer jobs and ask for workers.

The market

The market is the place where economic operators meet. This can be a weekly market, a retail shop, the stock exchange, the internet, or the so-called labor, capital, or real estate market. There are providers and those who ask for something.

The **price** for a **performance** is determined, among other things, by **supply** and **demand.** If demand is high and supplie is scarce, the price is likely to be high. If and at what price a business will actually result will be decided by the supplier and the customer at the end in agreement.

The supplier will regularly try to find a price at which he will make as much profit as possible or at least sufficient profit, perhaps also in terms of sales amount.

The customer will not accept every price and not every performance and will pay attention to a good price-performance ratio.

Both will consider the **competition.**

The economic order

Historical experience has shown that the **free capitalist market economy**, in which the state keeps out of the economy as much as it can, means that while the supply of goods is excellent, companies must ruthlessly exploit nature and workers to compete in the market. That is terrible.

They have also shown that the **communist planned economy**, in which all companies belong to the state and in which the state determines in plans what is to be produced how and by whom, can lead to relatively secure jobs, but people are only poorly and often inadequately supplied with goods and progress is slowed down. Because it does not motivate people to perform well if they only produce according to plan, and there is no competition, and in the end, everything will belong to the state. That, too, is terrible.

A **social market economy** is better, in which there is a basically free market with private ownership, but in which the state intervenes, again and again, to regulate, to adequately protect people and nature and also to help the economy, for example, with good framework conditions. It is sometimes difficult to say exactly what and how much the state, or the private sector, does better.

The individual company

If you have an **idea** of what you can successfully offer on the market, find sufficient **capital**, a suitable **location,** and competent **employees**, you can start a company if you meet the **legal requirements.**
The company will have to take care of four areas permanently:

1. The products on offer, such as **production**, service delivery, purchasing, and development.

2. **Sales** through distribution and advertising.

3. **Logistics and administration**, i.e., buildings, means of production, storage, transport, accounting, and human resources.

4. The leadership, i.e., management, strategy, controlling, and financing.

Many interests have to be taken into account: Those of the **owners or providers,** financiers or **sponsors** (profit, at least no loss, and image), those of the **customers** (price and performance), those of the **employees** (salary and working conditions) and those of the **community** (law and taxes).

The market should be observed, and the foundations of the company maintained or adapted.

Perhaps the company is operated as a "one-man business", as a partnership, corporation, or stock corporation; regionally or internationally.

And a small company can become a medium-sized enterprise and even a large international group with high profits, if it functions well and is successful in the market.

If not, it may happen that a company is no longer solvent or heavily indebted; then, often in **insolvency** proceedings, the remaining assets are distributed among the creditors, and the company or parts of it are sold or dissolved.

Earning enough money, in the long run, is, therefore, the most crucial goal in the economy. First, however, should be the clarity of what value the products offered by the company have for life.

Changes in the economy

With earned money, products can be acquired, whereby, again, someone makes money. **Cycles** are created. Growth occurs when things, knowledge, skills, or quality of life improve.

Economic fluctuations, phases of a boom, recession, or crisis are possible. Stability at a good level and sometimes even downsizing can also be valuable.

The task at the end of the chapter

Task 37 **My economy?**

What kind of economic system do you have locally?
What do you offer (manpower, jobs, products, ...)?
What do you ask for (which goods, services, ...)?
Which markets do you know and which do you use?

What can you do, what do you want and what will you do here?

37. My economy:

My economic order:

My offers:

My demands:

My markets:

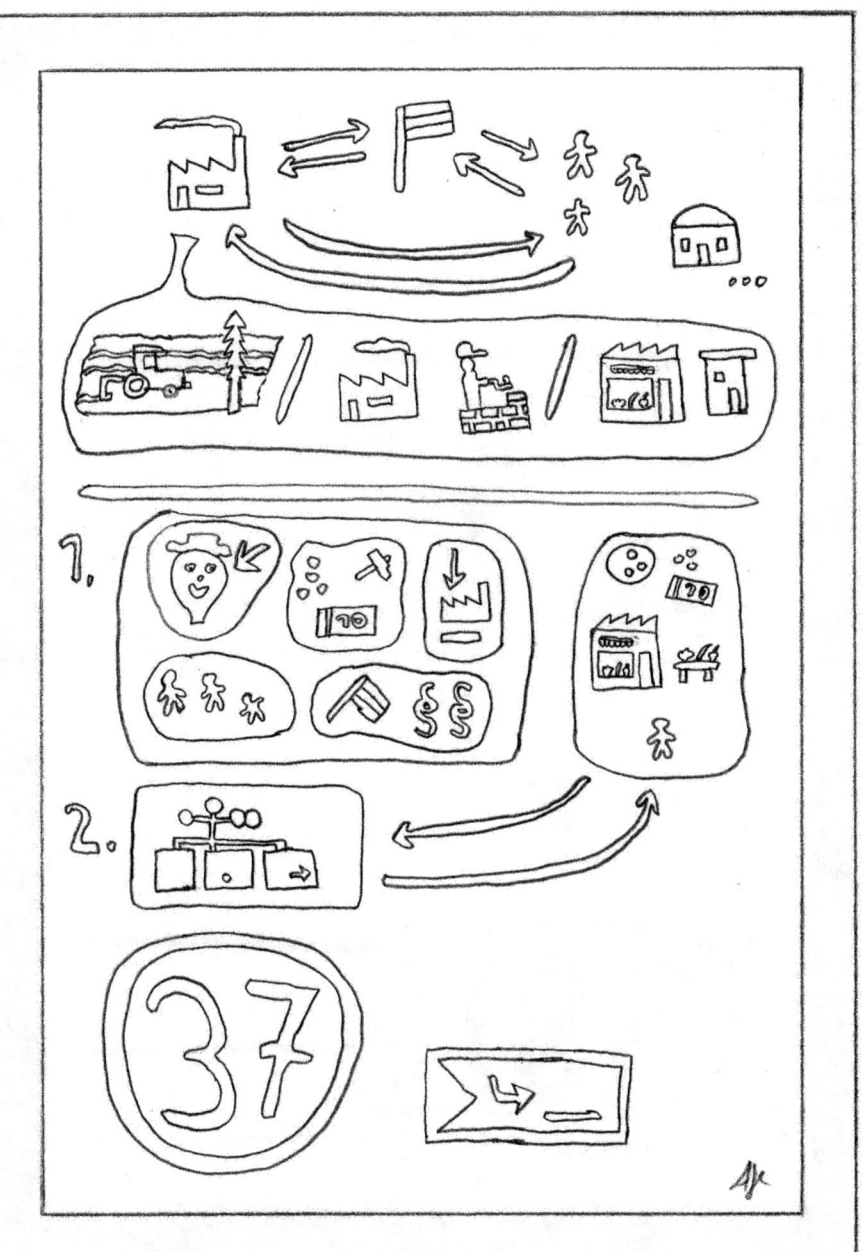

38. Chapter: Faith community and other communities

In addition to families, the state, and the economy, which were the subject of the previous chapters, there are other communities. We will close the topic of communities with the topic of faith community and other communities.

The essence of a faith community

In my opinion, the purpose of a religious community is to accompany its members through their lives and to help them to succeed in their lives by offering them a good lesson for **mental orientation** and also through the **community** of its members.

And it does this by offering regular **meetings**, perhaps in a faith center, in which faith is proclaimed and practiced and which, of course, is also a place of encounter with others.

This is actually something very valuable for everyone. On the other hand, no one can guarantee that the teaching of a particular faith community is right or at least helpful. This is especially true when the faith community focuses on spiritual or transcendental practices. Some things can only be suspected, trusted, or deeply convinced, i.e., believed. I find it more important than the absolute truth to ask how well a faith or a faith practice contributes to a good life. However, a realistic approach would be nice.

How can an existing faith community ensure all this? Well, by using this book and offering an assembly at least once a week, as described in the second chapter. ☺

In my opinion, this has four advantages:

1. It is guaranteed that the community will go through all **the essential world and life topics** once a year with the weekly impulses. And this in a way that I find beautiful, compressed, personal, and appropriate to the present level of knowledge of us humans. Most contents are, in fact, not my own but rather the summarized knowledge of many other people.

2. It is guaranteed that the religious community remains independent and **flexible**. The texts are only those of a person who can make mistakes. In every assembly, every community has the opportunity to clarify what it really believes or what seems to be really right for them locally and in their own time. And of course, there remains – even within the assembly – room for traditional, spiritual or transcendental elements, the way, the community considers this to be good.

3. It is ensured that the community members regularly have an opportunity to **meet.**

4. One contributes in this way to the human **world community.** When people see that "the others" are doing the same, it is a connecting element. A sense of "we in this one world for life" and mutual trust can grow and flourish.

And if there is no suitable local faith community, one could perhaps start one among the inhabitants of a place or a house.

The faith community as a faith congregation

Let us dream of a large congregation of believers that at least also use this book.

Imagine it has a fixed **faith center:** a place that is beautiful and comfortable. It is so close that most members can even reach it on foot. During the day, or at least in the evening, there is always someone there, so that even those who live alone or would like to leave their housemates from time to time, especially children, young people, or old people, have a place of encounter beyond the weekly assemblies. Maybe there is something to drink, a few books, board games, an instrument, or a songbook to sing. Perhaps you will find new friends, someone for personal one-on-one talks, or you will find a place in a discussion group.

Perhaps part of the faith center is also a very nice large room where the weekly assemblies can take place. If not, the congregation may use existing sports halls, festival halls, theaters, or the rooms of other communities, as long as the others are okay with it.

The congregation is well **organized.** Maybe it has a full-time leadership, an office and staff, and a council that supports and controls the administration.

There might at least be an open discussion group or a choir, orchestra, or preparation group to enrich the assemblies. Children's and youth groups and camps could be offered, nurseries, kindergartens, schools, or retirement homes could be run.

We can imagine that the members contribute something to the community mainly through free help, donations, or contributions within the scope of their possibilities. Each contribution will be recognized appropriately unless the donor wishes otherwise. The community tries to cover its costs.

The congregation probably offers professional **one-on-one talks** with its leader or a competent co-worker on personal issues. Perhaps once a year, and as needed.

Maybe there are ten different **events**:
1. The weekly assemblies.
2. A birth celebration on the occasion of the newly born children. The focus is on the children, the parents, perhaps godparents who want to be there especially for the child, and the question of how they want to deal with the children.
3. A youth celebration at the beginning of adolescence. Perhaps a visit of a one year accompanied youth discussion group precedes it. The focus is on young people and the question of how they want to use and enjoy their greater future freedom with manageable risk. Afterward, they may take over some tasks independently in the faith center.
4. An adult celebration for those who turned 18. The focus is on young adults and the question of what they want to do with their lives. Afterward, they may also be allowed to assume higher offices within the community, and to marry.

5. Individual wedding celebrations: The focus is on the bridal couple and the clarity that they belong together.

6. A midlife celebration, perhaps for those who turned 40 with a brief look back and forward.

7. A retirement celebration for all those who have just retired. The focus is on the new retirees, a review of their life achievements, and a look at their new phase in life.

8. Individual funeral celebrations: The focus is on the life of the deceased, the final farewell, and perhaps also the intention in the will.

9. Furthermore, regional celebrations such as Christmas, New Year, or inauguration, opening or closing ceremonies, in which the meaning of the celebration is the content.

10. Other events that fit the community, perhaps something spiritual or cultivation of customs and traditions.

Other communities

Communities for individual leisure activities or the achievement of goals such as sports clubs or interest groups can also be enriching.

The tasks at the end of the chapter

Task 38.1 **My faith community?**

Task 38.2 **My other communities?**

To which communities do you belong? What are your benefits and contributions? What can, would, and will you do?

38.1 My faith community:

38.2 My other communities:

305

39. Chapter: Norms

The last chapters were about communities, and in them there are norms, and we will now take a closer look at them.

Norms in general

A norm consists of a fact, a connection, and a consequence: If one thing, then the other.

Only if we know the norms well that apply to us, we can also well predict which behavior will produce which reactions. We realize clearer what we need to do (always), should do (unless there is an exception), or can do (we have the freedom to do so).

The laws of nature

Natural laws are norms that are **mandatory** for everyone, without anyone having to do anything for it. Their knowledge is, therefore, very important.

Example 1: If we jump upwards on earth without technical aids (facts), then we have to fall back to it again (consequence). The gravitational force of the planet forces us to do so. Above all, the electromagnetic forces in the ground and those in us prevent us from sliding through the ground.

Example 2: An action (fact) always has a reaction in which the total energy neither increases nor decreases (consequence). This is called the law of conservation of energy.

Example 3: A body on which no forces act (facts) retains its (movement) state (consequence) until changing forces act on it. This is called inertia.

First voluntary norm here: When I perceive the laws of nature, I remember them well. They are merciless.

The Law

If we **humans** attach legal consequences to a specific fact, which we **enforce** due to our power, law arises. Law then has the effect of natural law, even though it is not one.

Legal norms can be enacted, or created by habit, or case law, and they can be commandments or prohibitions. In **public law**, the state regulates its own affairs, and, especially in criminal law, it determines how to behave in the state. **Civil law** deals with the law between citizens. In **contracts,** people or groups can make arrangements with each other. Standardization is generally understood to be the definition of comparable parameters.

Legal norms can be interpreted according to wording, systematics, intention oft the legislator, and sense and purpose. Higher, more specific and more recent rules take precedence in the event of opposition. Legal gaps can also be closed by the analogous application of comparable norms.

Example 1: A state determines: If someone steals another person's property and the act can be proved to him (facts of the offense), he is punished appropriately for this (legal consequence).

Often the **police** clarify the facts, the judiciary, often judges or jurors, checks whether the offense is proven and determines the exact consequence. The **correctional system** implements this. Consequences can be, for example, coercion, fine, or imprisonment.

Example 2: The employer specifies that certain employees must be in the company on time for the start of work at 09:00 (facts of the case). If they do not do so, they receive a warning, and if they repeat it again, they are terminated (legal consequence).

Example 3: An area of one square meter, and the aspect ratio of 1 to the root of 2 (facts) is called A0 (consequence). The halved area A0 is A1, the halved area A1 is A2, and so on. This book is written in the original on page size A5, the illustrations are drawn on A4 paper.

Second voluntary norm here: I am aware of where rules apply to myself. I know the most important rules for my everyday life, and I remember them as soon as I hear them (legal basic and day knowledge). Otherwise, I can look it up or ask for help (detailed and specialized knowledge). If I myself set rules or make judgments, I strive for good law.

Example 4: If a seller has effectively contracted with a buyer to transfer a house for money to the buyer, the contract continues to exist, and is enforceable, because, for example, the payment is secured (facts), the seller must transfer the house (legal consequence). If he does not do this, the buyer can, in a constitutional state, sue the seller for transfer of ownership. If he can enforce his right in due time in the right court and can prove the facts, the rule of law will enforce the buyer's right forcibly, for example, by transferring the house instead of the seller.

A well-written contract usually has a **heading**, for example: Contract, purchase contract, exchange contract, gift contract, contract to produce a work, employment contract, rental contract, credit agreement, loan agreement, lending contract, articles of association, or marriage contract. It contains the exact names of the **contracting parties**, if possible, with their addresses. It includes a **contract text** which regulates understandably, and complete at least in the primary obligations, which unilateral or mutual rights and obligations the parties have. And it contains **place, date,** and **signatures**.

You can also conclude contracts verbally and declare things conclusively, it does not always have to be written or explicit. When interpreting an agreement, it is the concordant, recognizable, real will that counts. Some contracts may be valid, others void, contestable, terminable, or unenforceable.

Thirt voluntary norm here: I regularly check that I can settle very important legal matters in a written contract or, if necessary, have witnesses. Otherwise, simple documents such as receipts or a handshake or a verbal agreement are sufficient.

Morality

Morals can include **values** and **virtues.** The **custom** determines individual behaviors that are common in a specific place or within a particular framework. Morally correct behavior is regularly **not mandatory.** However, this does not mean that there are no consequences.

Examples: Someone lacks the courage to do an ordinary activity, or he dresses inappropriately, does not greet or say goodbye to others meaningfully, expresses himself inappropriately, never thanks, or eats in a very unusual way. He will usually get immediate reactions like weird looks that might trigger shame in him. And in the long run, he will struggle to find or keep good groups, friends, business partners, or the right life partner.

Fourth voluntary norm for this: I try to follow the essential local moral norms in a relaxed manner and as far as it makes sense.

The tasks at the end of the chapter

Task 39.1 **Where do norms exist that apply to me?**

Task 39.2 **Where do I give others norms?**

Task 39.3 **My main contracts?**

What is each? What can, would, and will you do in each case?

39.1 Norms that apply to me:

39.2 Norms that I give to others:

39.3 My contracts:

40. Chapter: Responsibility

The last chapter dealt with norms. Many should help us to act responsibly. Let us give more thought to responsibility in the following.

Responsibility in general

Those who have responsibility must respond as well and as correctly as possible to the being of what they are responsible for.

As adults, we have a fundamental responsibility for **ourselves,** and this includes our unconscious, our possession, and our property. In principle, we also have responsibility for the well-being of our non-adult **children,** as long as, and to the extent that, they cannot yet take responsibility. And in principle, we still have responsibility for the things for which we have **taken** responsibility; for example, for the completion of tasks at our workplace.

For this, I recommend the following **voluntary commandment:**

In my area of responsibility, I try to recognize the **good things** that are essential and I try to maintain or increase them as much as possible by naming, promoting, using, rewarding, or enjoying it.

I try to identify significant **weaknesses** in my area of responsibility and look, for example, through appropriate control, that, if possible, they do not become a problem. If there are **problems**, I try to solve them the best I can (chapter 14).

I regularly try to identify **mistakes** in my area of responsibility and deal with them correctly. (We make a mistake if we recognize or reproduce something incorrectly, or if we do something, overall seen, wrong despite a better alternative. Often there is a range of correct, good, or normal behavior.)

I try to avoid capital mistakes completely and always. (Capital mistakes are those that are obviously and seriously wrong.) I try to learn from mistakes and to deal with them in the right way, for example, to avoid further errors as much as possible. I accept that no one can be flawless, especially when confronted with new or difficult things. I therefore adequate risk making mistakes.

I expect the same from others towards my area of responsibility.

A mistake can be regarded as a violation of a norm and vice versa a violation of a norm as a possible mistake.

The violation of the norm

Much of what is presumably right or wrong, good or bad, we as human beings have defined in legal or moral norms. In the following, we will look at how we can respond responsibly to a possible norm violation from my point of view:

1. **Objective violation of a norm.** In the first step, we examine the external behavior of the person and ask whether this is an actual violation of the norm. We also think of incitement, aiding and complicity.

We also examine whether the behaviour is not justified by an **exception**, such as self-defense or state of emergency.

Example: In an unobserved moment, the offender takes away from the victim a valuable item of clothing that the victim had lying next to him to keep it. That might be theft. But if the garment was lent to the victim by the offender, and if the victim had to return it, but refuses and is perhaps on his way abroad to sell it there, then the removal is justified, because the right does not have to give way to injustice.

2. **Subjective violation of the norm.** In the second step, we examine whether the offender acted culpably, i.e., whether the offender can also be subjectively accused of the offense. This is usually the case if the offender acts deliberately or negligently. An offender acts deliberately if he knew what he was doing and wanted to do so. This does not necessarily have to be intention or certainty about the consequence; it is also sufficient that he accepts the norm violation approvingly. An offender acts negligently if, despite being able to do so, he does not recognize danger or does not act by this knowledge. Gross negligence is committed by those who violate their duty of care, especially severely.

It is not uncommon for both parties to have **contributory fault**, for example, in the genesis, amount or duration of the damage.

Example: Think of the case from earlier and change it, so that the garment belongs to the victim, i.e., the person who has it next to him, but it looks almost identical to the one the offender lent to the victim. If the offender knows this, he acts deliberately. If he assumes that it is his and takes it away without checking it carefully, he acts negligently. If he checked the garment very carefully and could not detect any deviation from his, he acts innocently.

3. In the third step, we examine the **consequences** of the violation.

I think that, in the case of small mistakes that are generally unavoidable, or those that happened a long time ago, which no one has noticed and which have not seriously harmed anyone, the **insight** is typically enough.

If mistakes of this kind can and should easily be prevented, then it is good if we also take care to **avoid repetition.**

If significant damage was caused, it should, as far as possible and reasonable, **be repaired**, for example, apologize, restore, or pay damages.

In the case of a severe violation of the norm, an appropriate **punishment**, such as a reprimand, fine, forced labor or imprisonment, should regularly follow. It should prevent further offenses by the offender or others and create appropriate justice.

Feeling guilty, shame and remorse motivate improvement.

Anger or a sense of revenge motivates one not to simply ignore violations of norms. It may be that we could not have behaved differently in the place of the offender, with his genes and his imprint. But even then, sanctions threatened and implemented, would help us to act by the norm.

In the example, the offender would have to return the garment if it did not belong to him. If, in the above case, he also acted deliberately, he should regularly receive appropriate punishment.

4. It is good if we forgive ourselves and others for the breach of the norm, at least if it was handled sufficiently well. This brings peace and quiet, especially within us.

The tasks at the end of the chapter

Task 40.1 **Dealing with violations of norms with me?**

How do you deal with mistakes or breaches of norms yourself?
How are you dealt with mistakes / violations of norms?
As suggested above in the text or differently?

Task 40.2 **My responsibility beyond that?**

Is the idea of responsibility in the text also yours, or what do you think is better?
For what concretely do you have responsibility?

What can you do, what do you want and what will you do in each case?

40.1 Dealing with mistakes or norm violations with me:

40.2 My responsibility beyond that:

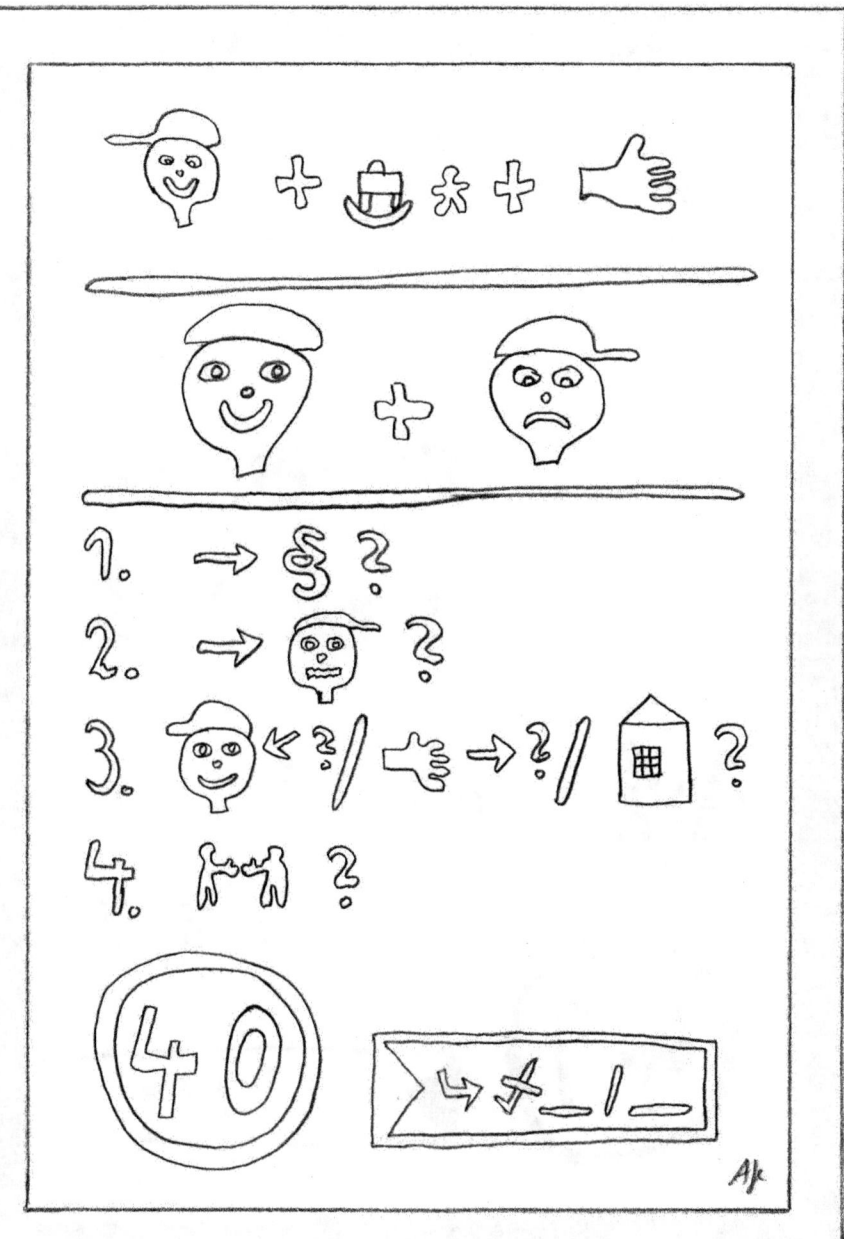

41. Chapter: Friends and acquaintances

The last chapter dealt with responsibility in general and before that it was about communities. Hereinafter, let us look at responsible dealings with individual parts of the world, and now especially at friends and acquaintances.

Acquaintances

Most people and most parts of the universe we do not know personally, some already.

We have **mutual** acquaintances, for example, from the areas of work, neighborhood, leisure, social media, or from parties or celebrations. Only we know **one-sided** acquaintances, but they do not know us; often, they are politicians, managers, artists, actors, or sportsmen.

Below are ten voluntary points on how we can deal well with others - not just people - from my point of view:

1. **Mindfulness.** I try to pay adequate attention to others and to know them well enough.

So it is clear how they will react and who or what about them might fit in well with us. It is probably impossible to assess the value or nature of another person as a whole. One would have to know all characteristics correctly, know why something or someone has gotten that way, and how he or she will become.

2. **Acceptance.** I try to accept others inwardly appropriately.

People and things are, at last at first, as they are and not as we would like them to be.

3. **Respect.** I respect others appropriately and can distinguish between who they are as a person and what they do in each individual case.

We, humans, tend to draw conclusions about the entirety out of individual cases. If we separate this, the other can feel respected, at least as a person, despite negative criticism.

And if there is something good about others, we may have the greatness to acknowledge it. If not remember: If we had the genes, the history of development, the current environment, and the expected future of the other, we would be, very sure, the same.

4. **Observe norms.** I try to adhere appropriately to the norms applicable to me, in particular to the applicable law and the applicable customs.

This makes our common behavior more predictable and avoids unnecessary irritations.

5. **Appropriate help.** If I need help or want something, I ask for it and let someone help me; if I want to offer something, I ask if it is desired. If necessary, I clarify an appropriate consideration or give or accept a no.

Life can only succeed in the long run with mutual help that does not overtax anyone.

6. **Appropriate criticism.** I try to criticize in a good way. If I recognize good things, I point it out in a proper way. In the case of bad things that I would like to communicate, I try to see if I can encounter the other person in

323

such a way that only he or she will notice the criticism. I then ask whether he or she is open to criticism and if so, I say what is wrong from my point of view.

When I talk about others, I try to do that truthfully and essentially complete. What I have been told confidentially, I keep, as far as possible, for me.

A smile, a nod, applause, praise, thanks, a gift, or the like can motivate to continue. Negative criticism expressed in such a way that it can be accepted, brings the chance to recognize and improve bad things, or to clarify something. And talking appropriately about other people is often important to learn to evaluate them thoroughly.

7. Solving conflicts well. I try to resolve a conflict, in particular an open dispute, appropriately, if necessary, with the help of others.

Conflicts are unavoidable. A frequent cause for conflicts, is **missing or wrong information.**

Also, everyone has their own **view of the world.** As if looking through invisible glasses, we seem to recognize some things more clearly and to suppress others (selective perception), or we interpret things in such a way that they fit in with the world view in which we believe.

Furthermore, almost everyone has a strong **will to survive good.** Especially in Prehistoric and Stone Age times, there were often famines. Who will the group let survive well? Or: Who will get a partner? Well, those who are particularly **valuable**, for example, because they can do, know or have something important, or simply because one like them, or because they fit well. Or those who have the power to enforce something, due to their mental, physical, or financial **strength,** or through their alliances. And in that, everyone is always also a bit of an opponent (and at times opponents are also helpers).

And some **nasty** people just like to argue.

There are four steps to solving conflicts:
I. First, clarify the **factual level:** What do both parties want? Example: Two are fighting over two coconuts.
II. Then, at a **meta-level**, clarify what they actually want. Example: One wants the coconut meat because he is hungry, the other wants the coconut water for seasoning.
III. If that doesn't help, then clarify on a **personal level** whether the two, or the groups to which they belong, are enemies. Reconciliation or a cease-fire could enable a solution.
IV. If necessary, **decide** the conflict. (See in particular chapters 35, 14, 39, 40, 15 and 13).

Friends

With some we can make friends and remain friends as long as it suits them both.

8. **Bond with friendly things.** For those who suit me well, and I want to, I try to make an appropriate bond.

Whether someone fits, we often find out well, when we inform ourselves with interest, and when we experience each other while doing things together. Emotionally bound, the feeling of belonging together arises, even if the other person is not there. You're happy when you see each other again, you're proud of each other, and you often want to be similar, or at least fit together well in the long run.

9. **Have good friendship.** For good friends, I am also there in difficult times, appropriately. This includes regularly listening to others appropriately, keeping secrets, perhaps giving comfort and help even when it may cost something.

Both, close friends, who, figuratively speaking, "swim in the same boat," and distant friends, i.e., those "from other boats," each have their own, slightly different, value.

Most friends will only be "normal friends," i.e., buddies or comrades who are there as long as it is nice for both of them. That also has its value.

10. **To cultivate friendship.** I cultivate existing relationships at least by keeping appropriate contact and by informing about essential new developments.

This way, we can maintain a valuable relationship successfully.

The tasks at the end of the chapter

Task 41.1 *My friends?*

Who are your friends? Who is a good one? Who is missing?

Task 41.2 *My acquaintances?*

From where do you know others, especially other people?

What can you do, what do you want, and what will you do in each case?

41.1 *My friends:*

41.2 *My acquaintances:*

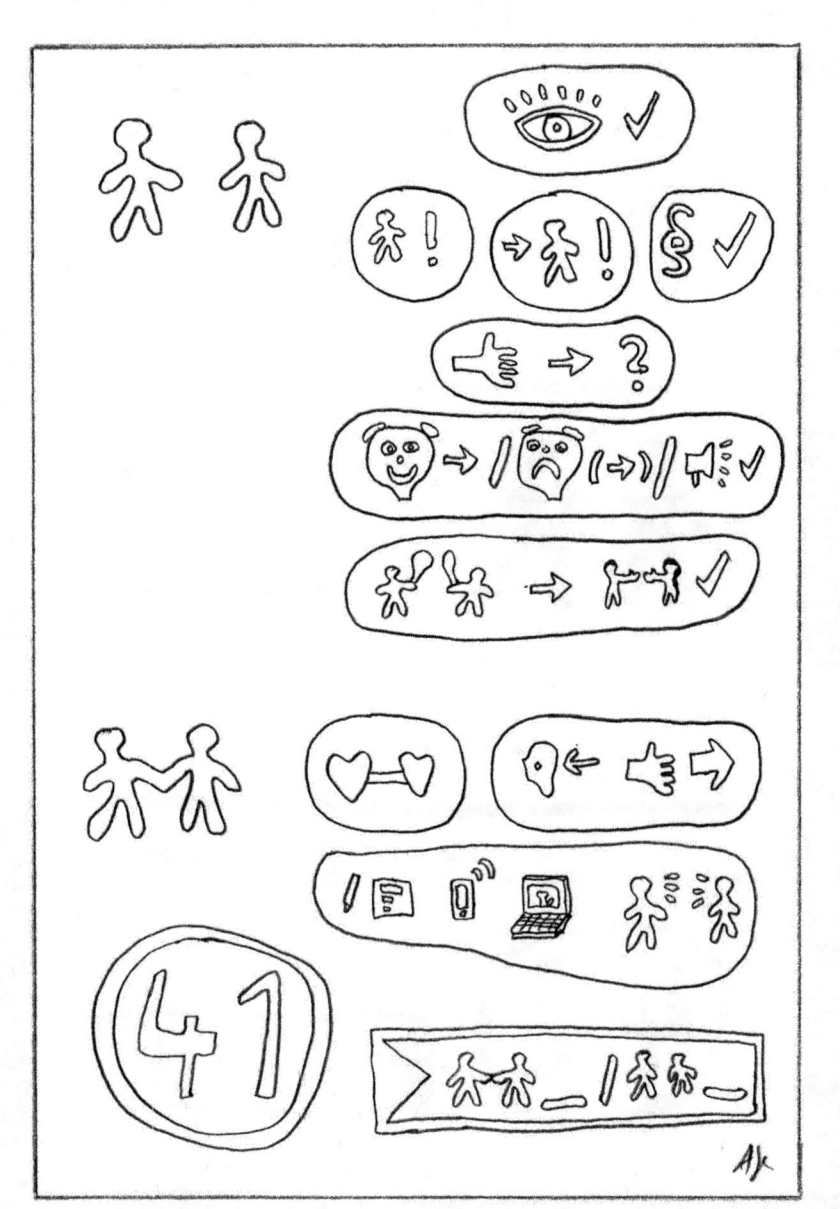

329

Chapter 42: Man and Woman

The previous chapter was about acquaintances and friends, now we look at two more different beings, man and woman. At the end, we will have a short look at differences in general.

The woman

Let's imagine it's Stone Age. The woman **gets pregnant and** then **breast-feeds** her baby. With a big belly or a baby in her arms, she will hunt, gather, and fight rather poorly. It is therefore optimal if she develops into a being that is particularly suitable for being in and around the camp: The emotional and loving contact with the small children, taking care of the children, of the others or the sick, diligently collecting and arranging things in the immediate vicinity, or also cooking, sewing or food processing. In the camp, the work is regularly somewhat simple and similar, and there is usually someone there to ask questions; on the other hand one needs to be able to cope with many different things at once. Comparatively good networking of the brain hemispheres helps here. A sense of beauty also makes sense at home, where others can see it. And knowing the other people in the camp, keeping good communication with them and staying in the group is also important. If she is a little smaller than he is, she does not need so many nutrients. With a bit more of fat in the body, there is still a reserve for the offspring even in rather bad times. Slightly soft and curvy in physique, higher voice and with her primary sex characteristics, she fits well to the children with whom she spends relatively much time. If she is more reasonable internally, this is also helpful for the survival of the family and for family planning.

The Man

The man then does the other tasks. Larger, with more muscle mass and thicker skin, he can fight more successfully to protect his female, or to protect the family or group. He can also hunt better, walk long distances to gathering places, and carry heavy food back to **provide** the family materially. A higher proportion of water in the body helps him to survive longer without drinking. And he must be able to solve complicated individual problems or difficult tasks: He should be able to search for and find new paths or campsites, develop new hunting techniques and weapons to be able to slay new animals or old ones at new sites and, if possible, tactically be better than his opponents. For that, he has a comparatively larger brain mass. In the camp he can, if he is already there and has time, take care of the physically or mentally heavier things and of course also of the children. To be successful in hunting or fighting together, hierarchy and questions of dispute must be clarified quickly. And when it comes to survival outside, one should sometimes be able to close oneself off emotionally; for worm emotions there is space again at the camp with the children and in the arms of the woman. And of course, he can explain a lot about the world out there to the older children and show it to them, as well as to the women. The joy of taking risks, courage and bravery make sense to him, along with wisdom. A deeper voice and a somewhat harder, more angular physique, along with more body hair and his primary gender characteristics, also go well with the role of the man.

The Couples

Basically, men and women complement each other well. And in principle, it therefore also seems to be good, if a man and a woman live together as a fitting couple, and, if possible, do this durable **heterosexually-monogamous.**

Together they can conceive and raise children, get fully involved with each other and perhaps love each other for being the most valuable person in their lives. And if you only have one partner, there is one partner left for almost everyone.

The most common form of living together in human history, however, is **polygamy**, in which a man lives together with several women. A genetically, economically, and humanly particularly good man can so have many, presumably good descendants.

The rarest thing in history is probably the form in which a woman is together with several men.

If women have to share a man, it may be advantageous if some of them have also developed a sexual affection for each other.

Likewise, **bi-** or **homosexuality** and **asexuality** have their own advantages besides various causes.

Also, some people feel comfortable with many different fixed partners, i.e., **polyamory.**

For some people, it can be good and right to stay alone as a **single** for a short time or permanently.

Women master the situation of living alone, mentally often better than men, but survival in the Stone Age was difficult for them alone, and over long periods of civilization his status determined that of the family.

I think everyone should see for themselves what suits them and what is socially possible. It is not so much a matter of free choice as of recognizing what is in and around one.

The "pairing" outside the partnership

Sexuality outside the partnership has an increased risk of contracting sexually transmitted diseases.

If he cheats on her, then, during the Stone Age, there was a danger that he would fall in love with the other, and would leave her and the children unprovided. If she is cheating him, then the offspring he took care of might not be his.

On the other hand, we are human beings, who are also able to find others than our own life partner attractive. If he cheats, during the Stone Age, this increases his chance of having more offspring. Together with a genetically better man, she can produce offspring, which will, in any case, make the group of her children more diverse. And a less attractive lover can be a relatively safe substitute if the own partner leaves.

A good life partnership with loyalty should be good, regularly. There may be exceptions here as well.

Further differences between people

Even differences that go beyond the sexes have the advantage that one can complement each other. The overweight, for example, may have been a fast-exhausted hunter or gatherer in luxuriant times, but he was particularly valuable in the famine.

It is typical that we regularly feel attracted to similar things and find the others rather dull; only in exceptional cases, these are more interesting.

Recognizing differences, and using them occasionally is probably usually good.

The tasks at the end of the chapter

Task 42.1 **My gender?**

What is it? What about you is male, what is female?

Task 42.1 **My love partner model?**

Hetero-? Homo-? Bi-? Asexual? ...
Monogamous? Polygamous? Polyamor? Single? ...

What can you, would you and what will you do in each case?

42.1 My gender:

42.2 My love partner model:

337

43. Chapter: Life partner

After having looked at differences in the last chapter, we now look at how it can still go well anyway, or actually because of this, with a life partnership.

The maturing process

Like fruits have to mature, children and teenagers before puberty are not yet physically and mentally developed enough for a life partnership.

As teenagers, we try to experiment with ourselves and get to know us as prospective adults. Who am I? What do I want to do with my life? Where should my place be in the world? Only when we recognize this to some extent, will it be clear to us which partner can suit us well.

As teenagers, we can, as long as society allows it, make **girl- or boyfriends** while perhaps still living with our parents. This is less than a life partnership and different from friendship. With girl- or boyfriends, we can learn whether, how or with whom life partnership is something for us.

Finding and bonding

From my point of view, there are four steps for us humans, how we find partners to mate on short term, or permanently and maybe to bond ourselves.

1. **Tempt.** We meet others at work, in our free time, or in social media, and we seem to be interesting.

Typically, men here, at first glance, will find beautiful and healthy-looking women of childbearing age attractive. Usually, women will pay particular attention to healthy, tall and physically, economically, mentally, and socially strong men who are also assertive and have a good linguistic and personal appearance. Whoever is like that, seems to be suitable for offspring.

2. **Flirting.** If the first impression fits and one is basically open for a relationship, one looks at, or smiles at one another invitingly, or one speaks to one another.

3. **Getting to know and conquer.** You talk, make compliments, do something together. Maybe you touch each other, kiss each other, and look at how the other one reacts. The question is: Does the other really fit me and with what I want? A life partnership, family, girl- or boyfriend, a child, or "just having fun"?

I think it's good if we ask ourselves the following questions: Does the other person **fit** sufficiently to me **as a person?** Is he approximately of **equal** value (age, wealth, profession, health, beauty, intelligence, and more)? If not, the clearly better may soon look for a better partner. And: Are we **similar** enough so that we can be mostly harmonious together? Being a little different is good because you can complement each other that way. For example, if she is a little younger, this can have advantages for both gender roles.

Then: Does our **vision of life and future fit** together well enough? Can we live our **everyday life** permanently as a couple (language, home, work, leisure time, loyalty)? Do our **family interests** fit? Do we want children, and if so, when and how many?

Last point: **The feeling.** Do our **personal preferences** fit adequately? Do we really **want** or **love** each other as partners? Caution psyche: Not every seemingly good provider is a good partner. And who, as a child, has not developed a secure bond structure, but an avoiding, ambivalent or chaotic one, or who had wrong role models, will often unconsciously continue the familiar or try the opposite. Most people, however, can bond themselves secure, and some things can be healed by love.

A **holiday** together, **everyday life** together, and a **short time of separation** could bring clarity. It is important to look whether there is something about each other that the other person will not be able to live with permanently. It is not uncommon for several partnerships to be necessary until one is clear who is really the right one.

4. **Mating.** Well, we are at the chapter life partner, and here it applies: If we want the other person to be our life partner, we could promise each other: **"We want to stay together durably as life partners and be there for each other appropriately."**

The essence of the partnership could be regulated in a contract. A wedding celebration makes, what is well, visible and able to experience. Those who wish, or should, can also undergo state or cultural rites.

Keeping

The life partnership also includes joint development, and this can also be some work.

Communication is very important. Talking to each other regularly, and being really interested in what the other person thinks, feels, and what moves him, is valuable.

(In the case of conflicts, we should especially remember chapters 41, 35, 14, 39, 40, 15 and 13.)

It is also important to make sure that we have a real **daily life** together. How can changes or wishes for change be reacted to? Do you do enough together, does everyone participate according to their possibilities, and does everyone have enough freedom? Life partners are not only people who happen to live together.

After all, mutual **love** is something that needs to be nurtured. Is there enough time to feel it again and again, also in tenderness and sexuality?

The Divorce

It is death at the latest that divorces life partners. One can also notice earlier that one was mistaken in the beginning and that the other never really suited them. Or that one has changed so much that it no longer fits or that someone else is obviously much better. Then it can be reasonable to get divorced.

Careful psyche again: It is not uncommon for partners, to fight each other as fervently after the separation, as they previously desired each other: The adored person, who should remain forever in their own life, can become the enemy, who is allowed to disappear entirely from the world.

Whoever has already settled the end for safety's sake is well off. In any case, compensation of assets and support should be appropriate also after the divorce, especially in the care of common children.

It would be better if we were to implement what is recommended in the text, so that if possible, there is no need for a "rose war," but so that we can enjoy a life partnership as a great source of happiness in the long term.

The tasks at the end of the chapter

Task 43.1 **My dream partner?**

Can you describe what your dream partner would be like?
Are you aware that fitting to you is more important than being great? Are you aware that the perfect partner does not exist?
Which people you know probably fit to you?

Task 43.2 **My life partner situation?**

What is your current situation with a life partnership?
Where are you, and what of the text do you implement how?

What can you, what would you, and what will you do each?

43.1 My dream partner:

43.2 My life partner situation:

345

44. Chapter: Love

After the life partnership in the last chapter, we now look at something that partners hopefully have enough of: spiritual love and its physical expression.

Spiritual love

Love is the strongest feeling of affection we know. When we love, we consciously or unconsciously perceive the beloved regularly as very **valuable** and very **fitting** to us, even if we cannot always understand it exactly. We are regularly happy when we can have what we love with us, think about it often and gladly, and we are motivated to preserve it well and therefore often deal with it lovingly. Sometimes we also feel love with little things or when we exceptionally recognize something bad, but love remains justified.

We regularly love our life partner, our children, or our parents. We can also love other people, animals, plants, things, or activities, entirely or in a specific role.

We are **fallen in love** when we perceive a few things about something or someone as very good and very good for us, and believe that everything else is definitely just as good. The feeling may be powerful, but only getting to know each other better, will show, whether it can become a lasting love or not.

The tenderness

We can **express** our affection **physically**. For example, we can lovingly look at another person, hug him, take him by the hand, kiss him, snuggle up to him, or tell him something loving.

The exchange of tenderness is regularly a good thing at any age if it is honest, and both want it.

Sexuality

Sexuality can be an **expression** of our **love** and affection **and** our **sexual desire,** at the earliest for adolescents after puberty; for some, it is also an expression of power.

The natural purpose of sexuality is to conceive children, and to strengthen and nurture the attachment to their partner, also to be able to raise children together. Therefore, our body often releases the bonding hormone oxytocin, which emotionally strengthens the connection to those close to us and the distance to others.

Sexuality is basically healthy, keeps organs fit and satisfies sexual desire and, like many other healthy things, should have a life-prolonging effect.

Consensual sexuality is typically our most potent natural source of happiness. The body releases, in particular, the happiness hormone dopamine, and for many, it is also a strong mental source of strength.

Without a mutual will, sexuality is rather disgusting, unpleasant, and sometimes traumatizing.

In **foreplay,** we go beyond the frame of tenderness by saying something sexually suggestive, by touching, stroking, kissing or smooching the partner, even at their erogenous zones, buttocks, breasts, or "pubic area". In foreplay, we recognize the partner's openness for more than tenderness, or we even arouse the openness.

We can increase the **petting** in manual or oral intercourse, and also anal intercourse is possible. Some like this area very much, others don't like it at all.

Finally, there can be **sexual intercourse**, thus vaginal intercourse, in which it can come to procreation.

The procreation

To explain the procreation, we begin with the woman. At intervals of about 28 days, she has her period. If we start counting on the first day of the menstruation, one of the **egg cells** present since birth **matures** in the ovary until the middle of the period and is fertile for a few hours after ovulation. An orgasm is not necessary but can be beneficial.

With the orgasm of the man, an ejaculation occurs. A small part of it are millions of **sperm**, which are newly **produced** in the testicles. If they enter the woman's vagina, they can swim from there to the fertilizable egg cell, one can penetrate it and fertilize it. Sperm survive in the woman's body for a few days, outside they die when they dry out, regularly within one day at the latest; males are faster, females more long-lasting. And some only have the function of eliminating another man's sperm.

After **fertilization**, one half of the man's genetic material merges with the other half of the woman's genetic material, thus forming the genetic material of the future child in the core of the first cell. Each half contains a complete construction manual, and each is a separate mixture of the two halves of the ancestor. Both leads to often very different children, who also have a lot from grandparents and their ancestors.

After fertilization, the first cell divides into two new cells. More and more cells are created by further divisions. To be supplied with nutrients, the cells have to migrate into the uterus and **settle there**, about five to 13 days after conception, but this does not always succeed. Successfully implanted, the menstrual period now remains off. During **pregnancy**, an embryo grows into a fetus and finally into a baby. It has its own blood circulation, is supplied by the placenta and umbilical cord, and floats in an amniotic sac.

Anyone who wants to have a child should have unprotected vaginal intercourse in the middle of the woman's period and not give up immediately. If it does not work in the long run, he or she can be infertile, or something else does not fit. A professional may be able to help.

And: If possible, no procreation between close blood relatives, since the risk of hereditary diseases in children is increased due to the similarity of the genetic material.

Contraception

Those who do not want pregnancy have several possibilities to prevent it. I would like to mention three:

1. The **contraceptive pill** brings hormones into the woman's body, which then thinks she is pregnant. As a result, there is no new ovulation. Advantage: Very safe. Disadvantages: Possibly unwanted side effects and no protection against sexual transmitted diseases.

2. A **condom** absorbs the ejaculation, sperm cannot enter the vagina. Advantage: It also significantly reduces the risk of infections with sexual transmitted diseases, if such a risk exists at all, though. Disadvantage: Can slip down or burst in exceptional cases, and is perceived as unpleasant by many men.

3. If you successfully **make sure** that no sperm can fertilize the egg cell during conception period, you will also be able to prevent pregnancy.

The tasks at the end of the chapter

Task 44.1 **My spiritual love?**

Who or what do you love? Who loves you?

Task 44.2 **My "physical love"?**

Where do you get tenderness from, and to whom do you give it? If you are old enough: What about your sexuality?

What can you do, what do you want and what will you do in each case?

44.1 My spiritual love:

44.2 My physical love:

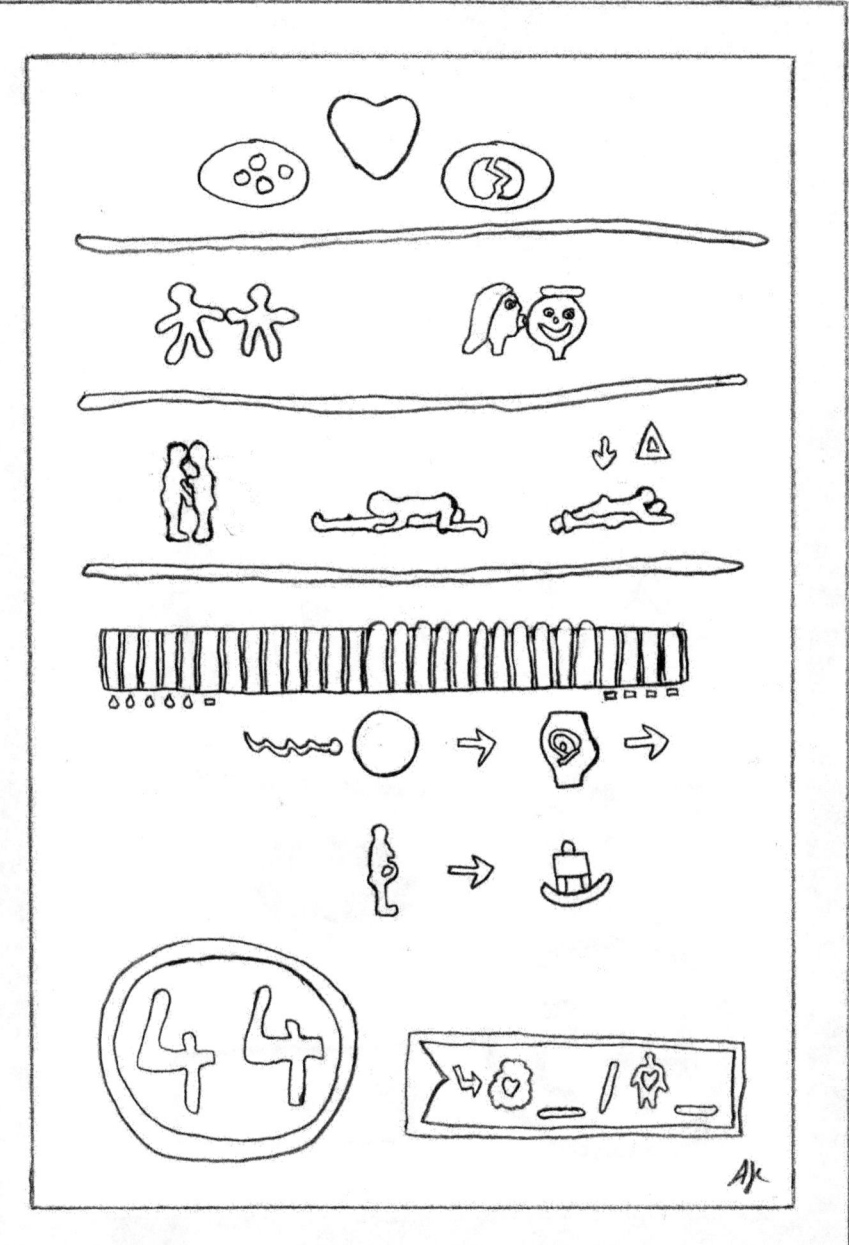

352

353

45. Chapter: Children

The last chapter dealt with the question of how children are conceived. In this chapter, we now look at how we can interact well with children.

Children are not small adults, but they have their own, the predominantly childlike psyche.

Children, and very essentially also the quality of life on earth, are dependent on adults. Good children can become good adults. Therefore it is essential how our children are and how we interact with our children.

Here are a few ideas how I imagine this:

The desire to have children

Anyone who is physically and mentally healthy, intelligent and beautiful, has a similar life partner and sufficient money together, is socially involved and likes children should definitely do the world a favor and have children. Otherwise, the good genes will die out.

Anyone who knows that he or she has severe deficits, which he or she would certainly pass on to his or her children, and anyone who certainly does not like children, should consider whether he or she can see his or her contribution to valuable life in the forgoing to have children. If so, others should appreciate it.

Anyone who has a child that will, for example, be severely handicapped or overtax the parents severely, should decide within the first three month.

The right time and number of children

Anyone who has two to four children at a distance of perhaps up to four years and at the age of maybe 21 to 40 with her and 25 to 50 with him, has children with siblings who can probably do something with each other, and who likely also have fit and already mature parents who are not overtaxed.

The overall circumstances are also important: Is there an overpopulation problem, or are you dying out locally? In modern societies, the population remains constant at about 2.2 children per woman on average. Too many people cannot cope well with nature, too few, and the markets, intellectual potentials, and securities are rather small.

We should bear in mind that after puberty one is capable of procreating, but not yet an adult; that in the case of a woman, giving birth from the age of 40, the health risk for her and the child increases significantly; and that she cannot have any more children on average from 50 to 52. In his case, fertility is basically maintained for the rest of his life, but it can decrease from around 40, and after death, he can no longer be there personally for the children and grandchildren.

The overall social, financial, and health situation is also important for the question of when, and how many children are suitable for a particular couple.

Often it is also good to simply accept what is coming.

Getting and raising the children

1. Already during the nine months of **pregnancy**, children need a mother who pays attention to her health because her child is directly affected by it.

2. Children need a good **birth.** It is good if you find the right place for it and someone to help you with it, and during the time before and after. The date of birth is often around the 280th day after the first day of the last menstrual period. It really starts when the contractions occur about ten minutes apart.

3. Children need a good **name.**

4. Children need good **health care** to maintain their health. For example, sleeping on their back the first three months, if possible breast milk in the first half-year and then gradually new food, initially unseasoned; diapers until they can go to the toilet, child-friendly play options, if posible with other children, clothing, accommodation, and protection.

Children need 5. **love,** 6. **secure emotional bonding** to at least one caregiver, and again and again 7. **quality time** in which one is entirely there for them. Children feel if you love them, feel connected to them, and value them. The tender touch of the skin is important right after birth. Talking to them is good. Without this, children die, as previous experiments have shown. If this is the case, they can feel safe and valuable, strengthen their basic trust, bond themselves securely and live motivated, also for others.

Children need 8. **freedom,** and 9. **limits.** Without sufficient freedom, they cannot try themselves out and develop into what they are. Spatial boundaries, prohibitions, commandments, and rituals, which are enforced in each case, provide security. Children should be challenged, not over or under challenged.

10. Children need **orientation.** Their most important orientation are other people as role models, they simply have to be copied. An appropriate, also emotional reaction to the behavior of the children is important. Just as appropriate praise and blame. Praise motivates more strongly and makes you confident, it should clearly outweigh. Harmful developments should be counteracted: The wrong action is criticized, not the child as such. Next time it can do better! And comfort when something went wrong. Children also need proper explanation and help so that they feel taken seriously and can act capable and motivated.

Children can often also help themselves or show what they want. And it does not necessarily have to be the parents who give them what they need.

After the first to the fifth year of life, it is good if **kindergartens** support parents who wish to do so.

From six to twelve, it could be useful if children go to a **common school.** It should prepare children well for local adult life, including appropriate selection, relieve parents, and contribute to beautiful childhood. School hours between 09:00 and 17:00, with lunch together, and as subjects the own language, the most important foreign language, basic math and subjects that deepen this book could be good anyway.

From the age of 13, the teenagers could go to **preparatory schools**, separated according to approximate career goals, which offer a good framework for puberty and a good preparation for career choice, training, or study.

Auxiliary and elite schools, also as boarding schools, could individually support the weakest and the strongest.

Letting the children go

Within the bounds of their possibilities, one is allowed to, and should give children their own responsibility. Letting them do it themselves, freedom in the game, small work tasks, or pocket money are possibilities. Especially in the youth, they should be given more freedom, and as adults they are responsible for themselves and should be treated accordingly. After all, children enter the world through their parents.

The task at the end of the chapter

*Task 45: **My children?***

Do you have children? Do you want some or more?
Yes?: Their names? When were they born? Who are they from?
What are they like? And how do you deal with them?
What do you like about them? What is exhausting for you?

What can you do, what do you want and what will you do?

45. My children:

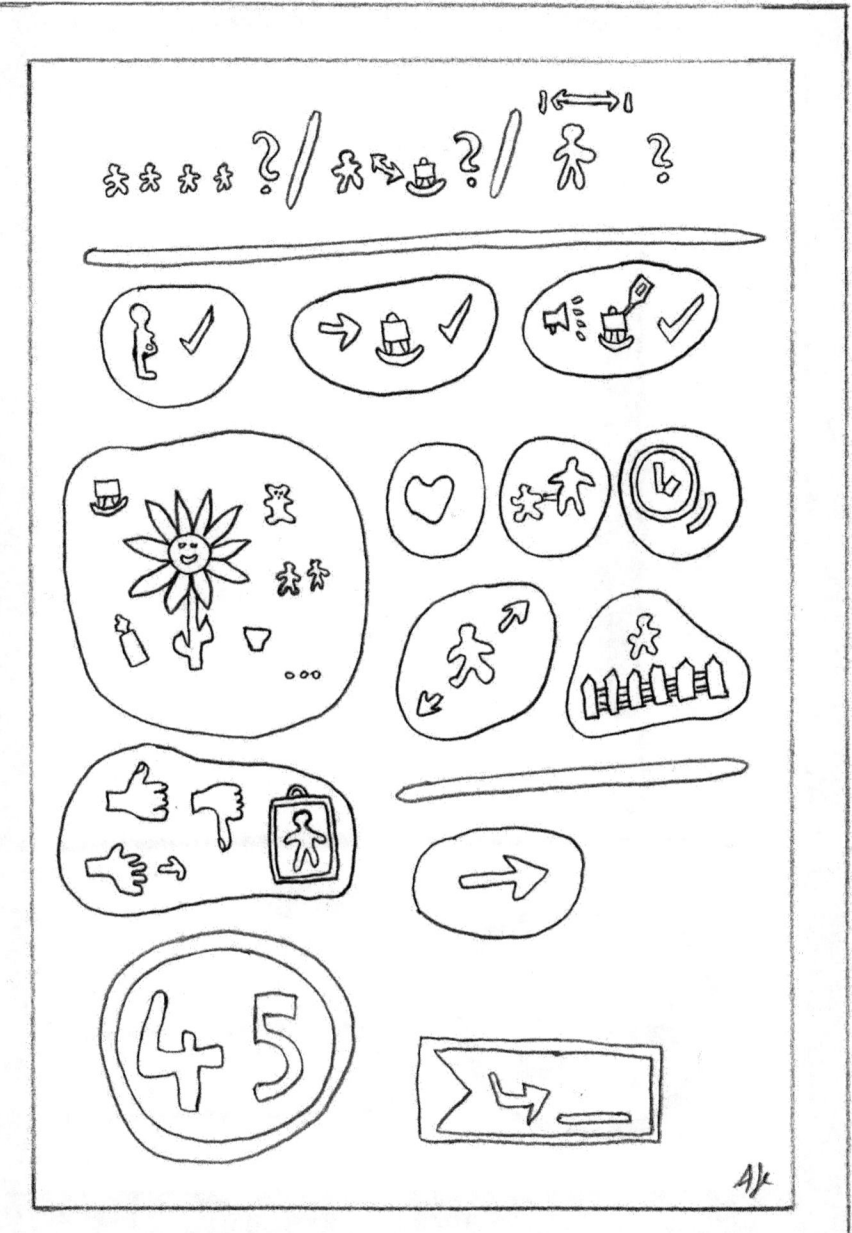

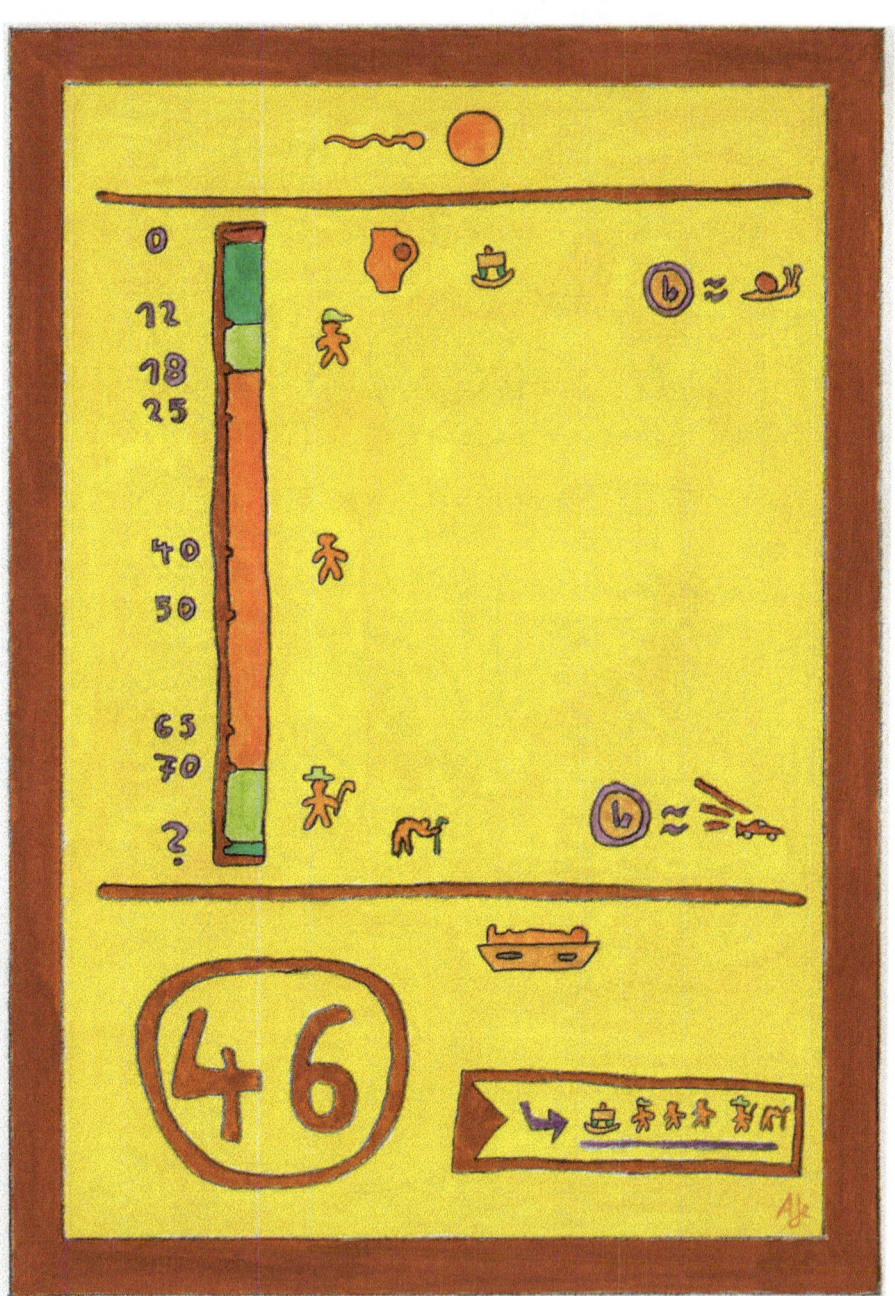

46. Chapter: Course of life

The last chapter was about children, and hopefully, they will grow old. This is the process we are looking at in this chapter, which is called: Course of life.

The time before birth

We look far back again. With the emergence of energy and the Big Bang, also the matter from which we are made of, came to existence. With the appearance of life on earth and in the course of its development over many generations, our parents and in them the egg cell and the sperm from which our **first cell** was formed, emerged. We grew in our mother's belly and regularly were born after nine calendar months.

The childhood

As a child in the world, natural **reflexes**, such as a grasping reflex, a search reflex, or a sucking reflex, which helps us to drink breast milk from the breast, initially help us.

We want to be able to do more and **learn** more and often be like the adults around us. We learn quickly, also through playful trial and error: Lifting our heads, turning, crawling, perceiving, and recognizing the world correctly and much more. And we continue to **grow.**

From the very beginning, we are dependent on the attention of other people. We, therefore, want to please parents or educators, and if something goes wrong, we relate many things to ourselves.

We don't need milk at night from about the age of six months and start sleeping through the night. The first milk teeth help us to eat new food. Adult teeth emerge from the age of six.

In the second year of life, we no longer put everything in our mouths, sometimes we can drink alone from a cup and eat with a spoon. Many a girl will already be able to go to the toilet alone. Sometimes it even takes up to the age of four.

In the second year of life, we begin to walk and also to speak: single words, two-word sentences, then more. Shortly before the end of the second year of life we can recognize ourselves in the mirror. Gradually the "me" and "you" work out better, and we develop awareness for our gender.

From the second to the fifth year of life, children can have **phases of defiance.** Sometimes it's about trying out the own will. Often the anger for something bad is behind it; still too small to clearly recognize or express exactly what it is, one reacts blanketly defiantly. During this time, we also notice that we can lie.

Around the age of three, we begin to consciously remember the things we experience.

363

Only from between eight and ten years, we can perceive our environment in such a good way, and control ourselves in such a way that we can cope safely in road traffic alone.

At the end of a healthy childhood, we know the basics and can live happily and bond safely without the constant presence of an adult.

The adolescence

Around the twelfth birthday, we change again considerably. Since girls tend to be one to two years ahead of boys in their development, it can be a little earlier for girls and a little later for boys.

During **puberty,** our **body** transforms into that of an adult. We grow again, get underarm hair and pubic hair, and the sexual characteristics develop more clearly. Girls, for example, regularly develop larger breasts and their menstrual period, boys a deeper voice and beard growth. Both develop adult genitals and become procreative.

Also, our **brain** reorganizes itself partially. Our risk assessment center develops relatively late, so as adolescents, we are brave but also careless. We test a lot, think black and white, are emotional, our daily rhythm is shifted into the evening, and we orient ourselves towards our peers, often in peer groups.

At the end of healthy adolescence, we will have reached our mental maximum, and we know to some extent what the world is like, who we are and what we want to do with our adult life.

The young adulthood

At about the age of 18 we are physically grown up. Till about 25, our **hormon level** is **highest**, we are physically most efficient, and our brain is still very much in a position to change.

As young adults, we will regularly still enjoy our freedom a little and then take our place in the world, for example, after school and training, we become familiar with our profession, find a life partner and our own home.

The older adulthood

As older adults, we mostly work in our profession and often have our own family with our own children. People of the same age seem much younger to us than in our childhood or youth. We are now particularly powerful for the community.

Although we are gradually deteriorating again, physically more than mentally, and the latter probably much less with high intelligence, we still often perform our best now, because we can counteract the decomposition for a while with practice and experience.

Women enter menopause between the early 40s and the late 50s, the body then destroys their fertility, which can be strenuous. After a permanent absence of menstruation, often between 45 and 55, women are no longer fertile. Some people now have a "midlife crisis."

All in all, however, we hardly change during this time compared to the time before and after.

The retirement age

How we feel when we have grown older, depends on our genes and especially on how healthy we have lived. Many people will gradually notice more clearly from the age of 65 that, due to their age, not so much is possible as it used to be. Time also seems to pass faster and faster.

Maybe at the age of 70, we could **retire** and be no more or much less employed. Perhaps we could help our children with our grandchildren, look for a volunteer work, or cultivate our hobbies as long as we can.

The old age

Not every person will get in **need of care** and thus becomes similar to a child again, but it can happen.

Most people can become around 80 years old. Women usually grow a few years older than men. A few can live to be over 100, in extreme cases at most 120.

The task at the end of the chapter

Task 46 **An overview of my whole life?**

What was essential or what will probably be: in my childhood, my youth, my young adulthood, my older adulthood, my retirement age, and my old age? If you like to, have a look at the tasks in chapters three to six and eight again.

46. My whole life at a glance:

My childhood:

My youth:

My time as a young adult:

My time as an older adult:

My retirement age:

My old age:

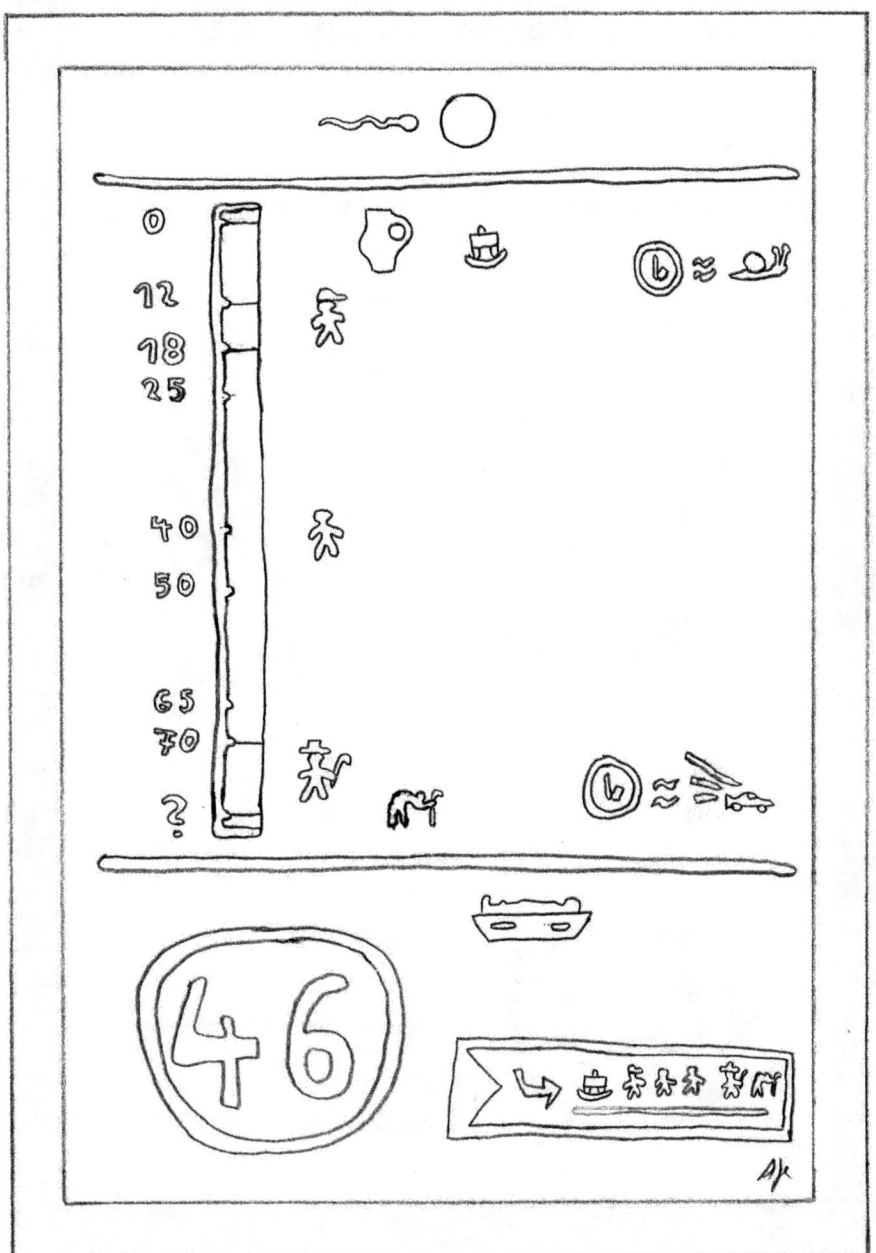

47. Chapter: Death

The course of life on this earth ends with what is the topic of this chapter: with death.

Every living being will die. Dead there is no more metabolism, no independent movement, no reproduction and no information processing.

Dying

Maybe someday we'll be old, demented, and in need of care. We become more forgetful, and at some point, we consciously may not even notice anything at all, possibly not even our own death.

Or we become old, and all of a sudden, a vital organ fails because it has become too weak. Maybe our heart isn't beating anymore. Dementia and care are then spared us and our environment.

We can die at any age. Perhaps because we are so severely injured or ill that we can no longer be healed. The gratitude that we were allowed to live at all, may then give us some consolation.

There are also people who kill themselves. Death is one of the things we don't usually have to take care of ourselves. We should basically use our life as long as we have it. If, however, it is foreseeable that our life will almost exclusively be burdensome, we should also be allowed to die.

What remains after death

The **energy** we consist of is preserved. The atoms and molecules we are made of can return to the cycle of nature and contribute to the lives of other living beings.

Half of our **genetic material** can live on in our children.

Things from ourselves can live on **in the minds of other** people: For example the love, the joy of life, experiences, or knowledge that we have passed on. And of course the memories of us, also those on pictures, sound recording media, or films.

Likewise, the **works** that we have created for ourselves or for others, or to which we have contributed, can remain long after us.

After our death, our **inheritance**, i.e., everything that belonged to us when we were still alive, including our debts, will still be there in its entirety. It is good when it is clear who is to receive it. Here is an example of a regulation:

"**Will:** In the event of my death, my spouse shall be the sole heir. If there are subsequent heirs, the heir should only be a provisional heir, i.e., be allowed to make use of the property, but should only be allowed to make dispositions with the consent of the subsequent heirs. Subsequent heirs in the event of the death of my spouse, or heirs if I do not (any more) have a spouse, are my children in equal shares. If one of my children has died, his descendants shall take his place in equal shares. Should my spouse, my children, or their descendants not live, my parents shall inherit in equal shares. If these also no longer are alive, the community or person who is most important to me should be the heir. If someone rejects the inheritance, he shall be treated here as not existing. My heirs must also take good care of my burial."

Burning, burying deeply, sinking in vast waters, or leaving to scavengers would be hygienically correct.

And a funeral ceremony, to which perhaps heirs, relatives, and friends are invited, and acquaintances are welcome, makes the change visible and a fitting farewell possible.

By the way, wise people will give their children, grandchildren, or other suitable people, groups, or legal entities a large part of their inheritance during their lifetime in such a way that they can still live well themselves. You can then notice a little what will happen to your estate without you. Also, one typically needs foreign assets as a young adult if one wants to build an existence and start a family, and not if one is already old, and the last parent dies.

And another regulation for a situation even before death makes sense to me; example:

"**Living will:** If I am still alive, but am no longer able to make my own decisions, I authorize my future heirs to settle my affairs for me. They should base their regulations on the question of what I would do if I were still in my right mind. If it must be assumed that I can no longer lead a self-determined life, I do not want any more life-sustaining measures. In the event that my brain is undoubtedly dead, my organs may be transplanted."

Good, if we clarify whether the authorized person also wants this. Important: We sign the will and the living will with place and date and inquire whether they meet the formal legal requirements required by the law. If something is invalid due to lack of form, the affected person should voluntarily and appropriately follow the last will. If the law already regulates the succession or representation in our sense, we would not have to do anything. It is good if we store the documents in a secure place where they can also be found. If we want to change or supplement something, we do that.

What else could be

Some believe that more of us will live on in this world or another. No one can know for sure. Near-death experiences with tunnel experiences can be a normal dying experience. Other ostensible experiences can be explained by psychotic reactions in extreme situations. Ostensible imprints from earlier lives can be evolutionary instinct knowledge. A dejavue experience can be the wrong impression that the current perception is at the same time memory. Faulty reconstructions, while remembering or memories of actual experiences, which one has forgotten as such, however, are further examples for causes of seemingly inexplicable.

With a view to today's knowledge and my own experiences with me, I think it is likely that with the death, our own consciousness ends forever. That is then also the final salvation from all our worries, but also the end of all our joys. This is not a problem: As long as we live, death is not there, and when we are dead, we lack the consciousness to be angry about it. That this fate affects everyone also contains a certain justice. And without the death of many of our ancestors, life would not have been able to develop into what we are allowed to experience today.

Whoever is helped by the idea of living on, be it to stay in contact with the deceased, or because they want it for themselves, may believe what is good for them during their lifetime. If consciousness does end, then we can't be annoyed about it anymore.

The certainty remains that not everything will be over with our death. Let us try to live our lives well together as long as possible. That might be the best thing, no matter what will really come.

The tasks at the end of the chapter

Tast 47.1 **My will and testament?**

Task 47.2 **My living will?**

What can you do, what do you want and what will you do here?

47.1 My will and testament:

47.2 My living will:

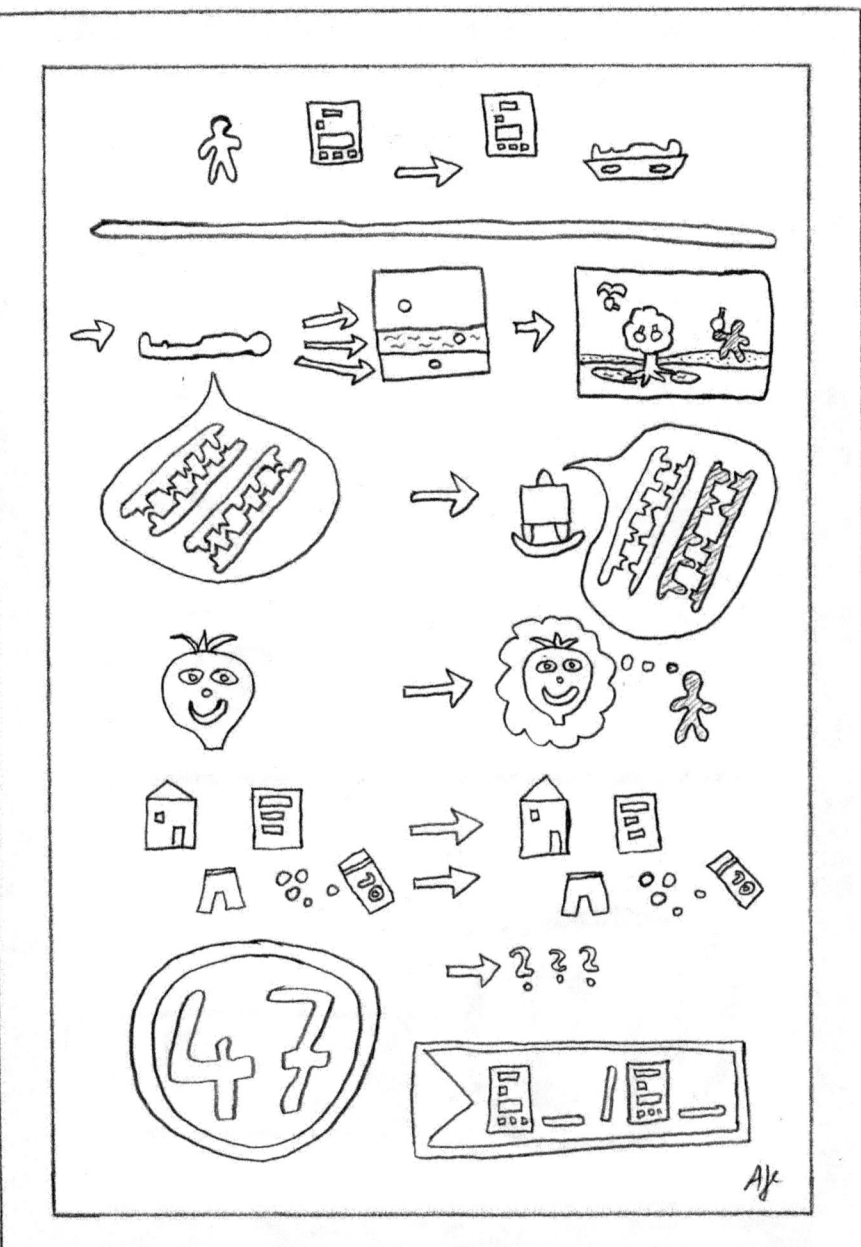

48. Chapter: Apocalypse

The last chapter was about death and also about how it continues afterward. How the world will continue and how it might end, is something we take a look at now: Apocalypse.

War

So let's think of what might be and start with the war. The weapons we humans have developed by the time I am writing this are enough to wipe out humanity. And the use of many weapon systems will contaminate the environment for a long time to come; and that in every place where the wind, rivers, currents, animals or travelers distribute the poison.

Wars are traumatizing, on both sides, no matter who wins. Traumatized people sometimes find life so difficult that they commit suicide. The environment also suffers, and children of mentally disturbed people often develop disorders themselves.

Wars are almost always wrong, even if they are fun for some and some earn money from it. We should, therefore, support peaceful politics with the long-term goal of having no war.

Environmental pollution

The dumping of pollutants into nature can harm life, including us, our food and environment, and even kill many things, inclusively us.

Soil sealing, monocultures, clearing of forests, overfishing, poaching, mining of raw materials without renaturation, and more reduces the habitat and can eradicate whole species of living beings.

In our own interest and responsibility as the most intelligent creature on earth, we should promote a policy and business enterprises that takes sufficient care of nature conservation, with the long-term goal of dealing sustainably with nature and the environment. And we ourselves should live in an environmentally friendly way appropriately.

Changes in our planet Earth

As in the past, there will also be **climate changes** in the future, i.e., it can become significantly warmer in the long term, but even colder.

Volcanic eruptions of extreme proportions could emit so much gas and ash that the Earth's temperature would drop significantly in the short term. So far, however, no eruption has wiped out life as such, and as the earth's interior cools, the probability of massive volcanic eruptions also decreases.

The **earth's interior** could **cool down to such an extent** that volcanism, mantle movements and with it earth plate movements would end. In the long term, erosion would wash any mountains into the sea. Probably the **magnetic field** would also **end**. Electromagnetically charged solar wind particles could then reach the earth unhindered, which would make life on the earth's surface extremely difficult or even impossible. This is not likely for the time being. If the magnetic field once again reverses its polarity, this should be less dangerous.

We should observe our planet well and counteract life-threatening developments as far as possible, for example by removing greenhouse gases from the atmosphere when it threatens to become too hot, or by deliberately producing them to prevent an excessively cold time.

Extraterrestrial dangers

A **comet, asteroid,** or similar could **hit** the earth and destroy life. Given our situation in our solar system, this is very unlikely, but not wholly impossible.

Aliens could attack us with hostile intent. Due to the size of the universe, it is likely, almost sure, that extraterrestrial life exists. Due to the extreme distances in space, it is expected that alien beings have never been on Earth or will never come on Earth. The fact that there are still no compelling explanations for a few unknown flying objects (UFOs), or some earlier human achievements does not mean that these surely point to extraterrestrial contacts or even to the afterlife. Of course, contact with extraterrestrials is not impossible. And perhaps they are friendly.

A neighboring galaxy, the **Andromeda Nebula**, is flying towards our Milky Way and is likely to collide with it around the year two billion. There will hardly be collisions, but gravitational forces could bring the Earth out of orbit or our solar system into a hostile part of the galaxy.

Supernovae, gamma-ray bursts, or black holes are rather no danger because of the long distances.

What is certain is that the hydrogen fuel of our **sun** will not last forever. Stars like the sun increase their activity in the course of their existence. According to calculations, it will become so hot on earth from the years 800 to 900 million that no higher life is possible. After the year five billion, the sun will expand into a red giant and then become a white dwarf. As a result, the earth's crust will probably liquefy because of the heat, before it permanently becomes too cold for new life.

We humans should observe space well and prepare ourselves together for possible dangers.

Under no circumstances should we completely abolish all our great weapon systems. We could use them to move comets or asteroids from their trajectory towards Earth or to impress aliens if they are not peaceful. Or does someone want to be a slave of aliens?

In the long run, we must be able to leave Earth permanently in giant spaceships or in space islands. Mars missions and space stations can be used for practice, space debris should be reduced. Perhaps genetic engineering or medical technology will be able to adapt us to a life outside the earth someday.

Final end and before it the Humanitarian Age

No star fuel lasts forever, and no particle is absolutely stable. In the long run, all stars will extinguish, atoms will decay, and matter will largely disperse into infinity. The end, especially the end of all life, it seems inevitable! What arose from nothing will become nothing again.

Maybe we humans can still spend many millions of generations in this world if we handle it well. Probably earthly life will only be able to survive once with our help. In any case, we can arrange our living space in such a way that it is more worth living with us humans than without us, and I believe we will create that together. However, we do not have to take ourselves and our actions too seriously. Nothing will last forever. Let us recognize the uniqueness of life on this earth, and what a privilege it is to be allowed to experience life.

The tasks at the end of the chapter

How will it probably continue if you die? What are the most beautiful things you have experienced so far? What are your most significant contributions to life so far? So:

Task 48.1 **The time after me?**

Task 48.2 **My most beautiful experiences?**

Task 48.3 **My most significant contributions to life?**

48.1   The time after me:

48.2   My most beautiful experiences:

48.3   My most significant contributions to life:

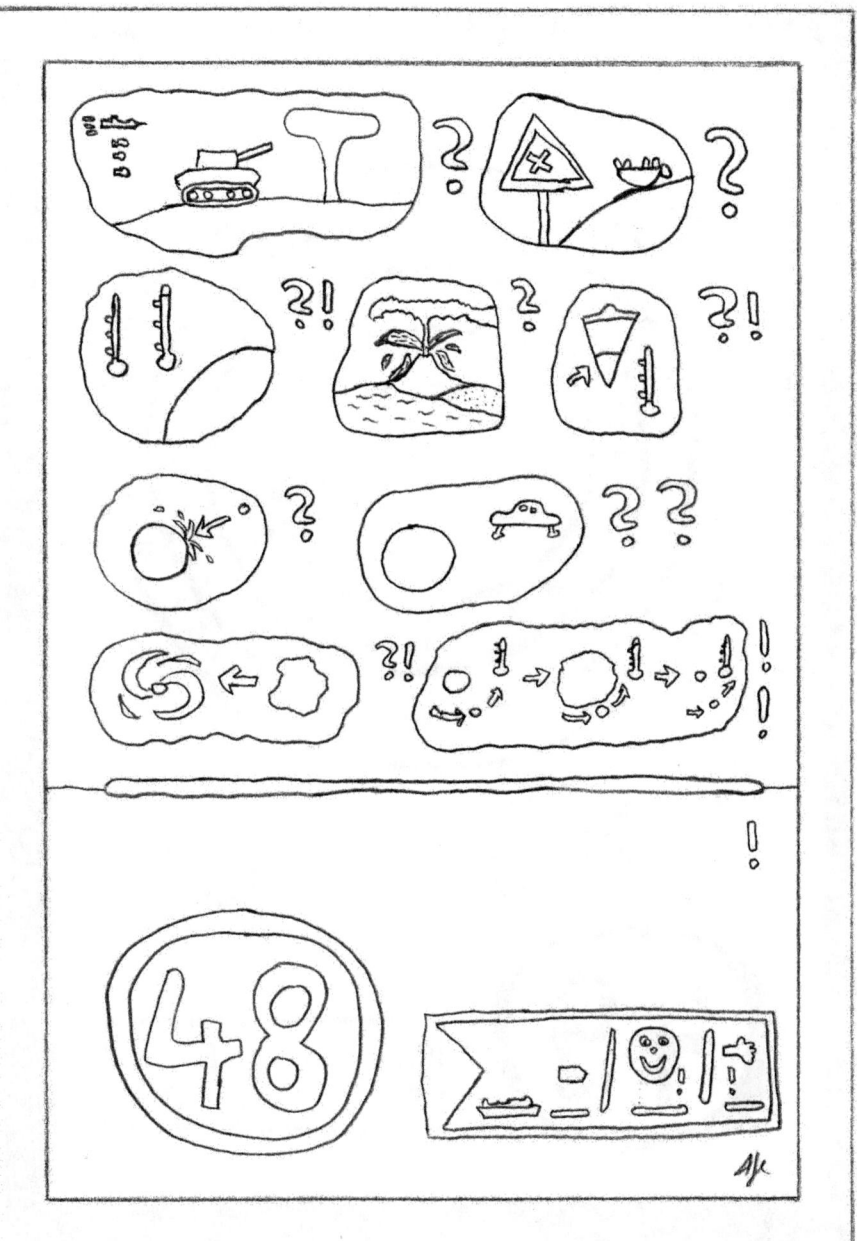

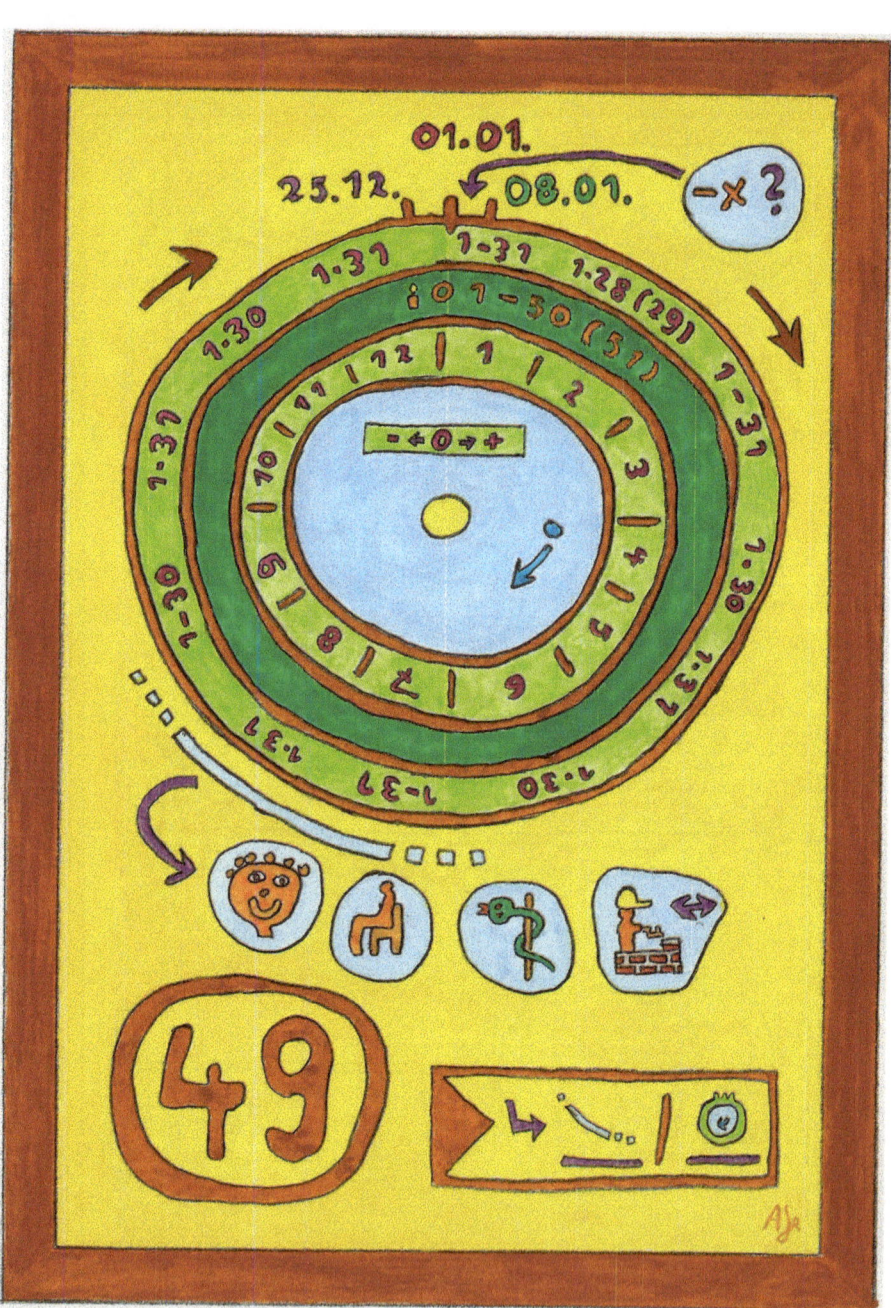

385

49. Chapter: Annual circle

It may take a very long time, before the end of the world which we have just looked at, will come, and there can be many more of those that it is about now: The annual circle.

The longest natural period that we can perceive well on earth is the year, i.e., the time that the Earth needs to go around the sun once.

The seasons

During the solar orbit, the earth inclines on December 21 at a maximum with the southern hemisphere against the sun. In the south is summer, and on this day as bright as never before or later in the year. South of the Antarctic Circle (66.56th latitude), the sun no longer sets. In the northern hemisphere, it is vice versa on that day: it is winter, on this day as short bright as on no other day, and north of the Arctic Circle it remains dark all day.

In the north the days then become longer, the temperatures first colder, then warmer again, it becomes spring, and in the summer, on June 21, the situation turns around: the days are now longest in the north, become shorter, and then it turns to autumn, winter and so on.

In some areas, there are rainy and dry seasons.

The year has altogether somewhat more than twelve moon phases and about 365.25 days, during which the earth rotates, as is well known, once around its own axis.

The annual circle

In the following, I would like to describe an annual circle, which we could let pass together in such a way.

In this annaul circle, we are with the current 49th chapter also in the 49th week after this book. Next week this cycle will end with the 50th chapter after 50 weeks and for some with the 50th discussion group or the 50th assembly.

In some years, there will have to be a **leap or Advent week** afterward. This is necessary because the year has more days than 52 seven-day weeks.

It follows the **Christmas week** with **December 25** as **Christmas Day.** Christmas now that I am writing this, is probably the most intensely celebrated day in the world for most people.

We should, therefore, celebrate on this day the most precious things together: 1. The birth or the emergence and consequently the existence of this world, of energy and, religiously speaking, of God, symbolized by golden balls. 2. We also celebrate the birth or the emergence and existence of life in this world, symbolized by green plants. 3. And we celebrate what is probably the most precious thing that has arisen and exists in life, the bright wisdom and warm love within us, symbolized by glowing red candles.

These are all gifts for us. Nice, if we also give something to a valuable person. A small symbol for the fact that the recipients and the givers are also valuable parts of what we celebrate.

4. Might we celebrate our family and relatives and, therefore, meet with those.

On **New Year's Day** on **January 1**, exactly one week after Christmas, the new calendar year begins in the **New Year's week.** Also this we can celebrate and at the same time our friends and acquaintances with whom we toast the New Year, and let it "bang" appropriately on a joint celebration.

We can implement good New Year resolutions immediately in a **fasting time** from January 1 at 18:00 (6 p.m.) till January 7 at 18:00. We can fast with at least one thing: 1. With something very dear, perhaps sweets or coffee, to see if we still have control over it. 2. With renouncing something that has become annoying to us, maybe some habits. Maybe we can get along with less or without afterward. 3. We may renounce something of which we are no longer conscious of its value, perhaps eating meat or a daily ritual. So we will appreciate it more after fasting. 4. Or we renounce the renouncing of something, i. e., we do something we would not do otherwise to see if something new is better. And of course we do not seriously harm anyone with our fasting, fasting is supposed to enrich our lives.

Again, exactly one week after New Year, on **January 8,** we could celebrate something in the **1st week:**
   1. The end of our short fasting time together.
   2. Our communities by opening their doors to the public from 10:00 to at least 14:00 and possibly offering something to drink and snacks to eat. Every active member of the community, in companies every employee, could de-

sign or get a tag that showes at least his photo, his name and his task in the community and it could be afixed where the community member often stays. So we can show each other where and what we do, when we are, for example, at work. At the same time, communities such as companies, authorities and clubs can use this to inform about their value, products and job opportunities. And if you can't see everything, or have to take care of visitors in the community on that day, you're hopefully to find another opportunity next year.

3. We can celebrate the restart of the 50-week cycle and this book, perhaps with a first assembly.

4. Chance or coincidence, on January 8, 1977, it is relatively sure that at 15:51, I was born. Whoever finds this valuable, may also celebrate this birth.

And then it goes on in the year. The months, beginning with January, have alternately 31 and 30 days. February, on the other hand, has 28 days, regularly every four years 29 days. It follows March, April, May, June, July, attention: August also has 31 days, and it continues with September, October, November, and finally, in December, we arriv again, with this chapter, in the 49th week.

In the annual circle there will be, depending on the place, custom and sometimes also group or person, different, other holidays, times and traditions. We are invited to use and cultivate what makes sense to us or at least gives us joy.

The holidays

Anyone who works full-time for 30 to 50 hours a week, takes appropriate breaks between work, is free after work and at weekends, finds appropriate balance, is an adult and healthy should actually be able to hold out permanently.

Nevertheless, I think that an employer should give his employee at least ten percent of his actual working time paid holiday. In the case of full-time work, that would be at least five weeks a year. This is an appropriate compensation for travel times or other private actions that also serve the employer. Self-employed people should allow themselves holidays.

We can treat ourselves to something fun during our **pleasure holidays.** We need **recreational holidays** when something has put us under extraordinary stress. **Healing leave** is mandatory if we need power to heal or do not want to infect colleagues. And **working leave** must or may be if we can do another job only at a time we should normally be at work, or when we want to do it.

The tasks at the end of the chapter

Task 49.1   My holidays / leave?

Task 49.2   My annual circle in an overview?

What does it look like for you in each case?
What can you do, what do you want and what will you do in each case?

49.1 My holidays / leave:

49.2 My annual circle in an overview:

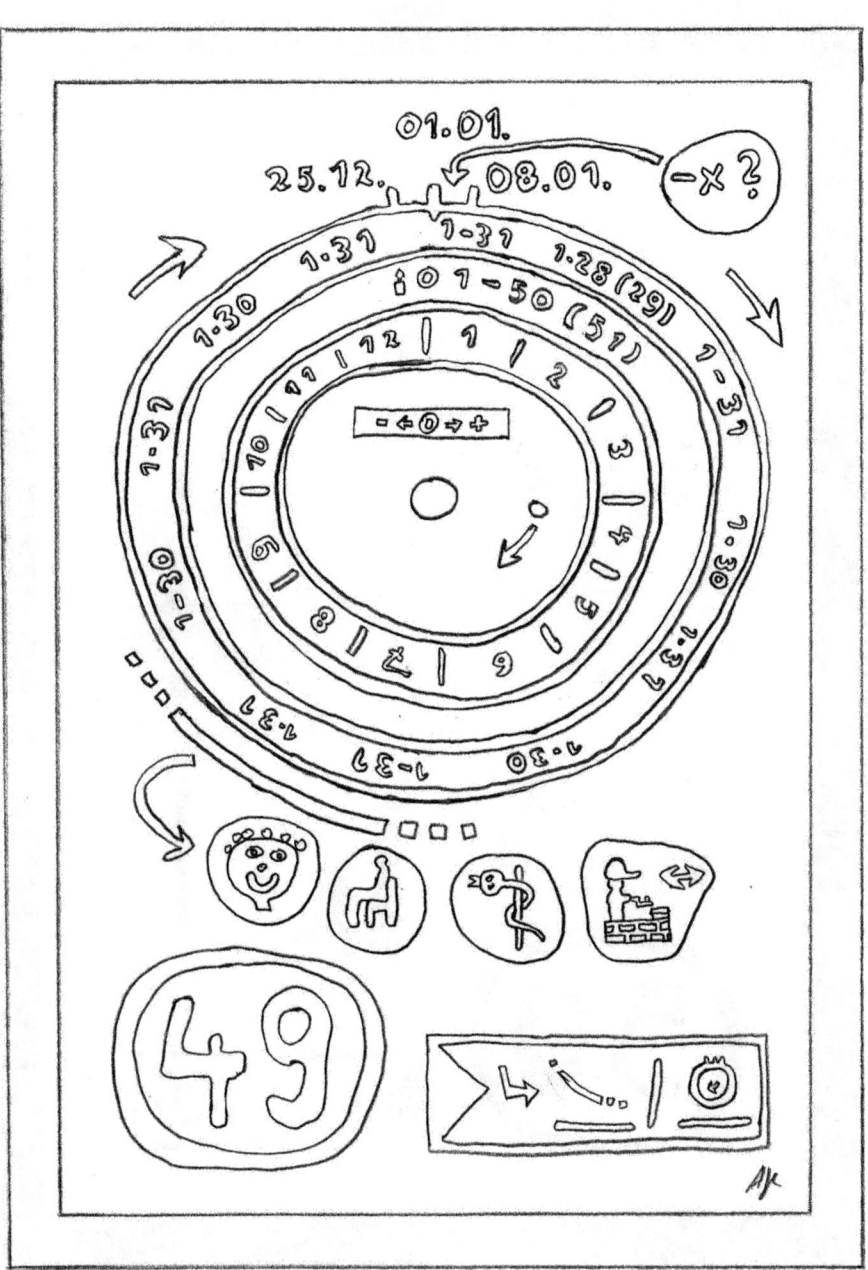

393

50. Chapter: End

The annual circle, the topic of the last chapter, ends after the 50th week, according to plan, with this chapter. In it, we look again, as in the first two chapters, at this book and now at how I and how it came into the world through me; and then, for the time being, it´s: The end.

My life up to the finished book

It probably began, as with everyone; with nothing out of which energy grew, which changed in the Big Bang, among other things formed our solar system with our earth, on which life also developed into what I am.

I was born, as is customary locally, in the hospital of a small Württemberg-Swabian town, I am German, and I am baptized Roman Catholic Christian.

My father was a carpenter who later worked as a wood mechanic in the industry. He was hardworking, and in the beginning, we were able to live in an apartment, since I was three years old, in our own detached house in a beautiful, quiet, somewhat rural residential area.

My mother was a commercial employee, who stayed at home starting with my birth, later delivered newspapers, and then helped half a day in a supermarket towards the family income and managed the household well.

My brother, one and a half years younger, was my playmate during childhood, later, when we were adolescents, we grew apart. He became a master craftsman.

However, love, adequate appreciation, good orientation, and often enough money seem to be missing. My mother came to me with her problems, I only went to her when it was so serious that she could immediately make an appointment with the pediatrician. I distance myself and suppress feelings. I also try to be safe and correct and to become exceptionally good.

As a child, I like to copy and optimize in the game. I live frugal. In communion with other children, I prefer to be the boss. In kindergarten and school I orientate myself towards educators and teachers. I function well, but I am asked why I never laugh.

I spend most of my early youth with mandatory schooling and watching TV. More than as a child, I suspect my happiness in the arms of a woman.

In late adolescence I become active: Student spokesman, editor-in-chief of the school newspaper, responsible for the class book, guitar lessons, dance lessons, first as a student, then as a teacher, part-time jobs to earn money, voluntary services in the church, supervisor at children's camps; going out on weekends, two friends, a girlfriend. I finish the highest school with an high school (Abitur) grade average of 1,0. I don't feel happy.

How should my life be? In any case, I want a wife and children; I am more emotionally open to both than usual. Professionally I want to become something big, valuable, and contribute to sustainably making the world a better place. My best school friend writes half ironically in the Abitur-newspaper: "Career wish: he volunteered for the still vacant Messiah's job of the church." Most others said priest, a few professor.

After my community service in the parish, I study law at a university in a neighboring state as a basis for becoming a politician, less out of interest, desire, or talent.

In doing youth politics, I recognize that politicians can only improve to a limited extent, and that I lack reform ideas. Nevertheless, I finish my studies, do my doctorate, both with a scholarship, do the legal traineeship, and pass the first state examination with a "grat", the second one with a "small predicate", with which I'm dissatisfied.

I look reasonable and controlled and attract girlfriends who don't fit. They are often surprised by my intense need for sensual, physical love, and they all want to live a "normal" life.

During my doctoral thesis, I have work blockade. I start to think about myself, the world, and a good life intensively. I write down my many ideas, also in subsequent years. After my legal traineeship, I make the first rough version of this book - again living entirely with my parents. There are more and more conflicts. For the completion of the book, I want to move out, find no optimal flat, believe I can't manage anything anymore, become restless, and at the same time so powerless that I fear to die, which I sometimes even wish for so that my misery ends.

With medical help, I become able to work again, work briefly as a lawyer, move into a one-room apartment in the state capital, do a specialist lawyer training, don't find a job, start a second draft and become depressed again.

I don't want to accept this, I want to heal it completely. I read many specialist books, work on myself, break away from my old environment and affiliations, write my life story, visit self-help groups, and use professional help. Seemingly healthy, I start the book for the third time and become depressed again. Nevertheless, I finish it in solitude.

After that I lie exhausted for further several years, most of the time lonely in bed. In the meantime, I have understood a lot, but I have no solution: I get depressed when my "soul" thinks that things can't go on like this for me. I am told that I cannot be placed on the job market. To become a judge the grades of my second exam are not enough. For me, there is no admission for medicine as a second degree. For priest I am not convinced enough of what I would have to do. Auxilary jobs do not satisfy me. The book was finished, but immature; for improvement, I lacked ideas and strength. I ask three people if I can live with them, all of them refuse. I live extremely sparingly, and yet it is foreseeable that my savings will end. I find no benefactor. For suitable women, I am not really attractive; other sources of strength hardly work.

I get enough strength to go on through renewed medical help and thanks to hope and aktivity through training and admission as a healer with permission and further training as a coach.

In my own practice, I initially lack clients. Two days a week, I work as an employed alternative practitioner in a medical practice for naturopathy. For individual courses I work as a lecturer at a naturopathic school.

I revise the book. My, in the meantime, also more experienced personality helps me to finish the book independently and with high quality.

And who knows, maybe that's how it should be.

Our common future

I think the most important goal for us humans should be to live well, together, in harmony with nature, and for as long as possible. It is important, despite and with our prehistoric and stone-age character traits and our influential past, to wisely overcome current challenges. This book wants to help us permanently.

Maybe this way will sustainably contribute to valuable life, and indeed also through me. If we use this book, we will make it together in the end.

The task at the end of the chapter

Task 50 **My time until the new beginning?**

What do I plan for Christmas? To whom do I give a book? What do I do New Year? With what will I fast afterward? How do I celebrate January 8th? And then?

What can I do, what do I want to do, and what will I do with this book?

Do you believe that this book can help you and us, humans, to understand the world and ourselves sufficiently well and to live together well on this basis for a long time to come?

We don't need everyone, but we can need everyone,
... also you ...
for a maximum of kingdom of heaven on earth!

50. *My time until the new beginning?*

Christmas:

New Year:

Fasting:

1/8:

More ideas to use this book:

399

403

I am here then.

When a **community** offers regular Lifebook assemblies, I'm happy to drop by if I can. I'm pleased to see discussion groups using this book. The use of this book within the community is free.

If someone wants to **translate** the book into another language, I believe this would be an enrichment in this language. If a visual artist or a photo-artist would like to create **new pictures** fitting to the chapters, preferably together with colorable versions, we can publish a book together. May my pictures be suitable for my purpose, from my point of view, seen purely artistic, much more is possible.

If someone produces or offers a **weekly calendar** with the pictures, **art prints, pieces of jewelry** with the symbol from chapter 18, **stuffed animals, clothing** or **accessories** that takes things from the book, this may enrich the market.

It is also an honor for me if someone as a coach, **life consultant,** therapist (behavior therapy), clergyman, or similar works with this book professionally with his clients, as I do.

If you are looking for a suitable **keynote speaker** or an **advertising medium,** you'll find a very good one in me when you convince me of the value or meaning of what it's about.

In principle, I am open to **further ideas**.

And of course, I am happy, really not least of all, when a **publisher** wants to print a version of this book.

In the individual case, we would, of course, have to agree on a profit, turnover, or flat-rate share that is appropriate for both of us.

See you soon
Dr. Andreas Jetter